Lotus

Illustrated DICTIONARY of MASS COMMUNICATION

Complied and Edited by:
Jack Williams

Lotus PRESS
4735/22, Prakash Deep Building
Ansari Road, Darya Ganj,
New Delhi-110002

Lotus Illustrated

DICTIONARY of MASS COMMUNICATION

ISBN 81 89093 46 0

Published by:

Lotus Press : Publishers & Distributors

Unit No. 220, 2nd Floor, 4735/22,
Prakash Deep Building, Ansari Road, Darya Ganj,
New Delhi- 110002, Ph.: 41325510, 09811838000
• E-mail : lotuspress1984@gmail.com www.lotuspress.co.in

Printed & Published by : **Lotus Press Publisher & Distributors,** New Delhi-02

PREFACE

Mass Communication includes journalism, programmes in radio and television broadcasting, public relations, communications arts, library science, programmes for technicians in museums and similar repositories, documentation techniques. Mass Communication is the transmission of messages which may be processed by gate keepers prior to being sent to large audiences via a channel of broad diffusion.

Approximately five hundred years ago a new form of communication arose. This 'mass' communication process, which makes use of permanent text that can be made available to millions of people at the same time, has quickly become an important factor in the lives of many human beings.

By removing words from the world of sound where they had first had their origin in active human interchange and relegating them definitively to visual surface and by otherwise exploiting visual space for the management of knowledge, print encouraged human beings to think of their own interior conscious and unconscious resources as more and more thing-like, impersonal and religiously neutral. Print encouraged the mind to sense that its possessions were held in some sort of inert mental space.

The most obvious difference between writing and speech is in their media. Whereas speech is carried by sound waves

in the air, writing is usually carried by one substance impressed upon another, as, for example, ink on paper. [Note] Even in its simplest form, the invention of writing produced significant changes in human communication.

This dictionary contains terms, be it simple or complex, of Mass Communication for the readers who are interested in this field.

■ 16:9 mode

TV signals coming from a Laser Disc or Camcorder in squeezed format can also be reproduced on 4:3 picture tubes without any distortion by manually switching to the 16:9 mode.

■ 4:3

aspect ratio of the NTSC TV screen, with '4' unit width corresponding to '3' unit height, proportionally regardless of the actual size of the screen.

■ 8-VSB

eight discreet amplitude level, 'vestigial side-band' broadcast transmission technology, VSB is an analog modulation technique used to reduce the amount of spectrum needed to transmit information through cable TV or over-the-air broadcasts used in the NTSC (analog) standard. 8-VSB is the ATSC digital television transmission Standard.

■ A.D.R.

Automated Dialogue Recording. This is just Dubbing, done in addition to or as a substitution for Location Sound. The term A.D.R., being something of a mysterious acronym, has a certain appeal, as it obscures the fact that dubbing was involved when it appears in the credits of your film. This might have something to do with the current prevalence of the term.

■ A.S.A.

A.S.A. stands for American Standards Association, the organisation that standardised the scale of measurement of film speed. This is the sensitivity to light of a particular type of film. It is the specific number used to measure Film Speed.

■ a4

the international standard paper size, 210 x 297 mm paper size or 8.3 x 11.7 inches. This size is supported by most printer manufacturers.

■ AAR

Automatic Alternate Routing.

■ ABC

Audit Bureau of Circulation. A service organisation that validates publishers' circulation claims through regularly scheduled audits.

■ ABEND

Acronym for Abnormal End of Task. It refers to software crashes or lossage. Derives from an error message originally on the IBM 360 mainframe. Common error message on Novell systems in current use.

■ absolute delay

the actual time taken for a signal to transit a Packet signal from end

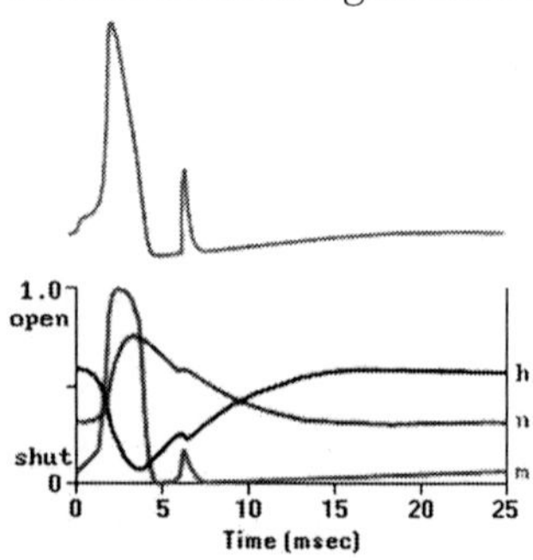

to end. It is affected by the actual circuit length and the 'propagation constants' of the type of medium used.

■ ac-3

the coding system used by Dolby Digital. The two terms, AC-3 and Dolby Digital, are often used interchangeably. See **audio**.

■ academy aperture

in 35mm this is the full frame exposed by the camera, with an aspect ratio of 1.33. When the film is projected there is a mask in the projector's gate to change the aspect ratio to 1.85 or 1.66, cropping the top and bottom of the image. Older films were not shot to be masked and should be projected without a mask. The Academy Aperture is sometimes called the Full Academy Aperture.

■ academy leader

this is standard countdown leader, counting down 8 to 3 and then with one frame of 2, at which point there is a single frame beep on the sound track. It is used at the beginning of a film for the lab to line up sound (using the beep) and later for the projectionist to know when to turn on the lamp and hopefully not miss the opening of the film. A common mistake is to count the footage from the 2, but actually frame zero is the one right before the first 8, a single frame with the words 'Picture Start'. Academy Leader is sometimes also known as S.M.P.T.E. leader.

■ ACAP

Application Configuration Access Protocol. A standard for accessing program configuration information from a remote server, allowing a user to use and change their configuration from any workstation by reading or writing the values on a central server.

■ Acceptable Use Policy (AUP)

a formal set of rules that governs how a network may be used. For example, the original NSFnet Acceptable Use Policy forbade non-research use by commercial organisations. AUPs sometimes restrict the type of material that can be made publicly available, many AUPs ban the transmission of pornographic material. The enforcement of AUPs has historically been very uneven. This was true of the NSFnet AUP: its limitations on commercial activity were so widely ignored that it was finally abandoned in 1994, thus actually enabling the development of today's commercial Internet.

■ access

the ability of media consumers to produce their own texts and to have those texts acknowledged by the agenda setting media. Also, the ability of media consumers to respond to the dominant media.

■ acculturation

in a media context, the tendency of reporters or other media professionals to adopt the ideas and attitudes of the groups they cover or with which they have a great deal of contact.

■ ACK

1. acknowledge. Used to confirm one's presence. An appropriate response to ping.
2. when one computer sends a block of data to another over a network, the second computer sends an acknowledgment code back to indicate that the transfer was successful. If there were errors detected in the transmission, the second computer would send a negative acknowledgment (NAK).
3. acknowledge. A handshake signal sent to the computer indicating that the printer (or other peripheral device) has successfully received a character.

■ active audience

an audience conceived as selective in their programming choices and interpretation, motivated by different demands and resistant to direct *media* influence, in contrast to the concept of mass audiences whom many perceived as passive and easily swayed. The concept represents a new way of thinking about audiences and their relationship to media communication.

■ active filter

a filter that uses an amplifier in addition to reactive components to pass or reject selected frequencies.

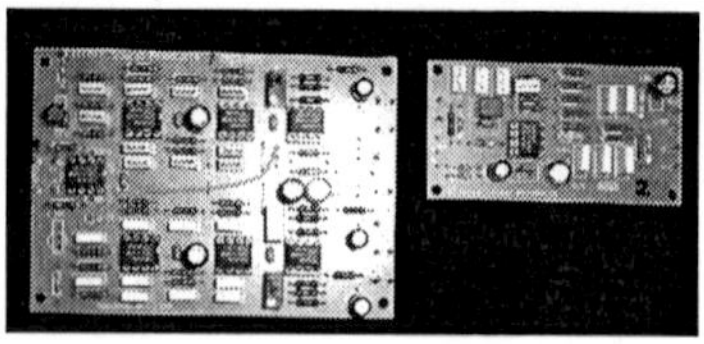

■ active matrix display

a type of flat-panel display in which the screen is refreshed more frequently than in conventional passive-matrix displays. The most common type of active-matrix display is based on a technology known as TFT (thin film transistor). The two terms, active matrix and TFT, are often used interchangeably.

■ actual damages

damages awarded to a plaintiff in a lawsuit based on proof of actual harm to the plaintiff.

■ actual malice

a fault standard in libel law: knowledge before publication that the libellous material was false or reckless disregard of the truth or falsity of the libellous matter.

■ actual size

a term used in scanning processes. It is the size of the original page when it was scanned, not enlarged using zoom or reduced using zoom out.

■ **actuality**

the term used in the media to refer to footage/film/tape of events as they happen. Semioticians see actuality as a key device for anchoring the preferred reading on the supposed 'facts' presented 'as they happened'.

■ **ad click rate**

sometimes referred to as 'click-through'. This represents the percentage of ad views that precedes an 'ad click.'

■ **ad clicks**

number of times users click on an ad banner.

■ **ad network**

a single entity that provides advertisers with a way of reaching a large number of users across several web sites with a single 'ad buy'.

■ **ad space**

space on a Web page that is reserved for ads.

■ **ad views**

a visitor seeing an ad. If the same ad appears on multiple pages simultaneously, this statistic may understate the number of ad impressions due to browser catching. An ad impression is not to be confused with a page view since several ads may reside on one page.

■ **adaptive routing**

in data networks, routing algorithms capable of adjusting message routes in response to changes in traffic patterns or transmission channel failures. e.g., alternate routes in the X-1J/X2 nodes.

■ **ADC**

an acronym for Analog to Digital Converter.

■ **ADCCP**

an acronym for Advanced Data Communications Control Protocol. An ANSI standard bit oriented data link control (DLC) protocol.

■ **additive**

a process or state whereby elements combine together, such as two primitive shapes combining to form a larger, more complex one. Additive is the opposite of subtractive.

■ **additive colour system**

a colour reproduction system in which images are reproduced by mixing appropriate amounts of red, green and blue lights.

■ **additive primaries**

the three primary colours: Red, Green and Blue. Colour systems use these primaries in differing amounts, working on the principle of adding spectral wavelengths to the light energy to create new colours. This system is used in lighting and computer display graphics. The complementary colours are the Subtractive Primaries: Cyan, Magenta and Yellow.

■ **add-ons**

1. add-ons are programs written to work in conjunction with an online service or your browser

that provide added functionality. They are generally written by third party companies or individuals and are often shareware, meaning you will need to register with the author and send in a fee if you decide to keep the program.
2. an optional, installable card that adds accessory functions to a computer. Add-ons might be, but are not limited to, sound cards, I/O cards, network cards, game ports, modems, controllers and real world interfaces.

■ address

in Packet Radio networks, it is the distinct identifier of a destination node or station.

■ addressable converter

a cable television box that can be supplied with 'programming' by a cable system providing pay-per-view events.

■ adjacent areas

surfaces that are separated on a multiview drawing by lines that represent a change of planes. No two adjacent areas can lie in the same plane.

■ adjacent view

orthographic views that are aligned to each other, allowing dimensional information to be shared. Examples are the front and top views or the front and right side views.

■ adjustable tray

in the case of printers, a paper tray that is able to adapt to more than one size of media. HP indicates that all trays used in the printers are adjustable, allowing varied usage.

■ ADN

an acronym for Advanced Digital Network. This refers to the backbone, usually a 56kb or faster, 'always on', network connection condition. This can be a leased line, a cable connection, xDSL, T1, T3 or similar.

■ advertisement

a paid public announcement appearing in the media.

■ advertising

an institutionalised process of persuasion in which both visual and

verbal *symbols* are manipulated to convince people to buy something, to foster *brand* loyalty or to buy into a consumer lifestyle.

■ advertising agency

a company that handles both the creative and the business side of an advertising campaign for its clients.

■ **advertising manager**

a client representative responsible for overseeing marketing efforts related to product, including budgeting, creative activities and liaison with agency.

■ **advertorial**

an advertisement that resembles a newspaper editorial or a television program but promotes a single advertiser's product, service or point of view.

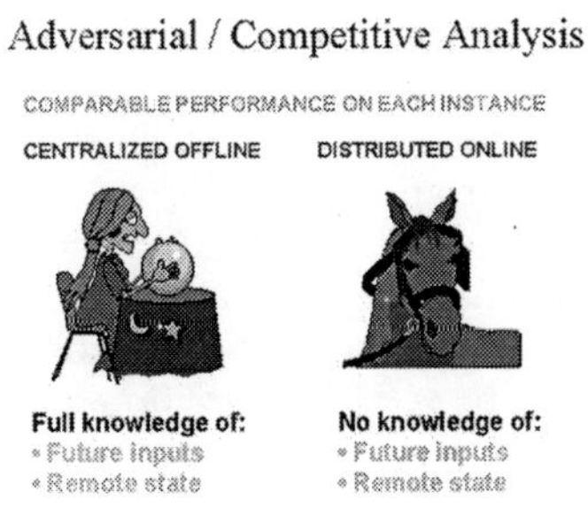

■ **AEA**

Advanced Electronics Applications Inc. AEA designs, manufactures and markets a wide range of amateur packet products as well as other amateur related items.

■ **aerial perspective**

a perceptual cue where objects farther away appear bluer and hazier. The cue is based on the effect of particles in the atmosphere blocking the passage of light.

■ **aesthetics**

the artistic qualities or aspects that elicit an emotional response to an object.

■ **affiliate**

a broadcasting station that aligns itself with a network.

■ **affiliate**

a partner website linking to a merchant's site in return for a commission.

■ **affiliate network**

a network aggregating affiliates the merchant programs. It offers easy access to a variety of programs and merchants' facilities to establish their own affiliate program.

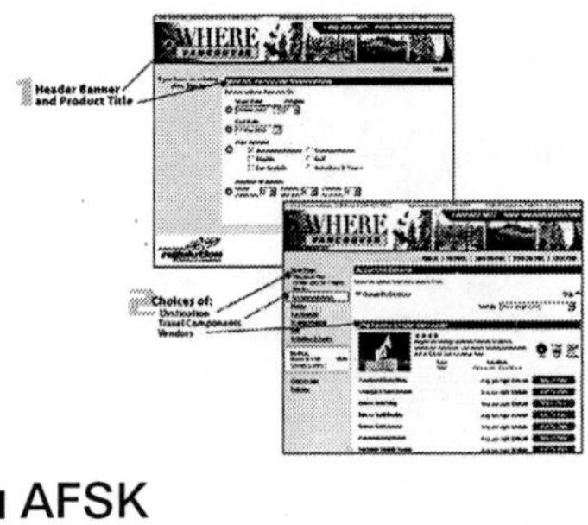

■ **AFSK**

Audio Frequency-Shift Keying. A method of digital modulation. This is a mechanism for sending digital information over a radio. A signal 0 (zero) is sent using one tone while the signal 1 (one) is sent using a different tone. This is the mechanism used by telephone modems and packet radio modems. When associated with VHF Packet, the audio frequency-shift is usually 1000 Hz. A 0 (zero) is one tone while a 1 (one) is a different tone.

■ AGC

acronym for Automatic Gain Control. Most often used in audio circuits, an electronic circuit which automatically increases the volume when someone is speaking quietly and drops the volume when someone is speaking loudly, to keep the transmitted signal constant. Can also be used with video and other raw signals.

■ age group

a target audience defined by age.

■ agency

the organisation that handles basic needs of advertisers.

■ agenda building

the ways the media decide what is newsworthy.

■ agenda-setting

the action of the *media* in influencing people's perception of what is important, acceptable or desirable. Attention is drawn to certain aspects of reality and away from others, thus influencing people in terms of what they should think about rather than what to think. This agenda-setting function in newscasting can be achieved deliberately or accidentally by the size of headlines order of appearance, choice of words and length of coverage. See also **democratic propaganda, frame**.

■ agenda-setting effect

the influence of the mass media created by emphasising certain topics, thus causing people to perceive those same issues as important.

■ aliasing

defects or distortions in a television picture or audio. In digital video, defects are typically seen as jagged edges on diagonal lines and twinkling or brightening. Aliasing is caused by insufficient sampling or poor filtering of the digital video.

■ alien and sedition acts of 1798

to avoid news broadcasts and newspaper or magazine stories that discuss the case or issues in the case.

■ aligned dimensions

a style of dimensioning in which text is placed parallel to the dimension line, with vertical dimensions read from the right of the drawing sheet. The aligned method of dimensioning is not approved by the current ANSI standards but may be seen on older drawings.

■ allowance

a tolerance measure used to describe the minimum clearance or maximum interference between parts. Allowance is the tightest fit between two mating parts.

■ aloha net

an early (1975) packet radio experiment conducted by the University of Hawaii. The Aloha net is known for its performance definitions for packet systems which have hidden transmitters.

■ **alphabet**

a group of letters used to symbolise each of the sounds that make up a word.

■ **alphabet of lines**

the standard linestyles established by ANSI to be used for technical drawing. The standards specify both the thickness and the design (i.e., dashed, solid, etc.) of the lines.

■ **alternate route**

a secondary communications path used to reach a destination if the primary path is unavailable.

■ **alternate use**

the ability to use communications transmission facilities for multiple applications - voice or data being the most common example.

■ **ambient**

used in electronics and electrical situations, it is usually used in the same way as, surrounding, average, native or enclosing.

■ **ambient light source**

a light source defined by its lack of orientation or location. Fluorescent lighting in an office is an example of ambient lighting. In renderings, an ambient light source is sometimes used as a default light source to give a baseline level of lighting to the model.

■ **ambient noise**

constant noise present in all forms of telecommunications paths, a condition that most Packet communications networks operate with.

■ **amplitude**

magnitude or size, voltage or power of an electronic signal.

■ **Amplitude Modulation (AM)**

modifying a 'carrier' signal by varying its instantaneous power to represent the information it carries, most commonly called 'AM'.

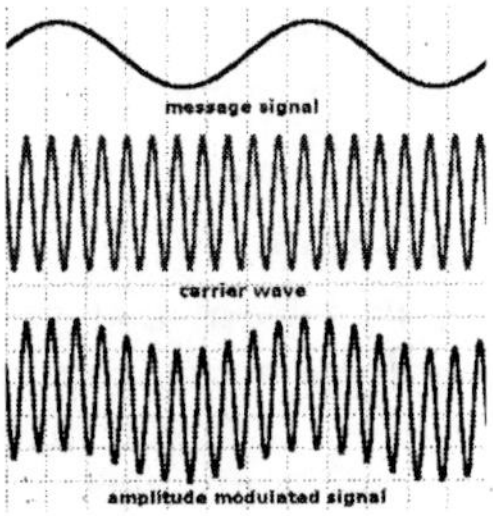

■ **AMPS**

All Media and Product Survey. Research to monitor the use of media (e.g. radio, television and print, etc.) and consumer products.

■ **AMRAD**

Amateur Radio Research And Development Corporation, is a non-profit group based in Virginia that has promoted many of the present day guidelines and practices that affect Packet Radio. AMRAD is one of the first organisations that was established to advance Packet Radio communications.

■ **analog**

media software which has a physical quality and presence.

■ **analog recording**

a recording in which continuous magnetic signals are written to the tape that are representations of the voltage signals coming from the recording microphone or the video camera.

■ **analog signal**

a signal in a form that varies in step with the actual transmitted information. The retransmitted analog signal is not always an exact replica of the input.

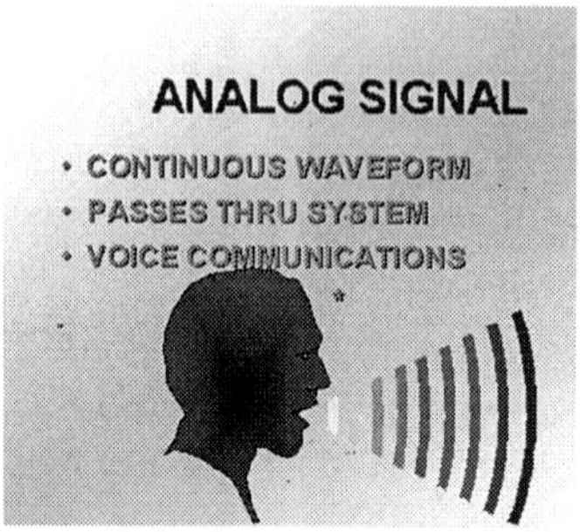

■ **analog transmission**

communications by transmission of continuously varying representations of the input signal, as compared to coded words in digital transmission.

■ **analogous**

a concept meaning similar or comparable in some respects. The concept is used to describe the extent to which a graphic representation compares with a real object.

■ **analog-to-digital**

the process in which a continuous analog signal is quantised and converted to a series of binary integers.

■ **anamorphic**

a method of creating a wide screen image with standard film, using a special lens on the camera and projector that compresses the width of the image that is exposed on the film and then expands it when projected.

■ **anchor**

the member of a news team who coordinates the reports.

■ **anchorage**

a term used by Barthes to describe the interaction of words and visual texts. A photograph, according to Barthes is *polysemic* (i.e. open to a range of possible meanings). Ordinarily text is added, perhaps in the form of a caption or an advertising slogan, to 'anchor' the meaning, to lead the reader towards the preferred reading of the visual text. More broadly, anchorage of an image's meaning can occur not only through words, but, say, through the juxtaposition of two images.

■ angle

the relative orientation of two linear elements with respect to each other. The angle is usually measured relative to the point of intersection or termination of the two lines.

■ angularity

an orientation control for geometric dimensioning and tolerancing. Angularity is a condition of a surface, centre plane or axis at an angle other than a right angle to a datum plane or datum axis.

■ ANI

acronym for Automatic Number Identification. A system similar to Caller-ID (CID), used by the telephone company and some classes of subscriber for identifying the caller. Unlike Caller-ID, ANI delivery is not blocked by * (star) codes.

■ antenna

a device that is the beginning point for getting radio, TV or similar signals, for the final point for transmitting them. The energy to or from the antenna is called RF. An antenna is a specialised transducer that converts RF (Radio Frequency) fields into AC (alternating current) or vice-versa. There are two basic types. The first is the receiving antenna, which intercepts RF energy and delivers AC to electronic equipment and the transmitting antenna, which is fed with AC from electronic equipment and generates an RF field. In computer and Internet wireless applications, the most common type of antenna is the dish, used for satellite communications. Dish antennas are generally practical only at microwave frequencies (above approximately 3 GHz). The dish consists of a paraboloidal or spherical reflector with an active element at its focus. When used for receiving, the dish collects RF from a distant source and focuses it at the active element. When used for transmitting, the active element radiates RF that is collimated (meaning to line up or in this case, to adjust the line of sight) by the reflector for delivery in a specific direction. At frequencies below 3 GHz, many different types of antennas are used. The simplest is a length of wire, connected at one end to a transmitter or receiver. More often, the radiating/receiving element is placed at a distance from the transmitter or receiver and AC is delivered to or from the antenna by means of RF transmission line, also called a feed line or feeder.

■ antialiasing

the process of reducing the visibility of jagged edges by using grey scale pixel values to smooth and feather contrasting intersections of bitmapped objects.

■ antique print

all prints printed and published before 1900 are considered antique prints. A modern reproduction of an old print is not itself an antique. The cut-off date of 1900 is not firmly fixed, however and in many circumstances original prints made before World War II are also considered to be antiques.

■ apparent motion

the sense of motion induced by rapidly displaying a series of images of an object to make the object appear to change location or shape. Animation techniques take advantage of this perceptual effect.

■ application layer

the topmost visible to the user presentation of a communications network. The user level of Packet Radio (AX.25) is Level 2.

Application-Layer Gateways

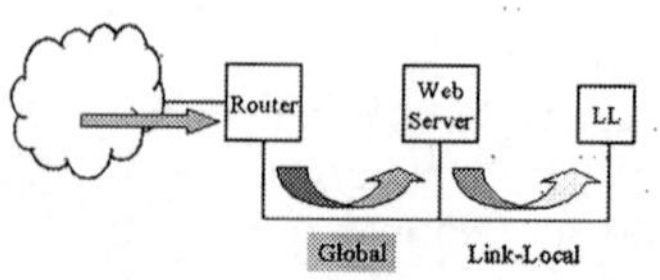

■ arbitron

the professional research organisation that measures radio audiences.

■ archival storage

storage conditions specifically designed to extend or maximise the lifetime of stored media. Generally involves the use of temperatures and humidities lower than access storage conditions. Temperatures and humidities are also tightly controlled within a narrow range and access by personnel is limited.

■ archive

offline storage of video/audio onto back-up tapes, floppy disks, optical disks, etc.

■ archiving

a term used to describe the storing and retrieval process for engineering documentation. Although originally involving paper documents, the term increasingly refers to the storage of computer-generated information on magnetic or optical media.

■ area rendering

a data visualisation technique in which the pixels in a 2-D area are each assigned a value. A colour lookup table maps a specific colour to each data value to create a rendered region.

■ ARQ

telegraphic code signal for 'Automatic Repeat Request' a time-honoured method of telegraphic error correction upon which most data transmission error correction is based. An error correction technique in AMTOR where the receiving station sends 1 character

ACK/NAK response to each AMTOR group sent. ARQ receivers check for errors and initiate an order to retransmit data blocks determined to be corrupted in transmission.

■ **art director**

the person responsible for the graphic design and creative positioning of an advertisement or campaign, the person in charge of an agency's production department.

■ **artifacts**

undesirable elements or defects in a video picture. Most common in digital are macroblocks, which resemble pixelation of the video image and pops and clicks in audio.

■ **artistic drawing**

a type of drawing used to express aesthetic, philosophical and abstract ideas. These types of drawings are not intended to communicate clear, concise information pertaining to a design.

■ **aspect ratio**

the proportions of the frame. In 16mm and 35mm the camera photographs a slightly square image, with an aspect ratio of 1.33 to 1. Aspect Ratios are usually shorted to leave out the '- to 1', taking for granted that it will always be in relation to 1 and so '1.33 to 1' can just be called '1.33'. In 35mm 1.33 is known as the Academy Aperture. In 35mm the image is usually shot with the Academy Aperture and then masked in the projector to produce a wider image: 1.85 in the U.S. and 1.66 in Europe.

■ **ASR**

telegraphic name for an 'Automatic Send/Receive' terminal station, typically one that has storage for outbound messages and holds them until called upon by the communications network to send.

■ **assembly drawing**

a drawing showing how each part of a design is put together. An assembly drawing normally consists of all the parts drawn in their operating positions and a parts list or bill of materials.

■ **assembly section**

a section view of multiple parts in an assembly. Differing section line designs differentiate between different materials or between similar materials belonging to different parts.

■ **assignment desk or news desk**

at broadcast bureaus and stations, the staff responsible for dispatching camera crews and reporters to cover news events.

■ **assignment editor**

staff member of a television or radio news team responsible for judging appropriateness of story ideas assigned to reporter for coverage.

■ **asynchronous**

lacking synchronisation. In video, a signal is asynchronous when its timing differs from that of the system reference signal.

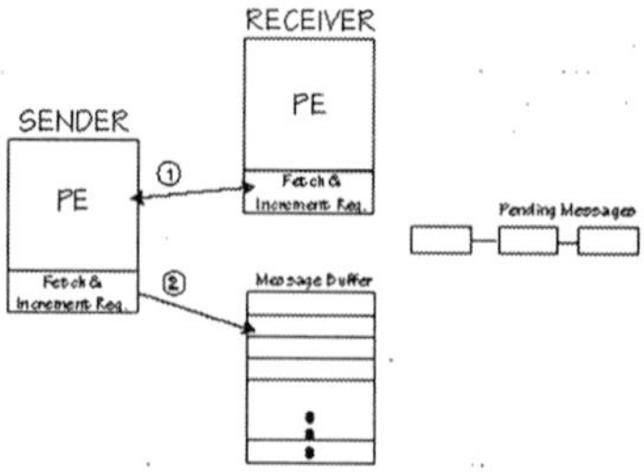

■ attenuation

term denoting a decrease in power between that transmitted and that received due to loss through equipment, lines or other transmission devices. Usually expressed as a ratio in dB (decibels).

■ audience

the group of consumers for whom the media text was constructed as well as anyone else who is exposed to the text.

■ audio

the audible or sound function of your multimedia interface. There are many types of audio currently available and while the Real Audio format is currently the standard, MP3 and others have made significant advancements and may well overtake the leader as the new standard. Some common terms and formats associated are 3-D audio, AC-3, AIFF, ASF, AU, audio scrubbing, digital audio, digitise, Dolby Digital (AC-3), fps, jitter buster, MIDI, MP3, MPEG (MPG), RealAudio, sampling, sound card, streaming, WAV, wave table and synthesis.

■ audio scrubbing

the process of moving within an audio file or tape to locate a particular section. The term originally comes from the days of reel-to-reel players, when rocking a reel would give the impression of scrubbing tape across the head. Many audio scrub tools today allow the user to drag a cursor across the waveform to audition different sections of an audio file.

■ audio track

a CD- DA track with digital audio samples encoded as 16 bit numbers.

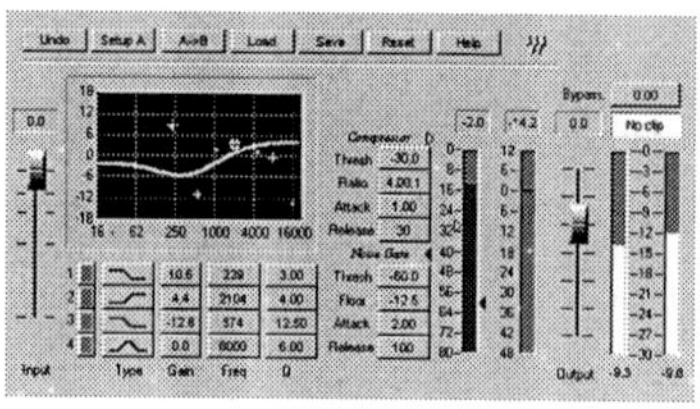

■ audiovisual (a/v)

pertaining to the use of recordings, videos, slides and other media for presentation.

■ audit

a formal unbiased check particularly of circulation of advertising media such as by the Audit Bureau of Circulations or Business Publications Audit of Circulation.

■ Audit Bureau of Circulations (ABC)

an organisation formed by advertisers and publishers in 1914 to establish ground rules for counting circulation data.

■ audit trail

the list of headers (R: lines) attached to every BBS message that is used to trace the path the message assumed from its originating BBS.

■ **auditor**

third party companies that verify ad deliveries and site statistics.

■ **author**

the creator of a text. Some texts are said to have a single author. Some texts have multiple authors, as in a television sitcom. In some cases authorship is unknown or ambiguous, as in Homer's epic poetry Ñ 'Homer' may in fact be a mythical figure which represents the many authors of the epics.

■ **authoring**

the process of using computer programming tools to assemble different media into an interactive presentation.

■ **authoritarian theory**

the prevailing belief that a ruling elite should guide the intellectually inferior masses.

■ **auto 16:9**

automatically switches the television to 16:9 full screen mode upon receipt of an encoded signal supplied by a broadcasting station.

■ **auto convergence**

by pressing one button on the front panel, the Rear Projector will automatically adjust the convergence to ensure true picture purity.

■ **auto label**

Auto Label utilises the additional information in the Teletext messages broadcast by individual stations. The identification label is used to automatically identify the pre-set stations.

■ **auto wide**

automatically switches the television to the appropriate zoom mode for either 4:3 or letterbox broadcast.

■ **autochanger**

a tape, CD, DVD or optical disc drive with the ability to change the media within it. Usually these are backup devices but not always. The devices also have the slang connotation of Juke Box by users that were around in the 50's and 60's.

■ **Automatic Alternate Routing (AAR)**

provision or function in a network to obtain a connection via secondary routes between two locations without need for user intervention. Compare to the NET X-1J4 nodes.

■ **automatic answer**

a function providing for a transmission control unit or station to automatically detect a connection and responding with a preset line of 'connect text'. Most commonly associated with personal mailboxes within the firmware of the TNC for Packet Radio use.

■ **Automatic Channel Installation (ACI)**

if this feature is provided in your cable network, your TV can be tuned automatically, including all channel indications and labels.

■ automatic route optimisation

in some Packet radio systems, this feature may denote added ability to adjust routing depending on traffic load or time of day. Some route adjustments may be accomplished by the System Node Operator (SNO) by locking routes to neighbour nodes at a higher quality number than that set in the nodes third parameter.

■ automatic routing

a means of internode data and traffic positioning through several network nodes that enables the fastest usable routing. This routing is usually determined by the node, however the node system operator may influence the routing by installing fixed or locked nodes and/or routes.

■ automatic trunk

a node connection whose destination is predetermined by the node sysop. It is the most commonly used feature of the X-1J4 TheNET firmware. This enables or initiates a connect to a programmed destination node.

■ automation

the use of machinery in place of human labour.

■ autorouting

a specialised software process that suggests routing connections between components on a circuit board. Autorouting is usually part of a suite of CAD electronics software functions that also include automated component placement, programming of CNC board drilling and component insertion equipment.

■ auxiliary view

a view derived from any image plane other than the frontal, horizontal or profile planes. Auxiliary views are usually termed primary or secondary, depending on whether or not they are perpendicular to one of the above-mentioned primary projection planes. Primary auxiliary views are termed depth, height or width auxiliaries, depending on the dimension transferred from the measuring view.

■ availability

refers to the extent to which an audience is able to make use of a mass communication medium. In order to use a newspaper, for example, a person must be able to read. Thus, newspapers are not available to illiterate individuals. Similarly, television is only available to those who possess TV sets.

■ a-wind and b-wind

this is the emulsion position of the film. There are two possibilities, just as there are two sides to a piece of film. Camera original is B-Wind. A print struck from it will be A-Wind. This is because film is printed emulsion against emulsion. To tell if a piece of film is A-Wind or B-Wind hold it up with the emulsion facing you. If it is A-Wind the image will read correctly, if it is B-Wind it will be mirror image. A-Wind and B-Wind material usually cannot be mixed, unless you don't mind things being mirror image or some material being soft in focus as a result of being printed base-to-emulsion (the solution is usually optical printing). But mostly, issues of A-Wind and B-Wind do not come up all that frequently. It usually only comes up when you have just completed your sound mix and the mixing house asks if you need a B-Wind track. If it is to be used with the negative from your camera the answer is 'yes'.

■ AX.25

the user level of Packet Radio (AX.25) is Level 2. The protocol or data 'envelope' set aside for use in Amateur Packet Radio. The envelope contains the callsign of the originating station, the callsign of the target Packet station, synchronising, addressing, control and error-checking characters. It is transmitted as a single 'frame' and designated as an AX.25 Packet. AX.25 amateur packet radio link level protocol that borrows the link layer from X.25 (also known as 'LAPB'), modifies it and tacks a datagram-style address/routing header on front

■ B2B

B2B stands for 'business-to-business' as in businesses doing business with other businesses. The term is most commonly used in connection with e-commerce and advertising, when you are targeting businesses as opposed to consumers.

■ back channel

a means of communication from users to content providers. Today, a simple type of back channel is an Internet connection using a modem.

■ backbone

1. a backbone is a system of links where nodes may communicate without interfering with or being interfered with by local access and where data may be passed in a fashion and with hardware that is optimised for passing data, rather than optimised for user stations.
2. a high-speed line or series of connections that forms a path to a large within a Network.

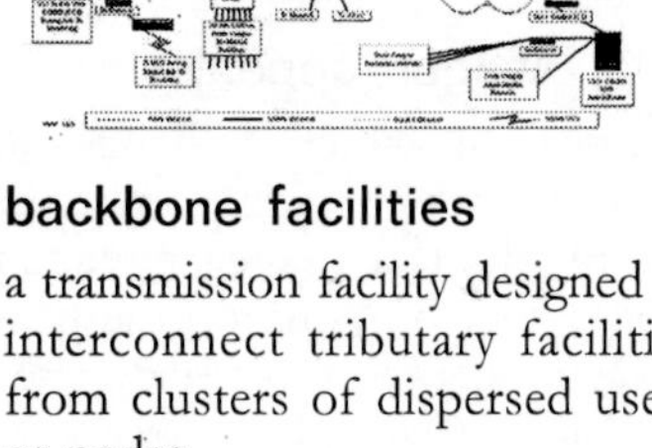

■ backbone facilities

a transmission facility designed to interconnect tributary facilities from clusters of dispersed users or nodes.

■ **backgrounder**

an in-depth document that explains a product, service or company in the context of its need, place in the industry and place in history, often supports and explains an accompanying press release.

■ **backwind**

rewinding film in the camera to shoot a Double Exposure.

■ **bait-and-switch advertising**

an illegal advertising strategy in which the seller baits customers by an advertisement with a low-priced model of a product but then switches customers who seek to buy the product to a much higher-priced model by telling them that the cheaper model does not work well or is no longer in stock.

■ **balance stripe**

a second stripe found on 35mm stripe mag stock and super-8 sound film to prevent warping.

■ **balun**

a form of impedance-matching transformer primarily to match radio antennas to unbalanced coax.

■ **band**

in analog transmission, it represents the range of frequencies between two defined limits.

■ **bandwagon appeals**

appeals in which audiences are urged to support a cause, purchase a product, engage in certain behaviour or 'jump on the bandwagon' because everybody else is doing so. (Example: A commercial urges children to buy particular toys because all of the children have one.)

■ **bandwidth**

1.it denotes how much information (text, images, video, sound) can be sent through a connection. Usually measured in bits-per-second. A full page of text is about 16,000 bits. A fast modem can move approximately 15,000 bits in one second. Full-motion full-screen video requires about 10,000,000 bits-per- second depending on compression.
2.the numerical difference between the upper and lower frequencies of a band of electromagnetic radiation, especially an assigned range of radio frequencies.
3.the complete range of frequencies over which a circuit or electronic system is allocated to function. In transmission, the U.S. analog and digital television channel bandwidth is 6 MHz. Bandwidth is the amount of spectrum available to each communications licensee.

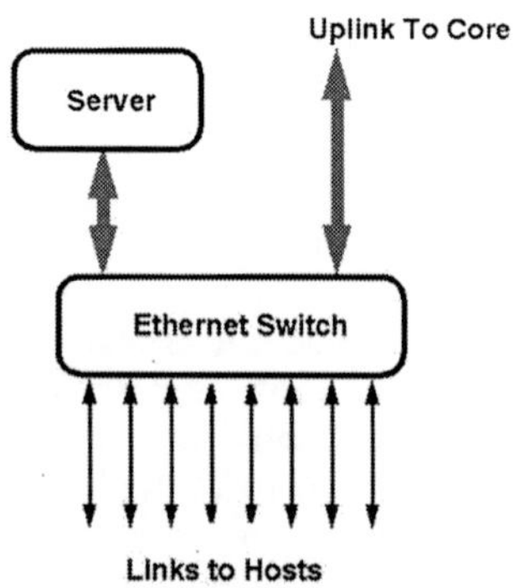

Edge-Switch Server Bandwidth

banner

a print media term for a headline for a story of unusual importance, stretching the entire width of the page.

banner ads

type of advertising found on web pages.

barney

a quilted cosy that fits around a camera to reduce camera noise. Generally it is only effective on a camera that is pretty quiet to begin with. The term comes from barney blanket, a kind of horse blanket.

base

film has two basic elements: The base is the clear, perforated strip and the emulsion is the thin, light-sensitive layer that is glued onto it.

base line

summaries of international development trend data.

base band

in Packet Radio communications, the total frequency band occupied by the aggregate of all the data signals used to modulate a carrier. In LANs, a physical transmission path using direct digital signalling, usually at a rate stated in megabits per second.

battery backup

usually associated with the internal TNC lithium cell used to maintain the information stored in the TNC's RAM. This battery backup holds the 'user configuration' while the TNC is OFF. Other forms of battery backup is the power source that supplies power to a station or site when utility power is removed or fails. This power source is sometimes called 'emergency or auxiliary power'.

baud

1. a unit of signalling speed. The speed in Baud is the number of discrete conditions or signal elements per second. If each signal event represents only one bit condition, then Baud is the same as bits per second otherwise, it is not equal to per second. Another method of expressing 'baud' is the unit of digital signal speed equal to the number of events per second.

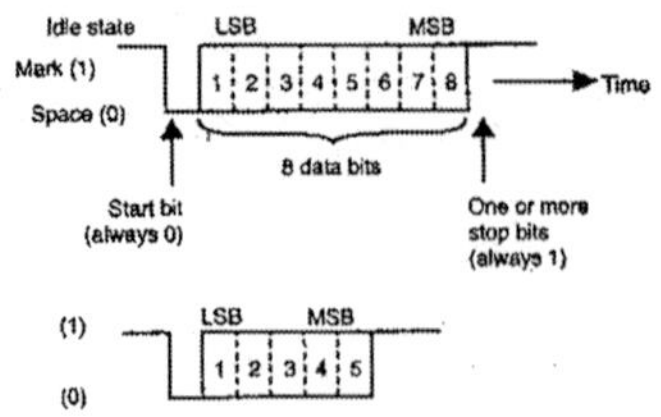

2. a unit of signalling speed equal to the number of signal events per second. Baud is equivalent to bits per second in cases where each signal event represents exactly one bit.

■ baud rate

the speed at which data is transmitted over a communications line, used to transmit data between devices, such as computer-to-computer or computer-to-terminal.

■ baudot

a 5 bit code used in RTTY communications. Named after J. Baudot, an early French inventor of telegraphic instruments. Compare with: ASCII which is an 8 bit code capable of coding 256 characters instead of 32 for Baudot.

■ bayonet

a type of lens mount commonly used with heavier lenses, such as zoom lenses. In contrast to screw-mount lenses, bayonet lenses are attached to the camera with a locking mechanism. Bayonet lenses can typically be changed much faster than screw-mount lenses.

■ BBS

Bulletin Board System. This is a server which is accessed by packet stations to be a repository for messages and files. These messages and files can be accessed by a packet operator who connects to the BBS. BBS also have a capability called Forwarding which may be used to transfer files between BBSs.

■ beam

a directional antenna. Beams are usually made of aluminium and are constructed from a horizontal length of tubing having between 4 and 16 1/2 wave length aluminium elements. Beams for packet radio usually cost between $50 and $100. The key features of a beam are:
1. Directionality
2. Gain.
In this case, Gain means less power and signal is wasted in the direction away from where the beam is pointed. The main lobe power is concentrated in the direction the beam is pointed.

■ bench-bar-press guidelines

informal agreements among lawyers, judges, police officials and journalists about what should and should not be published or broadcast about a criminal suspect or criminal case before a trial is held.

■ best light

similar to a One Light, but by implication, the timer has gone through the film more thoroughly in selecting a timing light that will agree with the majority of the footage.

■ best-seller list

ranking of best-selling books based on retail sales.

■ betacam

an analog video taping system using a 1/2-inch tape cassette. Digital versions include Digital Betacam and Betacam SX.

■ beware surveillance

a media function that occurs when the media inform the public of short-term, long-term or chronic threats.

■ bias

an inclination toward something that is either deliberately inserted or is systemic, that is, reflects the logical if unintended consequences of how information is arranged.

■ bias cutting

the second step in the manufacture of film. Process of cutting oriented film in a continuous spiral to obtain molecular orientation at a 45° angle to the roll. Similar to peeling an apple in one piece.

■ bid

Bulleting Identification: Usually applied to BBS bulletins that are forwarded across a Packet network. The purpose is to identify or track the bulletin (—e.g., source).

■ billboard

a large outdoor printed sign. Costs for a specific billboard are determined by the amount of traffic that passes its location, plus the board's size and visibility.

■ billings

total sale of broadcast airtime.

■ biltmore agreement

settled the press war between newspapers, which had refused their services to their electronic competitors and radio.

■ bin

see **trim bin**.

■ bipolar

in communications, the predominant line signalling method used for base band digital, zero and one values are represented by positive and negative voltages respectively, as in ' polar ' telegraph circuits. In high-speed integrated circuit electronics, a similar technique used for transmission within a CMOS chip is typified by the Bipolar CMOS .

■ bit duration

the time taken for one bit to pass a point on a transmission link. Also called: bit length, bit time, bit interval, bit period.

■ bit oriented

descriptive of data communications protocols using a control byte rather than embedded control characters or control messages as well as having a high degree of transparency to codes used for messages. Typified by IBM's SDLC and the CCITT's HDLC of X.25 packet networks.

■ bitcasters

'radio stations' that can be accessed only over the World Wide Web.

■ black leader or black emulsion leader

black leader is black, opaque film, often specifially called black emulsion leader. It is what the negative cutter uses when preparing A&B rolls. It is very important that it be emulsion leader rather than plastic leader when used for A&B rolls, since plastic leader cannot be cement spliced. It also must be very opaque, not any black piece of film will do.

■ blanking

the brief period in the television scanning process when the electron beam returns from the right to left or from the bottom to top of the screen, rendering the video signal invisible. It is during the blanking interval that closed-captioning and teletext occurs.

■ bleed

printing to the very edge of the page so that there is no margin around the add. Some publishers charge a 15% premium for this type of printing since it reduces the speed of the press and creates printed waste material.

■ blimp

a fibreglass housing used to encase a noisy camera to make it suitable for sync sound filming.

■ blimped camera or self-blimped camera

the term is used not to mean a camera in a blimp, but a camera that is designed with internal soundproofing without the need for an external blimp. For instance, with an Arri BL the 'BL' stands for 'blimped'.

■ blind spot

an area where radio reception is weak or nonexistent.

■ blind stamp

a blind stamp is an embossed seal impressed without ink onto a print as a distinguishing mark by the artist, the publisher, an institution or a collector.

■ blister pack

a display package in which clear plastic seals the product, which rests against a 'backer' sheet, usually made of card stock.

■ block

a (wood) block is a piece of wood used as a matrix for a print. Wood blocks are used primarily for woodcuts or wood engravings.

■ block booking

a policy of major film studios that required theatre owners to show several of a studio's low-quality films before they could receive the same studio's top-quality films.

block error rate (BLER)

the ratio of number of blocks transmitted to the number of blocks containing errors, a user-oriented measure of data transmission quality. Synonymous with 'frame error rate' in digital communications line systems.

blow down

the actual term for the opposite of a blow up is a Reduction Print, but this term has been coined by Colourlab in Rockville, Maryland, for a reduction print made from super 16mm to regular 16mm, as an alternative to the much more expensive process of blowing up super 16mm to 35mm.

blow up

an optical enlargement of a film from one gauge to another, such as 16mm up to 35mm. The opposite of a blow up is a Reduction Print.

blur

to distort the current selection or image by reducing contrast along object lines with gradients.

boilerplate

1. a brief paragraph stating who you are, what you do and how you do it, usually used as the first paragraph in a biography or last paragraph in a news release.
2. standard wording about a company that usually appears near the bottom of all company-issued press releases.

bond, bonding

a large sum of money given by a publisher to a government to be held to ensure good behaviour. Should the publisher violate a government rule, the bond is forfeited to the government and the newspaper or magazine cannot be published again until a new bond is posted.

book

a talent agency's listing, with pictures of actors and models.

booker

the staffperson at a TV, radio or cable station who responds to pitch letters when an appearance needs to be arranged or 'booked'.

booking

a scheduling of the talent and staff that will work on a shoot or photo session.

boot

to start a computer or system, to load an operating system into a computer and begin operation.

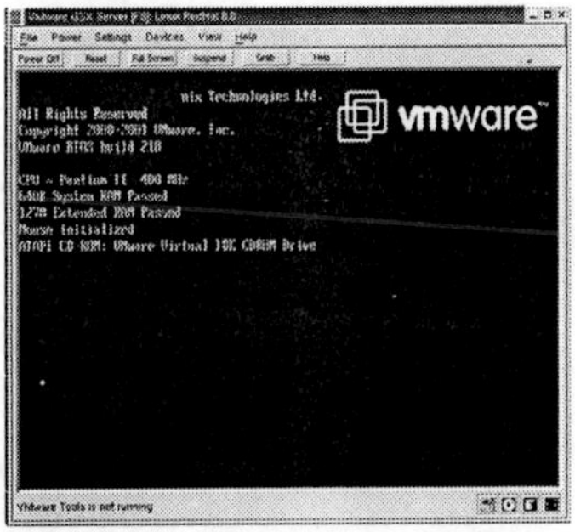

BPA

Business Publications Audit of Circulation, Inc. A non-profit organisation, which audits specialised business publications.

BPP

bits Per Pixel. An acronym for the number of bits used to represent the colour value of each pixel in a digital image colour format. example: CMYK=32bpp, RGB true colour =24bpp,256 colour & greyscale=8bpp, 16color=4bpp, B&W line art=1bpp.

bracketing

the filming of several takes of the same shot at different f-stops to achieve the desired result. Usually this technique is applied to shooting titles much more than anything else. (It is a good idea to film a few frames of black in-between, since it is sometimes difficult to tell where the camera was stopped.)

brand/branding

branding is applying a value to a commodity that is distinctive and valued. Brands are certain highly valued images that become associated with a particular manufacturer or distributor of goods.

break

in Packet and data transmission systems, a timed interruption of about 300 milliseconds, often intended to interrupt a distant transmitting station.

breakout node

this is a node that is capable of handling multiple links. In many cases packet nodes have been installed in places where several radios or backbone links are not allowed, such as on high mountains of great commercial value. A breakout node holds no special purpose except it is a node that has proven to be expandable.

bridge

in Packet networks, a set of nodes (2 or more) may be interfaced to form a bridge or gateway (node-stack) between frequencies or baud rates. In LANs, an electronic device providing a logical connection path between two LAN segments.

brightness

refers to the reflectance and whiteness of a sheet of paper. Higher brightness papers are more expensive to produce and are usually associated with higher quality.

brightness & contrast balancing

the process of adjusting the density and intensity of an image.

broadband

increased bandwidth for Internet connections, which speeds up downloads.

broadcasting

producing and designing media content to appeal to a broad audience segment and offered on airways to a large number of people. The technology of broadcasting only applies to content carried through the airwaves.

■ broadsheets

full-size newspapers. They are thought to provide more serious coverage, compared with *tabloids* or half-size papers that are perceived to be more sensationalistic in coverage.

■ brochure

a folded leaflet with an advertising or promotional message.

■ b-roll

film or television footage that plays while an announcer speaks over it.

■ browsers

type of software that lets individuals search for content on the World Wide Web.

■ BSQ

a digital/data communications protocol used to send binary files via packet radio.

■ bullet theory

a commonsense theory, much debunked, that people are passive recipients of media information. That media can touch people and change them directly.

■ Bulletin Board System (BBS)

a communicating computer equipped so as to provide informational messages, file storage and transfer and a degree of message exchange to allow use by Packet Radio users. e.g MBL, FBB, AA4RE etc. BBS programs.

■ bumper sticker

an advertising strip attached to an automobile bumper.

■ burst

in data communications, an event containing a number of elements, as in a burst of errors in other communications, a term descriptive of the intermittent occurrence of errors.

■ bus

a common physical conductor, to which several units of compatible type are connected in parallel, sharing use of the bus.

■ bus card

an advertising poster attached to the side or back of a bus.

■ Business Reply Card (B.R.C.)

a pre-printed postcard enabling direct mail recipients to respond easily. Direct mail offers that include BRCs have a much higher response rate.

■ Business-To-Business (B-To-B)

communications or commerce between companies (as distinguished from dealings between a company and a consumer), frequently conducted through trade journals.

■ business-to-business advertising

advertising directed not at the general public but at other businesses.

■ busy hours

prime time, that period of hours when connections are most in demand in a Packet Radio network.

■ button

an Internet advertisement that is smaller than the normal banner ad.

■ buzz

media and public attention given to a company, its products or services.

■ byline

the name printed below the title of a newspaper or magazine article, crediting the author.

■ bypass

the connection of two customer locations circumventing use of the Packet Switched Network, particularly locally.

■ c -band

a portion of the electromagnetic spectrum used heavily microwave and satellite transmission frequencies in the region of 4 to 6 Gigahertz.

■ C.R.

abbreviation for Camera Roll.

■ C.T.B.

stands for Colour Temperature Blue. This is an abbreviation for the colour correction gels used in lighting to convert the colour temperature from tungsten to daylight. They come in gradients: Quarter Blue, Half Blue, Full Blue.

■ C.T.O.

stands for Colour Temperature Orange. This is an abbreviation for the colour correction gels used in lighting to convert the colour temperature from daylight to tungsten. They come in gradients: Quarter Orange, Half Orange, Full Orange.

■ cable guards

metal shields or 'skirts' on a camera pedestal that sweep cables out of the way so the camera doesn't roll over them.

■ cable modem

1. a data modem that uses the bandwidth of a given cable system. Because cable modems provide Internet access over cable, they are much faster than modems that use typical phone lines.
2. device which converts computer data to a high-speed signal

that be carried by cable TV system.

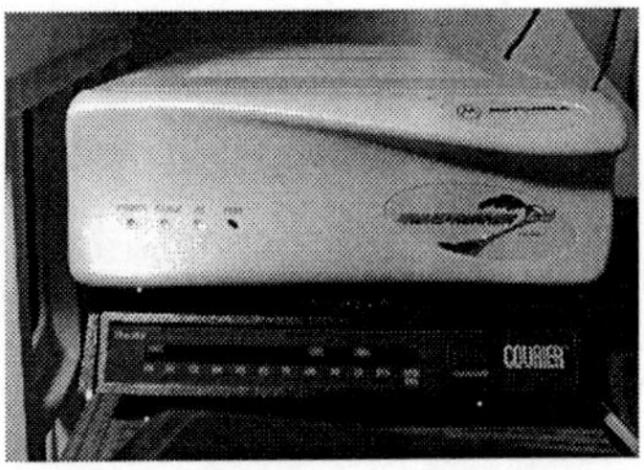

■ **cable ready**

TV or VCR with a tuner able to pick up the added cable TV channels without the need of a converter box.

■ **cable sync**

a somewhat archaic method of sync sound shooting, where a cable runs from a Pilottone generator in the camera to the tape recorder.

■ **cable television**

non-broadcast, point-to-point transmission of television programming by coaxial or fibre optic cable. Used for programming intended for a more limited audience than over-the-air broadcast television.

■ **cable TV**

a television system by which a single, with antenna or satellite dish receives signals from distant stations and transmits those signals by direct cable to the persons subscribing to the system.

■ **cablecasting**

the delivery of media content through underground or overhead cables. Refers only to the technology of cable, but content production and design resembles narrowcasting.

■ **cache**

1. a quick buffer - high-speed memory that is used to store data quick access.
2. storage of digital data (video, audio, text, etc.).

■ **calliper**

the thickness of a sheet of paper or other print media.

■ **cam**

computer-aided manufacturing, the operation of a machine controlled by a host computer.

■ **cam head**

a type of pan head for a camera mount. Commonly associated with studio cameras. Pan and tilt actions are controlled by variable drag adjustments.

■ **camcorder**

an all-in-one *cam*era and re*corder*.

■ **camel's-hair brush**

brush made of soft camel's hair, often used for removing dust from lenses.

■ **cameo background**

a totally black background.

■ **cameo lighting**

the use of special lighting with a dark background so that subjects appear as if they are being photographed against a totally black background.

■ **camera blocking**

working out camera and talent positions and movements prior to the taping of a show.

■ **camera car**

a car or truck with a camera mount, used for the taping of scenes while the vehicle is in motion.

■ **camera cards**

graphic cards designed to be picked up by a camera.

■ **camera chain**

a complete camera system: camera, cables, video controls and power supply.

■ **camera core**

a 2 inch Core.

■ **camera cue light**

tally light. A red light on the camera that indicates when it is or-the-air or being recorded.

■ **camera head**

the actual television camera which is at the 'head' of a chain of camera-related electronics.

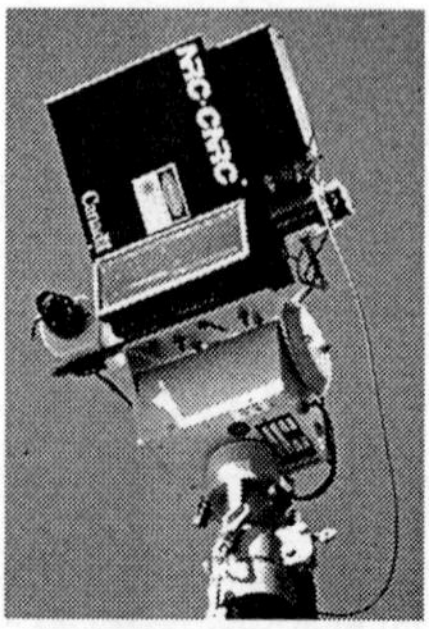

■ **camera jib**

remotely-operated, crane-like camera mount which can typically move a camera from floor or ground level to a height of 10 or more feet.

■ **camera left and right**

directions given from the camera's point of view. The reverse of 'stage left' and 'stage right', used in theatre.

■ **camera light**

a light normally mounted on the top of a camera to provide added illumination.

■ **camera noise**

the sound of the camera running. Even supposedly quiet cameras will make some noise.

■ **camera of record**

videotaping an event as it happens, generally without effects or production embellishments. Intended only as a 'raw record' of the event.

■ **camera operator**

the person who records and frames the images in the video or film production process, usually with the guidance of a director.

■ **camera original**

a slightly more adamant way of saying Original.

■ **camera prompter**

an electrical device for displaying a script that can be read by talent during a production. Also called

TelePrompTer.

■ **camera rehearsal**

rehearsal using cameras, designed to make final checks before a production.

■ **camera reports**

a form of paperwork used to log shots and takes and put down any notes either to the lab or for future organisation in the editing stage. There is generally one camera report per camera roll. Camera reports can be used to communicate specific timing requests to the lab (for instance, if a shot if lit with unusual colour gels, this can be noted to let the timer know not to correct the colour). Camera reports are extremely helpful to analyse any problem with the footage, since they provide a written record of the coverage (the least of which is that if the slate has the wrong information written on it, which happens now and then, a note can be made in the camera reports to keep the assistant editor from getting confused.

■ **camera roll**

each roll that you shoot becomes a camera roll. It is often helpful to label them with a number in the order that they were shot. The usual way is with the abbreviation C.R. followed by a number. The lab will then assemble and print them in that order. This makes things less confusing when you first get back your footage.

■ **camera stock**

this is film. It is also called camera stock to distinguish it from Print Stock.

■ **camera tape**

cloth tape specifically for use on film shoots, much like gaffer's tape. Camera tape is typically 1 inch wide and white so that it can be used together with a sharpie for labelling magazines with the emulsion type and camera roll number. It is valid to use the terms gaffer's tape and camera tape interchangeably (they are both really the same type of tape) depending on how the tape is being used. It is designed not to leave a sticky residue behind on the camera.

■ **camera tube**

the primary light-sensitive glass tube in a tube-based video camera that converts the light image from the camera lens into an electrical signal.

■ **campaign**

the total planned, coordinated sales

effort on behalf of a specific client or product, often multimedia in nature and run over a period of time. Motto Advertising has created numerous award-winning campaigns for its clients.

■ **candidate access rule**

section 312 of the Federal Communications Act, which forbids a broadcaster from instituting an across-the-board policy that denies all candidates for federal office the opportunity to use the station to further a political campaign.

■ **canned**

the term to describe material that is recorded for repeated use on television or radio.

■ **canon connector**

a shielded, three-pin audio connector. Generally used with professional microphones. More commonly called an XLR connector.

■ **canted camera**

camera angle achieved by turning the camera slightly to one side causing the subject matter to run up or down hill. Result is also referred to as *Dutch angle*.

■ **canvas drop**

a canvas background that can be lowered into place from the studio grid.

■ **cap up**

to cover the lens of a camera.

■ **capacitor**

electronic device that can store an electric charge. A central part of a condenser microphone.

■ **capstan**

a motor-driver roller and rotating shaft in the VTR that pulls the tape over the heads.

■ **captioning service**

organisation that encodes open or closed captions (text) into TV video - often for display and reading by hearing impaired.

■ **capture**

digitising segments of analog video for editing on a non-linear editing system. Sometimes relates to acquiring or displaying the beginning and ending frames of scenes for on-screen reference.

■ **cardioid pattern**

a microphone with a heart-shaped pattern of sensitivity.

■ **carrier sheet**

the sheet to which labels are temporarily attached. Usually this sheet has a 'slick' feeling or appears shiny.

■ **carrier system**

a transmission system capable of providing multiple communications channels over a single physical path.

■ **carrier wave**

an electromagnetic wave modulated with audio or video information used to broadcast radio and television signals.

■ cart cartridge

a plastic container with audio or videotape that threads automatically when inserted into a record or playback machine. In contrast to a cassette, the tape is commonly in a continuous loop.

■ cascading

the flow of a signal through a sequence of electronic stages, each stage adding an additional effect.

■ case reporter(s)

a book (or books) containing a chronological collection of the opinions rendered by a particular court for cases that were decided by the court.

■ cassette

a plastic container with a supply and take-up reel of audio or videotape that threads automatically when placed in a record or playback machine. Unlike the cartridge, the tape is not in a continuous loop and must be rewound.

■ catadiatropic lens, cat lens

a telescopic lens that uses an internal mirror to reduce the physical length of the lens.

■ catalogue

an illustrated booklet listing products or services available.

■ catalogue albums

albums more than three years old.

■ catalogue raisonne

a documentary listing of all the works by an artist which are known at the time of compilation. It should include all essential documentary information.

■ catchlight

a small, concentrated reflection from a major light source which appears in a subject's eyes.

■ Cathode Ray Tube (CRT)

any video screen employing an electron gun used for displaying information. TV sets, computer monitors and vectorscopes all have CRT's.

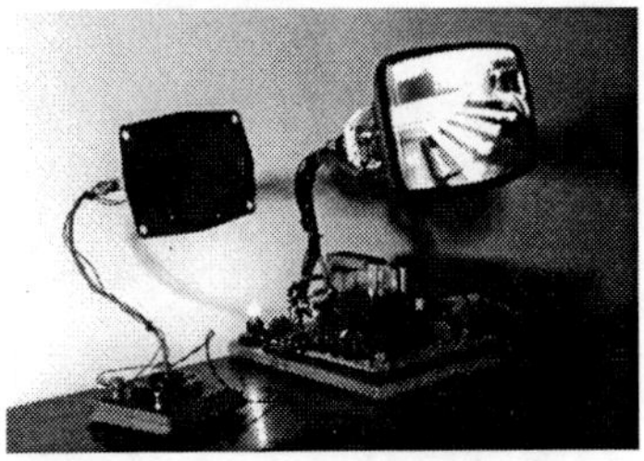

■ CATV

Cable Television. Relaying a television service using optical fibre or coaxial cable.

■ causality

the arrangement of scenes in editing to suggest cause and effect relationships.

■ c-band

the frequency band from 4-6 Ghz, used mainly for distribution of television signals to terrestrial relay transmitters.

■ CCD

Charge Coupled Device. A solid-state camera imaging device that has a number of advantages over camera tubes.

■ c-clamp

c-shaped clamp with tightening set screw that's used to hang lighting instruments from the ceiling grid of TV studio.

■ CCTV

Closed Circuit Television. Any wired system for television distribution.

■ CCU

Camera Control Unit Electronic. Controls for a camera where colour correction, luminance, etc., are adjusted. CCUs for studio cameras are generally found in the video control room.

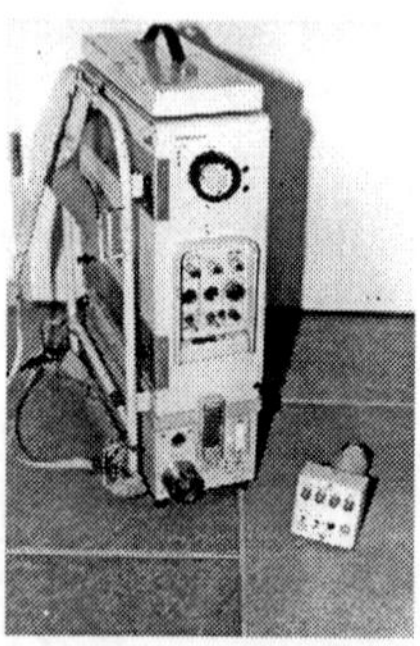

■ CD

Compact Disc. An audio recording and playback medium that uses digitally encoded information on a laserdisc. The sound is decoded by optical laser for high-quality audio playback.

■ CD- DA track

a track on a compact disc containing audio information encoded according to the CD-Digital Audio specific.

■ CD-I

Compact Disc Interactive. An interactive audio/video/computer system developed by famous companies for the consumer market.

■ CD-ROM

Compact Disk Read Only Memory. A device that uses a rigid disk to store information in a form that can be read by a computer.

■ CD-ROM XA

Compact Disc Read Only Memory Extended Architecture.

A format for recording compressed digital audio at lower qualities, allowing capacity increases on a single CD from four to 19 hours.

■ CD-RTOS

Compact Disc Real-Time Operating System. The name of the operating system used in CD-I players.

■ CD-WORM

Compact Disc Write Once Read Many times. A type of CD-ROM disc named for the process used to create data on the disc. CD-WORM Discs perform identically as CD-ROM discs. The difference being a laser is used to 'burn' the reflective layer to create the data tract. The cost of 'WORM Burning' is considerably less than glass master production for a single disc. CD-WORM Disks can be used to transport CD-ROM titles for mastering and replication.

■ CD-WREM

Compact Disc Write Read Erase Memory. A data storage system commonly referred to as 'Magneto-Optical'. It incorporates laser technology to 'Burn' a magnetic layer on the disc, this produces a reflective surface that can then be read. This magnetic layer can be burned many times giving the medium read, write and write over capability not found in CD- ROM & CD-WREM. This advantage comes only with considerable cost for Drives and Disc Cartridges. As a result this technology has not caught on in the home consumer market. It has great potential for multimedia, pre-press publication and other digital graphic applications.

■ cease-and-desist order

a Federal Trade Commission order notifying an advertiser that a certain practice violates the law. Failure to comply with a cease-and-desist order can result in fines being levied against the advertiser.

■ cel

a transparent sheet for use in animation on which individual drawings appear. Multiple cels (cel sandwiches) may be overlaid to build scenes and to eliminate the need to redraw areas.

■ cel animation

animating portions of an image through the use of multiple layers (cels) of transparent acetate sheets. Specific types of content are confined to specific cell layers.

■ cell

one frame of animation, usually a single cartoon or picture.

■ cement splice

a type of splice used primarily by negative cutters. In a cement splice the two pieces of film overlap each other and are fused together with film cement.

■ censorship

the practice of suppressing a text or part of a text that is considered objectionable according to certain standards.

■ centre spot filter

a diffusion filter with a clear central area. Gives a clear central area and slightly diffuses surrounding areas.

■ CG

Character Generator. A device that electrically creates letters and symbols for TV titles and other graphic displays.

■ CGA

Colour Graphics Adapter. A relatively low-resolution colour display system for PC-type computers.

■ CGI

Common Gateway Interface- a specification for how information can be transferred between web server and a CGI program. CGI-script is among other used for websites that offer input from users e.g. a questionnaire.

■ CGMS

Copy Generation Management System. Copyright protection method of making it impossible for most people to copy a DVD.

■ challenge for cause

the request by a litigant in a criminal or civil case that a juror be dismissed for a specific reason.

■ change of venue

moving a trial to a distant community in order to find jurors who have not read or viewed prejudicial publicity about the defendant.

■ changing bag

a double chambered black bag with a zipper on one end and two elasticised arm holes on the other side, used for loading film into magazines.

■ channel

the pathway by which a message travels from sender to receiver.

■ channel surfing

the practice of scanning a series of television channels to find something that catches the eye or to avoid commercials. Made possible by the remote control, it now occupies some viewers for entire evenings, wreaking havoc on advertisers and programmers. Surfing is one reason programming practices such as seamless transitions from one show to the next and splitting 30-second commercials into two 15-second halves have become prevalent.

■ channelisation

division of a larger capacity channel into a number of smaller channels for use by multiple functions.

■ chapter / chapter stop

a code, embedded in a videodisc that indicates where segments begin. While scanning, the player will sense these, which speeds the process of locating segments.

■ character

a unit of typographic information, usually variable as part of a language. Because data is handled and transferred as a series of characters the term also can mean one bit pattern in a specific data code. Often referred to as a 'word' in the computer programming sense. In their nature, these characters are 8-bit 'words' conveying the instantaneous amplitude level of their transported signal.

character make-up

make-up (generally accompanied by hair pieces, etc.) designed to change an actor's appearance into that of the character being played.

character oriented

descriptive of a Packet Radio communications protocol or transmission procedure that has control information transmitted in the form of special bytes called control characters.

characterisation

the development of characters in a narrative. Characters can be well developed (round characters) or poorly developed and stereotyped (flat characters).

charge back

charging studio costs to another division of the same company.

charger

an electrical, AC-to-DC device which replenishes (recharges) battery power.

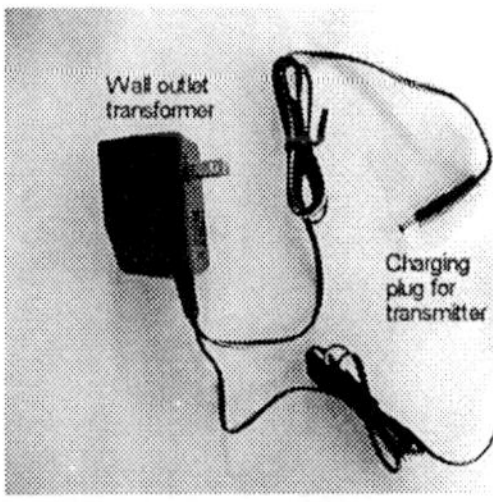

cheat

when the camera is set up for a second shot at a different angle it is possible to move things around a little to improve the new composition, the difference in perspective and angle of the two shots hiding the fact that things are not exactly in the same place. Both actors and furniture on the set can be cheated. The term is often used as cheating something 'into' a shot or 'out of' a shot, as in telling an actor 'We're going to cheat you in a little' and having them stand a little to one side so more of them is in the shot.

check print

this is a print made from an internegative or an optical to verify the quality and success of an effect.

chiaroscuro woodcut

a form of woodcut involving several blocks in which one or more of the blocks is used to print large areas of tone. Typically, a chiaroscuro woodcut will involve a line block to indicate the outlines of the composition and tone blocks with areas carved out to create highlights by allowing the white of the paper to show through. The final effect is similar to an ink wash drawing with highlights and line drawing.

child-resistant packaging

packaging that accomplishes the purpose of the Poison Prevention Packaging Act of 1970, to protect young children from accidental ingestions of potentially hazardous household products. Valéron Strength Film is considered the benchmark in child-resistant packaging, offering proven performance and an extremely sturdy, tear and tamper-resistant package. Film-based package fails to meet federal child-resistant protocol standards.

■ chine applique (chine colle) prints

a chine applique or chine colle is a print in which the image is impressed onto a thin sheet of China paper which is backed by a stronger, thicker sheet. China paper takes an intaglio impression more easily than regular paper, so chine applique prints generally show a richer impression than standard prints. Proof prints are often done as chine appliques.

■ chip camera

a camera that uses one or more CCD's.

■ chip chart

a test chart consisting of shades of grey from TV white to TV black used for setting up cameras.

■ chroma

colour.

■ chroma channels

the separate light-sensitive pickup devices or colour circuits in a TV camera. Typically there are three channels: red, green and blue.

■ chroma crawl

an undesirable moving colour artefact or pattern in an NTSC picture. Generally caused by a television set decoding colour information as high-detailed luminance information.

■ chroma gain

camera control that controls the amounts of colour in a picture.

■ chroma key blue

a deep shade of blue commonly used in backgrounds which is intended to be keyed out and replaced with other video. See **chroma key**.

■ chroma keying

facility to replace selected colours in a video image with others that allows the creation of different scenes against the background. Some video boards contain such capabilities.

■ chroma processor

a computer program associated with desktop editing programs that can subtly or drastically alter colours and colour balance in sources of video.

■ chroma resolution

as distinct from luminance detail, the amount of detail in colour channels.

■ chroma key

an electronic matting effect that keys out or removes a portion of video of a specific colour. Another video source is then substituted for the removed area. Generally, a deep, saturated blue is used as a keying colour.

■ chromatic aberration

colour fringing or other colour

abnormalities caused by imperfections in a camera lens.

■ chrominance

signals of an image system that represent the colour components of the image such as hue and saturation. A black and white image has chrominance value of zero.

■ chromolithograph

a colour lithograph usually involving a large number of lithographic stones to allow a complex colour separation (at least three colours). The term is often used to describe late nineteenth-century colour lithographs that emulate or reproduce paintings.

■ chyron

a piece of equipment that allows video editors to insert text and graphics over the video picture or within the video frame.

■ CI forums

electronic discussion forums initiated by The Communication Initiative.

■ cinch marks

not to be confused with sync marks. Cinch marks are small vertical scratches on a roll of film that are caused when the end of the film is pulled to tighten the roll, causing any dust on the film to make a small scratch. Too much drag on the supply while rewinding is one common way that cinching can occur.

■ Cinching

The wrinkling or folding over, of tape on itself in a loose tape pack. Normally occurs when a loose tape pack is stopped suddenly, causing outer tape layers to slip past inner layers, which in turn causes a buckling of tape in the region of slip. Results in large dropouts or high error rates.

■ cinemascope

the first modern wide screen movie format. It achieved a 2.35:1 aspect ratio by using a 2:1 anamorphic lens.

■ circuit

as applied to Packet Radio. A path including any needed supervisory and signalling or conditioning equipment for the transmission of digital signals. In the network a circuit is an assigned connection between two nodes. Each of the two nodes has information to the effect that the circuit exists. The two nodes also have a routing table from which the first element on the path to the other node may be realised but the two nodes do not know all of the intervening nodes. The circuit exists until the destination user or server or the originating user or server disconnects or until one of the two nodes decides that data cannot be sent any longer (due to L4 retry time-out or unchoke failure) or if no data is passed across the circuit during the time set by the no activity time-out. In the recommended network the L4 retry time-out is 5 minutes times 2 retries and the no activity time-out is two hours.

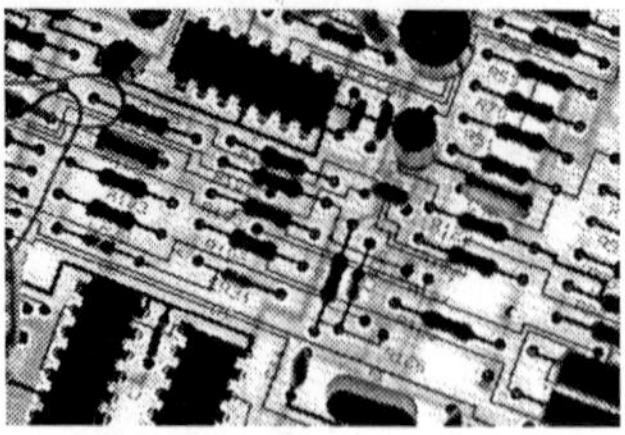

■ **circuit breaker**

an electronic 'fuse' that can be reset after it is overloaded.

■ **circulation**

the total number of copies of a publication delivered to newsstands, vending machines and subscribers.

■ **citation**

the reference to a legal opinion contained in a case reporter that gives the name, volume number and page number where the opinion can be found. The year the opinion was rendered is also included in the citation.

■ **civil complaint**

a written statement of the plaintiff's legal grievance, which normally initiates a civil suit.

■ **clamp light**

a type of lighting fixture designed to hold a screw-in light bulb, with a not-so-dependable spring clamp for mounting on the side of an open door, etc. Often includes an aluminum reflector dish as well.

■ **clapper or clapstick**

the Slate or just the two sticks that are struck together to mark a sync sound take.

■ **classified ad**

a brief listing appearing in a periodical of items for sale and/or services offered, usually arranged by category. Motto Advertising has extensive experience in writing and inserting effective classified ads in newspapers, magazines, on television and the internet.

■ **clean edit**

an edit with no accompanying electronic noise, distortion or other disruption.

■ **clear / in-the-clear**

non-scrambled satellite TV programming.

■ **clearance**

the process of getting permission from a copyright holder to use copyrighted material.

■ **click**

a click is the opportunity for a visitor to be transferred to a location by clicking on an advertisement.

■ **click rate**

the percentage of the ad views that resulted in click throughs.

■ **click through**

a click through occurs when a user clicks from the host Web site through to the advertiser's Web site.

■ **Click Through Rate (CTR)**

this is the percentage of ad views that resulted in an ad click.

■ **client**

an organisation that employs an advertising agency to create advertisements.

■ **client list**

a list of a company's key clients, sometimes includes contact information.

■ **client pays' wire service**

client pays to have his or her own news or feature stories transmitted through print and broadcast media newsrooms at no cost to the media.

■ **cliff edge effect**

an RF (Radio Frequency) characteristic that causes DTV reception to deteriorate dramatically with a small change in signal reception. Bit error rate increases to the point where video cannot be obtained by the receiver. The picture and audio are lost entirely.

■ **clip**

to cut off video levels above a certain point in order to stay within a set contrast ratio. A problem that commonly results in 'chalky whites'.

■ **clip art**

professionally made drawings, generally available on CDs, that can be used in newsletters and various media.

■ **clip bin**

editing screen display in a window that shows video clips that have been digitised and ready of use.

■ **clip link**

DVCAM approach for marking in/out points of raw footage while it's in the camera. Resulting thumbnail images and time code numbers can then be downloaded to the non-linear editor as a guide in digitising only the selected shots.

■ **clip-on mike**

a small personal microphone that can be attached to clothing.

■ **clipper gain knob**

a knob on a video effects unit used to set the threshold level for colour or luminance keying.

■ **clock hour**

radio format that specifies every element of the program.

■ **clock speed**

The speed in MHz at which the computer's central processing unit operates.

■ **clocking**

Repetitive, regularly timed signals used to control Packetised transmissions.

■ **clone**

to duplicate a portion of an image to another location. This is a cornerstone to the editing of digital images. This effect is useful in the process of retouching photographs.

■ **closed captioned**

printed words and dialogue intended for hearing-impaired viewers broadcast along with a TV signal. The term 'closed' means that a special electronic device must be used to decode and display the information.

■ **closed captioning**

text stream included in broadcast signal that provides narrative description of dialogue, action, sounds and other elements of the picture. Most often used by the hearing impaired and in environments where audio is undesirable (such as in restaurants).

■ **closed circuit**

non-broadcast programming. Television that goes to an audience by a direct, point-to-point distribution system.

■ **closed set**

a television studio that is closed to all but specific crew and talent involved in the scene.

■ **close-up lens**

attachment. A lens element that fits over camera lens, allowing it to focus closer than normal.

■ **close-up lens attachment**

a lens element that fits over camera lens, allowing it to focus closer than normal.

■ **CLUT**

Colour Look-Up Table. A table containing all the colours that may be used in a particular picture. Each entry provides an RGB value. The picture may then be encoded using the table entry addresses rather than the direct RGB value.

■ **CMD**

an on screen prompt which is displayed by the TNC. This prompt informs the user that the TNC is in the 'command' mode.

■ **c-mount**

a common type of camera lens mount used on 16mm motion picture cameras and on some video cameras.

■ **co2 powered**

propelling a device with a cylinder of compressed carbon dioxide.

■ **coated lens**

lenses and lens elements having a magnesium-fluoride coating designed to reduce light reflections.

■ **coaxial cable / coax**

an electrical cable designed to carry video signals. It has a central wire core surrounded by an insulator and a braided wire shield.

■ **co-axial magazine**

a type of magazine with two chambers side by side, with the supply and take up rolls rather like wheels mounted on either end of the same axle.

■ **co-channel interference**

interference caused by two or more stations using the same channel (frequency).

■ **code numbers**

inked-on edge numbers, usually added to a workprint and mag track after syncing, so that corresponding sound and picture can always be properly aligned during editing. They are also used for the general organisation of the footage. Sometimes the term edge numbers are used and although this is not incorrect, care should be taken that it is understood that you are talking about the inked-on numbers and not the Latent Edge Numbers.

■ codec

coder-decoder. An electronic circuit for compressing and decompressing video, generally for transmission by telephone lines.

■ codec coder-decoder

an electronic circuit for compressing and decompressing video, generally for transmission by telephone lines.

■ codes

a system of signs whose rules and conventions are shared with others, thus allowing meanings to be generated, circulated and interpreted. The existence of codes enables viewers to distinguish different types of programming from each other (sitcoms from soap operas) or to distinguish programming from *advertising*.

■ coercivity

The level of demagnetising force that would need to be applied to a tape or magnetic particle to reduce the remanent magnetisation to zero. A demagnetising field of a level in excess of the coercivity must be applied to a magnetic particle in order to coerce it to change the direction of its magnetisation. Coercivity is the property of a tape that indicates its resistance to demagnetisation and determines the maximum signal frequency that can be recorded by a tape. Hc is the common abbreviation for coercivity.

■ COFDM

Coded Orthogonal Frequency Division Multiplexing. COFDM can transmit many streams of data simultaneously, each one occupying only a small portion of the total available bandwidth. The DTV standard used in Europe.

■ coherence

a descriptive dimension of light that characterises its hardness or softness. The harder a light source is, the more coherence it is said to have. Professional photographers refer to coherence as light quality.

■ cohesive force

The force that holds a material to itself or together.

■ cohesiveness

See **cohesive force**.

■ collateral bar rule

a rule which bars someone who violates a court order from trying to defend this action by arguing that the court order was unconstitutional.

■ collision

simultaneous transmissions on a Packet LAN that interferes with each other in a contention-based access scheme. It occurs when two or more terminal node controllers (TNC) attempt to transmit at nearly the same instant.

■ colour balance

to adjust the chroma channels in a video camera so that whites in a scene will be reproduced as true white.

■ colour bar generator

device that creates colour bar test signal.

colour bars

a series of coloured bars of established properties used as an electronic standard for adjusting brightness, contrast, colour intensity and colour balance.

colour burst

the colour timing information contained in the TV signal. A 3.58 MHz subcarrier frequency timed to a quarter millionth of a second is used to synchronise colour information to the luminance signal.

colour compatibility

the ability of different colour subject matter to translate into a black and white picture and maintain adequate contrast and separation.

colour conversion filter

a camera filter used to convert light from indoor to outdoor colour temperature.

colour correction

adjustments that alter and correct the tonal and colour qualities of video.

colour lcd

a flat, liquid-quartz-type display which can reproduce a full colour image.

colour phase

as shown on a vectorscope, the electronic phase difference in degrees between the colour standard and specific colours reproduced by video equipment.

colour resolution

the degree to which the combined colour channels in a system can reproduce fine details.

colour separation

a traditional photographic process that uses four film negatives to ultimately create a full-colour printed product. Recent computer innovations have obviated the need for separated film negatives in certain applications.

colour standard

a colour criterion or reference used to set-up colour video equipment.

colour temperature

it is a measurement of the colour of light and important in that film is much more sensitive to colour temperature than our eyes are. It is measured on scale that takes its name from the scientist Lord Kelvin.

colour temperature metre

a measuring device that indicates colour temperature in degrees Kelvin.

colour under

heterodyne-type colour process used in most videocassette recorders. To facilitate recording (with some loss of quality) the basic 3.58MHz colour frequency is converted to a lower frequency.

coloured filter

a glass or plastic material placed either in back or in front of a camera lens to subtract certain colours of light. Used to alter the colours in a scene.

colourimetry

characteristics of colour reproduction. In TV, the range of colours that a system can reproduce.

■ **colourist**

the timer of a video transfer.

■ **colourisation**

adding or modifying the colour in a video image.

■ **colouriser**

an electronic circuit that generates colour which is added to or made to modify an image.

■ **colourising control**

a knob which can move through the entire range of colours. Used to select colours for electronic effects.

■ **colour-subcarrier**

a sub-channel of a broadcast signal designed to add colour information to a basic black-and-white video signal.

■ **column inch**

a unit of space one column wide and one inch deep.

■ **combining**

a production process used to join or add materials together in a permanent or temporary fashion (e.g., glue, nails, screws, welding, soldering).

■ **comet tail**

a smear or black trailing image in video cameras used under certain conditions caused by subject matter in motion.

■ **commentary**

articles, interviews, opinion pieces from people working in development and/or communication.

■ **commercial**

an audio or video advertising announcement, usually presented on television, radio or in a movie theatre.

■ **commercial appropriation**

a legal aspect of invasion of privacy relating to the unauthorised used of the name or likeness of a well-known individual for the personal or economic gain of a third party.

■ **commercial speech doctrine**

the legal doctrine that states truthful advertising for products and services that are not illegal is normally protected by the First Amendment to the U.S. Constitution.

■ **commercial television**

television programs broadcast by local stations whose income is derived from selling time on their facilities to advertisers.

■ **commodification**

a belief that all entities have (or should) a material value and be judged on that basis. Audiences are also regarded as commodities by media industries for sale to advertisers.

■ **common control system**

(a Packet node) an automatic switching system that makes use of common equipment to establish a connection. Once connection is made, the common control equipment is available to establish another connection.

■ **communication**

a transaction involving the meaningful exchange of information between sender and receiver. It entails a process by which messages are encoded, transmitted and decoded and how the message is transformed by this process. The focus in this text is on communication that is 'mediated' by a technology that allows the few to communicate with the many.

■ **communication for development news**

summaries of news articles pertaining to communication with a direct impact on development issues and/or news articles pertaining to using communication for development purposes.

■ **communication process**

conveying a message or idea to someone, in technology education the focus is on the use of visual and electronic media.

■ **communications audit**

a systematic survey of members of a target audience (often members of the media or potential customers) to determine awareness of or reaction to a product, service or company

■ **communist theory**

theory of the press that holds the media and should promote the goals of the ruling political party.

■ **companding**

compression-expanding technique used by audio devices such as wireless microphones to increase dynamic range.

■ **compatibility**

a property in data processing and telecommunications systems permitting exchange of information directly and in usable form. IBM compatible implies identical or interchangeable signals and methodologies on a non-IBM PC as that of a 'true-blue' IBM PC.

■ **compilation editing**

commonly used editing style in documentaries. Continuity can jump around and not adhere to any logical or time-based sequence. In compilation editing continuity is usually provided by narration.

■ **complementary colours**

colours that are opposite to each other on the colour wheel.

■ **complexity editing**

assembling shots with a primary regard to building story or dramatic effect rather than following a logical or temporal sequence.

■ **component**

refers to the use of independent, individually controlled audio or video elements in a single television or audio system. A TV system having a separate monitor, tuner and audio system would be an example.

■ component recording

videotape recording in which the colour information is recorded separately from the luminance and synchronisation information.

■ component signals

In contrast to a composite signal, non-encoded video signals. Typically, refers to separate luminance and chromanance signals.

■ component television

home television systems that consist of a separate video monitor, tuner, audio amplifier and speakers.

■ composite master

final, end product of an editing session including all program elements and special effects.

■ composite signal

a video signal that contains all of the necessary synchronising pulses. A video signal in which the luminance and chrominance information have been combined using a standard such as NTSC, PAL or SECAM. The composite video format is also used for consumer video recording systems.

■ compositing

the process of combining multiple layers of special digital video effects to achieve complex special effects.

■ comprehensive layout

the finished model of a print ad.

■ compression

a digital process that permits data to be stored or transmitted using less than normal the number of bits. Compression is critical for displaying audio and moving video fast enough on desktop computers. Some compression standards for still images are formulated by JPEG, for moving video by MPEG and for telecommunications transmission.

■ computer graphics

the creation of still and animated video through the use of computer-type equipment.

■ computer network

two or more computers linked together with the ability to interact and exchange data.

■ computer platform

a basic desktop computer. Many editing and special effects hardware and software products use a computer as the basis of their systems.

■ **computer program**

a set of instructions in a language understood by a computer, used to direct the operations of a computer.

■ **Computer-Assisted Reporting (CAR)**

skills involved in using the Internet to aid reporting.

■ **concept**

the general idea behind a slogan, pitch or campaign.

■ **concept story**

feature story designed to pique the interest of a certain demographic audience.

■ **concept testing**

a type of feedback in which a one- or two-paragraph description for a new series is presented to a sample of viewers for their reactions.

■ **concurring opinion**

a written opinion by an appellate judge or justice in which the author agrees with the decision of the court but normally states reasons different from those in the court opinion as the basis for his or her decision.

■ **condenser microphone**

a microphone that detects sound by amplifying changes in electrical capacitance between two, closely-spaced plates.

■ **confidence heads**

VCR audio and video playback heads that immediately play back signals after they are recorded. In this way signals can be monitored for quality as recordings are being made.

■ **conflict**

a basic psychological ingredient in news and dramatic productions which has the power to capture and hold audience attention.

■ **conformations**

progressive versions of a film in the editing stage are known as conformations, often identified by date. Conformations are only of any significance on a large production where different editing departments should be sure to be working with the latest conformation.

■ **conforming**

the word to describe the negative cutter's matching of the original to the work print.

■ **conglomerates**

corporations that contain many companies who conduct business along a wide variety of fronts. Linkages among these companies provide both vertical and horizontal monopolistic control.

■ **connected**

the condition that occurs when two Packet stations are described as being 'connected'. The state in which the two station read only those Packets from each other when MCON is OFF.

■ **connote/connotation**

a description of value, meaning or ideology associated with a media text that is added to the text by the audience.

consensus

the word means a generally shared agreement. The term is used in particular by Marxist critics of the media, who argue that the media operate to create a consensus in society (or at least an illusion of consensus) that the norms, laws and rules in the society are the only 'right' ones, which any right-thinking member of society must accept. Thus, for example, those who might operate outside the consensus, such as union 'activists' or 'terrorists' do not normally have their ideas and views presented by the media as if they are 'reasonable'. In order to strengthen the consensus the media periodically whip up moral panics against those deviants ('folk devils') who are deemed to lie outside the central cultural system, e.g. 'welfare scroungers', 'union activists', 'travellers', 'ravers' etc.

consent

a defence in both libel and invasion of privacy cases that provides that individuals who agree to the publication of a libellous story or the appropriation of their name cannot then maintain a lawsuit based on the libel or the appropriation.

consent order or decree

a document in which an individual agrees to terminate a specific behaviour, such as an advertising campaign or to refrain from a specific action, such as making a certain advertising claim.

consequence

the importance or weightiness of a news story.

conservation

using energy efficiently, finding alternatives to existing energy forms, improving energy conversion methods (e.g., reducing friction, engine tune-ups).

consortium

a partnership of a number of TV stations or productions facilities that exchange programming or services. They are generally linked by satellites.

conspiracy theory

with particular reference to the mass media, this view assumes that a small and powerful and often hidden, elite are able to use the mass media to condition and persuade passive audiences into conforming to the powerful elite's wishes. It depends very much on the notion of all-powerful media and easily duped audiences. It is difficult to find evidence that the media really are that powerful and 'conspiracy theory' is often dismissed because it would otherwise sound like some kook who takes the X-Files literally. Nevertheless, it's something close to this that underlies much left-wing criticism of the media.

construct or construction

the process by which a media text is shaped and given meaning through a process that is subject to a variety of decisions and is designed to keep the audience interested in the text.

■ **construction of reality**

in media studies, this idea emphasises that there is no single 'reality', rather a range of definitions of 'reality'. Reality as presented by the mass media is therefore not a picture or reflection of 'reality', but, rather, a constructed interpretation of reality. In the view of 'radical' critics of the media in particular, the mass media plays a crucial role in 'constructing reality' for the rest of us. In the view of many representatives of post-structuralism and post-modernism, just about every aspect of reality seems to be considered a social construction.

■ **consumer**

a private individual at whom advertisements are aimed, a buyer.

■ **consumer advertising**

advertising directed at the general public.

■ **consumer culture**

see **consumerism**.

■ **consumer equipment**

relatively inexpensive audio and video equipment intended for 'home' or non-professional use.

■ **consumer market**

a defined group of consumers.

■ **consumerism**

a lifestyle in which the purchase of commodities is indicative of individual worth and social status. Also implies that the acquisition of material goods may solve personal problems, help achieve goals and foster an identity. A consumer culture can flourish in a society where people are judged on the basis of appearances (what they look like) or possessions (what they own).

■ **contact**

a person who knows about an event and its location and can assist the production team during a telecast.

■ **contact printing**

the method used by the lab to copy film. A contact print is made on a machine called (sensibly enough) a Contact Printer, in which the original film and unexposed print stock are sandwiched together, emulsion against emulsion and are run at a constant speed past a light which shines through the original, exposing the print stock with the same image. All work prints, answer prints and release prints are contact prints. The only other type of printing is Optical Printing, which is usually done to add an effect or to blow up or make a reduction print.

■ **content**

information

■ **content analysis**

the statistical analysis of a range of texts. The results are usually compared with a different set of results from the same range of texts e.g. what proportion of reports about men in the tabloid press represents men as victims and what proportion represents women as victims? or with some 'objective' standard, such as official statistics e.g. what proportion of women in soaps is shown as housewives as against the proportion of women in the population who are housewives. The most serious problem with content analysis is the initial selection of categories. The second most serious problem is where to find your objective standard.

■ contested sites

institutions that are challenged because of demographic, social and political changes. Both society and its institutions are seen as domains ('sites') in which nothing can be taken for granted but everything is up for grabs. For example, the media may be interpreted as a kind of battleground ('site') in which opposing groups with conflicting visions compete with each other over who gets to define content, structure or outputs. Reference to a 'contested site' portrays a reality that is subject to negotiation, compromise and change.

■ contingency fund

a percentage added to the cost of a production budget to take care of delays and production problems.

■ continuity

the seamlessness of detail from one shot to another within a scene. Continuity refers particularly to the physical elements, rather than to the choices in coverage that can result in a lack of seamlessness. Elements of continuity include any actions of the actor, the placement of props, the lighting, the costumes and so on.

■ continuity cutting

an editing approach based on either a temporal or logical sequence that centres on maintaining a smooth flow of events.

■ continuous white balance

automatic camera white balance mode that makes moment-by-moment adjustments in response to changing light conditions.

■ contrast

ratio of light and dark on a scene.

■ contributing reporter or writer

often used to describe a freelance writer.

■ control

methods used to regulate a system or device.

■ control c or ctrl c

this is used to bring a TNC to the 'command' (cmd:) mode from the 'converse' or 'transparent' mode. It is executed by holding the 'control' key down and pressing the 'C' key. In most TNC's it is not necessary to press after executing a Ctrl C.

■ control character

a character inserted into a data stream to notify the receiver of a special function to perform or to identify the purpose of the data or message associated with it. An example of a control character is the Control G. A control 'G' will ring the bell of the connected or target station.

■ **control device**

any device that senses, switches or regulates an operation (e.g., switch, valve, brake).

■ **control mode**

permit command or control actions to occur.

■ **control room**

a room associated with a production studio in which a director, technical director, audio engineer and others work to coordinate and control various sources of audio and video during a production.

■ **control signals**

signals passed between parts of a communications system to oversee operation and configuration of the system.

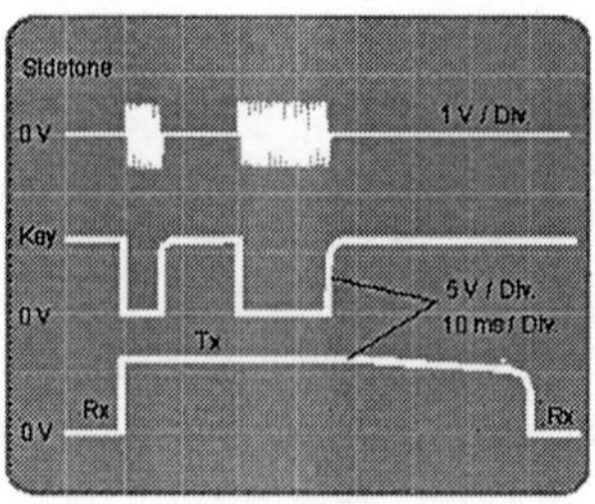

■ **control system**

a system that senses, switches or regulates an operation.

■ **control track**

the portion of a videotape signal consisting of timing pulses associated with video fields and frames. Used in editing and maintaining playback synchronisation.

■ **controlled circulation**

a type of circulation in which publications are sent free or distributed to a select readership, such as airline passengers or motel guests.

■ **convergence**

the merging of previously separate communication industries such as publishing, computers, film, music and broadcasting, made possible by advances in technology.

■ **conversational currency**

topic material presented by the media that provides a common ground for social conversations.

■ **conversational mode (chat mode)**

interactive data communications carried on between Packet stations, as in data or keyboard conversation.

■ **conversion filter**

a lens attachment designed to convert the colour temperature of outdoor light to indoor colour temperature or vice-versa.

■ **converter standards converter**

an electronic device that changes one international broadcast television standard to another.

■ **convertible camera**

a video camera that can be quickly switched between use in the studio and in the field.

■ **cookie**

a flat board, like a flag, but full of irregular holes used for creating a pattern of shadows when put in front of a light.

■ **cool**

a television picture that has a slightly blue or green cast.

■ **co-op**

the practice of a national brand subsidising local advertising costs incurred by a company that sells its product. Typically, the national brand has stringent rules about the advertisement in which the product appears.

■ **cooperatives**

groups of broadcast stations and production facilities that exchange programming- typically news segments.

■ **copy**

headlines and message in an ad.

■ **copy editor**

last professional to see and approve written material before it is delivered to an audience by a media outlet. Responsible for its accuracy, grammar and length.

■ **copy protection device**

a system designed to foil attempts to make illegal copies of copyrighted audio or video recordings.

■ **copy stand**

device for holding flat artwork and a camera. Used for photographing artwork under controlled conditions.

■ **copyright**

that body of law that protects the works created by writers, painters, photographers, performing artists, inventors and other persons who create intangible property.

■ **copyright notice**

the words 'Copyright ©2003 by Don R. Pember,' for example, which indicate to a user that a work is copyrighted by the author or creator.

■ **copywriter**

a person responsible for writing advertising copy and generating creative concepts, often in collaboration with an art director or creative director.

■ **core**

a plastic hub used to hold film without a reel. There are 2 inch cores (small cores) and 3 inch cores (large cores). 2 inch cores can also be called camera cores.

■ **coring out**

the process of removing video noise by converting the analog signal into a digital signal and then back again.

■ **corner insert**

a square or rectangular key insert into a segment of a background picture. Generally used in news to show graphics behind a newscaster.

■ corporate identity

a company's name, logo, typeface, colours, slogan, etc., are elements that help comprise its corporate identity.

■ corrected print

same as a timed print.

■ corrections

further changes in the timing of a print are known as corrections.

■ corrective advertising

rules established by the Federal Trade Commission that require an advertiser to correct the false impressions left by deceptive advertising in a certain percentage of future advertisements.

■ Cost Per Click (CPC)

1. a reward based per click through to a merchants program, e.g. 2 percents per visitor sent to your site.
2. the advertiser pays only for clicks received.

■ Cost Per Lead (CPL)

a CPL is where the advertiser pays only for those clicks where the user clicks through and generates a lead for the advertiser by filling out an online sales contact form or other means.

■ cost per minute

it is the production costs divided by total production time. Costing out is the process of figuring out the costs of a production. The count down starts from Visual cues to talent - usually from ten seconds to start or to the end of a production or segment.

■ Cost Per Sale (CPS)

where the advertiser pays only for those clicks where the user clicks through on the banner or ad and actually purchases a product on the advertiser's site.

■ Cost Per Thousand (C.P.M.)

the cost of advertising per thousand potential customers reached by a given publication, broadcast or outdoor advertisement. This figure is often used in media planning.

■ cost per viewer

it is the production costs divided by the number of viewers. It reflects the cost per measured results- comparing the costs of a production with the intended results. In commercial television this could consist of comparing increased sales revenue with the costs of doing a commercial.

■ Cost-Per-Impression (CPM)

CPM is the cost per thousand for a specific site and is used to either an ad site or to measure the exposure of the ad against the cost. e.g. affiliates are paid a flat fee based on every thousand impressions. The CPM rate is sometimes used to compare the cost of using one site against another.

■ countdown leader

similar to Academy Leader in film, a visual, (and sometime aural) second-by-second countdown from 10 to 3 seconds. Use cue at the beginning of segments for playback.

■ counterproofs

in printmaking, impressions taken from a print or drawing by passing it through a press against a damp sheet of paper. The image appears in reverse.

■ court's opinion

the official opinion of an appellate court that states the reasons or rationale for a decision.

■ cover

re-recording of one artist's music by another

■ cover positions

a print term denoting premium positions. They are:
1st Cover - Outside front cover
2nd Cover - Inside front cover
3rd Cover - Inside back cover
4th Cover - Outside back cover.

■ cover shot

an establishing wide-angle or long shot of a set used both to establish the relationships between subject matter in a scene and to momentarily cover problems with lip sync or mismatched action.

■ coverage

coverage is used to describe the architecture of breaking down a script into the shots that will allow the scene to be cut together. Although coverage addresses the bare-bones question of getting shots that will cut together smoothly, it is important not to be too distracted from bigger aesthetic question of getting the right shots for the scene to work.

■ CPU

1. the Central Processing Unit that controls data flow and 'thinking' function within a computer. When supported by a 'MATH Copressor', it can perform computations at greater speeds.
2. the heart of a computer that processes information according to the instructions received from software.

CPU 500

■ CR (Carriage Return or [enter])

a control character causing the print or display position to move to the first position on the line, drawn from the typewriter and teleprinter function with similar action.

■ crab dolly / crab

a camera mount with steering controls that can move the camera in any direction.

■ crabbing

moving a camera sideways or in arc on a crab dolly. Also referred to as trucking.

■ cradle head

a heavy, cradle-shaped camera pan head consisting of two half-circle elements.

■ **crane camera crane**

a camera mount capable of booming to a high vantage point.

■ **crash edit**

an assemble edit made by manually switching the VTR into record. The resulting edit may not be frame-locked and may leave a slight glitch or distortion at the edit point.

■ **crawl**

the movement of credits or other graphic material across the screen.

■ **creative boutique**

advertising organisation that specialises in the creative side of advertising.

■ **creative compromise**

including and excluding elements in a production based primarily on budget concerns. An example would be eliminating a top star in favour of enhanced special effects or an exotic production location.

■ **creative team**

the art director, copywriter and artist, working together to develop an advertisement or campaign.

■ **credibility**

the trust that the audience holds for media that perform surveillance functions.

■ **credits**

used in electronic media to identify and acknowledge the cast, crew and production staff of film and television products.

■ **critical**

a reflective position on the meaning, biases or value messages of a text.

■ **critical autonomy**

the process by which a member of the audience is able to read a media text in a way other than the preferred reading. Also used to describe the ability of media literacy students to deconstruct texts outside the classroom.

■ **critical end**

to label your film when turning it in at the lab when the roll ran out during a very important shot and you want to make sure you get every last frame possible.

■ **critical viewing**

the ability to use critical thinking skills to view, question, analyse and understand issues presented overtly and covertly in movies, videos, television and other visual media.

■ **critical/cultural approach**

Analytical technique that examines power relationships in society and focuses on meanings people find in texts.

■ **crop**

to cut an image, usually a photograph, down to size so that it fits into a prescribed space. To cut out unwanted portions from a photograph.

■ **cross back lights**

using two back lights a few feet apart in such a way that when viewed from the camera position the light very slightly wraps around the sides of the subject.

cross connection (x-connect)

in Packet Radio communications systems, a bit stream addressed between two ports of a node or routing unit.

cross fade

the process of bringing down one audio or video source while simultaneously bringing up another.

cross light

the use of two keys on opposite sides of a subject often at a 180-degree spacing.

cross modulation test

sometimes called 'cross mod' for short. This is a test the Mixing House will do in conjunction with the lab you plan to use to make sure the optical track is exposed and developed for optimal sound quality.

cross processing

a technique used much more by still photographers. Cross processing is the use of colour reversal film stock to be developed as a negative. A positive print struck from that negative will have strange and rich colours, intense contrast and on overall yellowish hue.

cross talk

unwanted energy (speech, tone or digital pulses) transferred from one transmission path to another. Comprises part of the 'noise' observed on analog communications circuits.

cross-cut

to cut back and forth from one scene to another, often to follow action happening at the same time in two different places.

crossing the line

a 180-degree or more shift in camera position resulting in a reversal of on-screen action or audience perspective. 'The line' is also referred to as the imaginary line and the action axis.

cross-laminate

a patented process of laminating two bias-cut films with their directions of strength at right angles to one another. This third and final step in the manufacturing process produces one sheet of high strength, puncture and tear-resistant film.

cross-laminate

a patented process of laminating two bias-cut films with their directions of strength at right angles to one another. This third and final step in the manufacturing process produces one sheet of high strength, puncture and tear-resistant film.

crosstalk

the inadvertent induction of a second, interfering signal into a primary signal.

CRT (Cathode Ray Tube)

a TV-like monitor screen.

crystal sync

specifically, a way of recording Sync Sound where the camera runs at correct speed with a quartz crystal-governed motor and tape recorder records its pilottone using a built-in quartz crystal pilottone generator. The crystal is much like the kind used in a quartz watch. Unlike cable sync, the camera and tape recorder are not attached.

crystallisation

the sharpening and elaboration of a vaguely held attitude or predisposition.

c-stand

a type of light stand with fixed legs that swing out or together when not in use, usually equipped with an arm and typically used to hold a flag.

cu

a close-up shot.

cube flip / cube spin

a special effect in which pictures appear to be glued to the sides of a cube.

cue cards

large white cards used by on-camera talent to help them remember dialogue-black markers are normally used to write material in large letters.

cue sheets

a road map, of sorts, for the mixer to find the sounds on your tracks during the mix. It is laid out as a grid with each track forming a column and time moving ahead in rows measured in 35mm footage (even if your film is 16mm you must convert the footage to 35mm).

cue track

a videotape audio track that can be used in several ways: to record SMPTE/EBU time code, to record the PL line conversation or in-house identification or cues or for a second audio track.

cultivation analysis

an area of research that examines whether television and other media encourage perceptions of reality that are more consistent with media portrayals than with actuality.

cultural dopes

the view that the readers of media texts are the more or less willing dupes of the media producers. This view is now not widely accepted, since greater emphasis is placed by media researchers on the active meaning-producing work of readers. A more 'modern' view of audiences is presented by Fiske: A homogeneous, externally produced culture cannot be sold ready-made to the masses: culture simply does not work like that. Nor do the people behave or live like the masses, an aggregation of alienated, one-dimensional persons whose only consciousness is false, whose only relationship to the system that enslaves them is one of unwitting (if not willing) dupes. Popular culture is made by the people, not produced by the culture industry. All the culture industries can produce a repertoire of texts or cultural resources for the various formations of the people to use or reject in the ongoing process of producing their popular culture.

■ **culture**

common values, behaviours, attitudes and beliefs that bind a society together.

■ **curl**

the level of curvature or wave that a sheet has before or after printing.

■ **cursor**

a marker such as a line or rectangle that indicates specific positions on a computer screen.

■ **curvature error**

A change in track shape that results in a bowed or S-shaped track. This becomes a problem if the playback head is not able to follow the track closely enough to capture the information.

■ **cut**

1.: what the director says to end the filming of a shot.
2.: the cutting apart of 2 shots at the frameline or the point where the shots have been cut apart.
3.: in the different stages or at the completion of editing the edited film itself can be referred to as 'the cut' or 'the edit'.

■ **cutaway**

a shot, usually a close-up of some detail or landscape, that is used break up a matching action sequence and is often very helpful in editing to rescue you from an impossible break in continuity or coverage. A cutaway, as the name implies, is a shot that does not focus on some detail of the shot before or after it but cuts away from the action at hand, unlike an Insert Shot. However, the two terms are sometimes used vaguely or interchangeably, although this is not always a useful practice. The best cutaways are the ones that have some logic to them, that relate to the scene.

■ **cut-edge condition**

condition of the edges of paper, which can affect paper's ability to feed properly.

■ **cut-in shot**

the use of a close-up shot of something within a scene in order to show added detail.

■ **cutline**

the caption to a picture or other graphic element of a story.

■ **cut-outs**

any portion of the media that has been removed, including binder holes, notches or square cuts.

■ **cutting**

editing tape or film.

■ **cutting in the camera**

shooting scenes in the desired sequence so that little or no editing is required. Often used in covering news stories where there will not be enough time for editing.

■ **cutting on the action**

changing shots at the moment when some action is taking place.

■ **cutting on the beat**

editing shots in time with music. Generally cuts begin at the start of a measure of music or on any beat within a measure.

■ **cyan**

Blue-Green- A secondary colour in the television additive process a primary colour in the subtractive printing process.

■ **cyberspace**

a space created by a network of linked computers where online interaction occurs. Cyberspace consists of a fictional (virtual) reality with widely accepted protocols that allows people to orient themselves to each other through communication in an environment that is virtual rather than real.

■ **cycle**

in all-news radio, the amount of time that elapses before the program order is repeated.

■ **Cyclic Redundancy Check (CRC)**

a powerful error checking method for data and digital communications. The transmitting terminal computes a numeric value representative of the number of marking bits in the associated block of data and sends that value to the receiver, where the number is recomputed to compare against the block as received. Values of CRC-8 and CRC-16 are adequate for most AX.25 messages, while CRC-32 is needed mainly for very long blocks of tens of thousands of characters as noted in Internet type environments.

■ **d5**

a tape format that is non-compressed component digital video which has provision for HDTV recording by use of about 4:1 compression (HD D5).

■ **dailies**

the work print, before it has been edited, so called because the minority of labs will have it ready later the same day it was dropped off (if you are a client to whom they give some type of priority). Also known as Rushes.

■ **damages**

money awarded to the winning party in a civil lawsuit.

■ **data**

multiple units of information- singular is ' datum '.

■ **data circuit**

Packet Radio Communications channels provided specifically for the exchange of data as compared to voice or other information forms.

■ **Data Communications Equipment (DCE)**

the device or TNC which provides signal conversion so that data communications can be established, maintained and discontinued. Some DCE are controlled through local or remote software commands. Standards body term for devices that perform signal conversion at the extremities of a data circuit. A data set (modem) or a CSU are common examples of a DCE. Contrast to DTE.

■ **data compression**

a technique that provides for the transmission or storage, without noticeable information loss, of fewer data bits than were originally used when the data was created.

■ Data Encryption Standard (DES)

a cryptographic standard defined by the National Institute of Science and Technology (NIST) for the general public to encrypt and decrypt digital and data transmissions.

■ data link

a serial data communications pathway, generally between two adjacent nodes without an intervening node.

■ data link control

synonomous with link layer data protocols related to AX.25 Packet Radio. The second layer of the ISO Reference Model for Open Systems Interconnection (OSI).

■ data rate

the basic rate at which data is transferred on a circuit. Often referred to as 'baud rate'. A more correct statement is, bits per second or bps. See **baud**.

■ data set

a telephone industry name for a modem.

■ data terminal

a station in a system capable of sending and/or receiving data signals.

■ data terminal equipment

the standards-body term for a computer, user terminal, workstation or personal computer used for data communications. Data Terminal Equipment is another name for the computer used to send and receive data in digital form at its comport (I/O) port to and from a Terminal Node Controller (TNC).

■ database

a collection of data that is structured and organised into a chosen format, a computer database makes it easy to create, retrieve and resort data stored electronically.

■ datacasting

enhanced options offered with some digital programming to provide additional program material or non-program related resources, allowing viewers the ability to download data (video, audio, text, graphics, maps, services) to specially equipped computers, cache boxes, set-top boxes or DTV receivers.

■ dataengine

a TNC manufactured and marketed by Kantronics. The DataEngine has two HDLC radio ports and one serial port. The

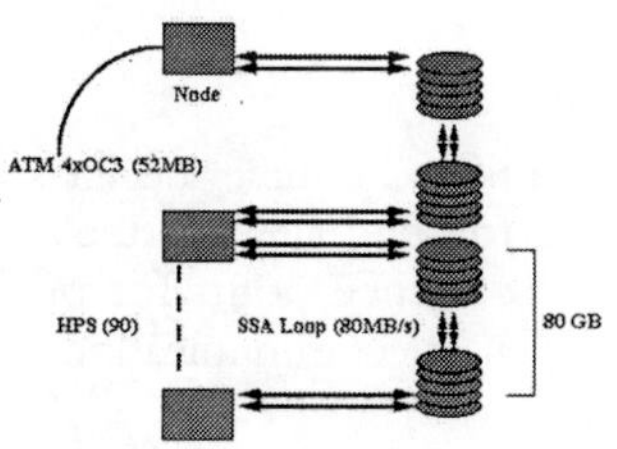

modem are plugged in and provide a useable on-air data-rate from 300 to 19.2 Kbps.

dateline

a line at the beginning of a printed news story or news release giving the place and date of the story's origin.

daylight balanced

the colour temperature of daylight which is 5,400K on the colour temperature scale (it does vary during the day, being higher at noon and lower in the earlier and later parts of the day). Colour film for outdoor shooting is balanced for daylight, otherwise the image would appear blue in hue. If daylight balanced film is used indoors without a correction filter the image will have an orange hue.

daylight spool

an aluminium spool holding 100 feet of film with solid, opaque sides, painted black, which will protect the film from becoming completely exposed when loading a camera in daylight. The name daylight spool comes from the fact that the film may be loaded without total darkness. There are also 400 foot daylight spools, but these are very rarely used as they do not always work very well in a magazine.

dbm

1. identifier meaning 'decibels referred to one milliwatt,' the common reference point for power levels in telecommunications circuits.
2. a data signal should then be 13 dB lower or -19 dBm.

dbm0

1. identifier meaning 'decibels referenced to one milliwatt and corrected to a Zero dBm effective power level'- used to state the relation of a signal level on a transmission line at other than a one-milliwatt point.
2. at a carrier modulator input where test tone level is -16

dbm0p

identifier for CCITT psophometric - weighted noise measurements adjusted to a relative 0 dBm transmission level point. Example: An absolute measurement of minus 40 dBmp noise at a carrier channel output point would mean a signal-to-noise ratio of about 47 dBm0p exists at that point on the circuit.

dbrn

identifier meaning 'decibels above reference noise,' the reference commonly used being 90 decibels below one milliwatt.

dbrnc

identifier meaning 'decibels above reference noise measured through a (filter) weighting network approximating a type C voice message channel'- the common North American nomenclature for a DDD trunk channel and having a reference of 90 decibels below one milliwatt of power.

dbrnc0

commonly pronounced 'de-brink-o' identifier meaning 'decibels above reference noise with C message weighting adjusted for equivalence to a 0 dBm (one milliwatt) equivalent circuit point'. Example: a direct measurement of 49 dBrnC0 at the nominal +7 dBm output of a carrier demodulator would mean the noise had been offset by 7 dB, thus the reading in DBrnC0 would be 42.

DBS

1. 'Direct broadcast satellite.' An alternative to cable and analog satellite reception utilising a fixed 18-inch dish focussed on one or more geostationary satellites. DBS typically uses MPEG-2 encoding and QPSK transmission.
2. the programming services that are available to home satellite-dish owners. The services include RCA's DSS small-dish service, PrimeStar and Full View TV.

dce - dte

interfaces, most typically RS-232 type.

DDE

Dynamic Data Exchange. A communication technique for Windows and OS/2. DDE Applications can send and receive data once a communication path is established.

DDS

Digital Data Service.

de novo

new or fresh. In some instances a court of general jurisdiction will hear an appeal from a case from a lower court and simply retry the case. This is a de novo hearing.

dead air

a technical error in which no signal is fed for broadcast.

dead spot

a zone within the range of a radio transmitter where little or no radio signal can be received.

decibel

The unit of measure used to indicate relative changes in signal intensity or sound volume. The actual expression for calculating the difference in decibels between signal A and signal B is
decibel (dB) = 20 logbase10 (signal A amplitude/signal B amplitude)
+6 dB represents a doubling of the signal or a 100% increase
+5 dB represents a 78% increase
+4 dB represents a 58% increase
+3 dB represents a 41% increase
+2 dB represents a 26% increase
+1 dB represents a 12% increase
+0 dB represents no change-signals are equal
-1 dB represents a 11% decrease
-2 dB represents a 21% decrease
-3 dB represents a 29% decrease
-4 dB represents a 37% decrease
-5 dB represents a 44% decrease
-6 dB represents a halving of the signal or a 50% decrease

decibel (db)

1. the logarithmic unit or measure of a ratio between two powers, P1 and P2. The equation is: db = 10 log10 P2/P1
2. a unit of measurement representing the logarithmic ratio of two voltages, currents or power levels, used in telecommunications to express transmission loss or gain, defined as one-tenth of a Bel, hence the appropriate notation is dB, shown here.

■ decoding

the activity in the communication process by which physical messages are translated into a form that has eventual meaning for the receiver.

■ deconstruction

a mode of analysis predicated on two assumptions. First, that there is no such thing as reality, only constructions (or discourses) about reality. Reality is treated as any kind of text that can be exposed in terms of those biases and premises that went into the construction process. Second, that there is nothing natural or real about this constructed social reality, since it is created by individuals who make choices within broader contexts. The creation of media products allows it be deconstructed by unpacking of those assumptions, agendas and outlooks that created the text.

■ dedicated link

a point-to-point link between two dedicated ports for the exclusive use of those ports or nodes or for the use of stations passing through the network, using those two nodes.

■ dedicated port

this is a port designated for a specific purpose, usually a link to another network or application hardware. Other stations which would connect through the network might pass across the link that use the dedicated port. No user station would access the dedicated port on the dedicated port's frequency.

■ defamation

any communication that holds a person up to contempt, hatred, ridicule or scorn and lowers the reputation of the individual defamed.

■ definition

explains a point, concept or thing by stating what something means. The definition may be taken from a dictionary (literal/denotative meaning), may come from common understanding (connotative meaning) or speakers may create their own meanings.

■ demo

a demonstration tape used to sell a musical performer or group.

■ democratic propaganda

persuasion inadvertently built into media messages or embedded within the normal functions of media structures in open societies with free expression. The outcome reflects consequences rather than intent—in contrast to conventional forms of propaganda, which involve deliberate attempts to indoctrinate ('brainwashing'). The cumulative if unconscious effect of these largely one-sided messages may have a controlling effect by defining some aspects of reality as acceptable or normal, others as irrelevant or inferior.

■ demographics

measurable characteristics of media consumers such as age, gender, race, education and income level.

demurrer

an allegation made by the defendant in a lawsuit that even if the facts as stated by the plaintiff are true, they do not state a sufficient cause for action.

denote/denotation

a description of a media text indicating its common sense, obvious meaning.

density

relative darkness of print.

depoliticisation

the process of taking something that resonates with danger or challenge and transforming (neutering) it into something that is relatively harmless, marginalised and private/personal.

depth of field

while a lens focuses on a single plane of depth, there is usually an additional area in focus behind and in front of that plane. This is depth of field. Depth of field increases as the iris is closed. There is more depth of field the wider the lens and less the longer the lens. There is a deeper area in focus the further away a lens is focused than there is when a lens is focused close. Depth of field does not spread out evenly, the entire area is about 1/3rd in front and 2/3rds behind the plane of focus. To factor together all these variables it is best to consult a depth of field table.

deregulation

the process of removing or diluting the rules which govern the operation of certain companies or areas of industry. In the media, this refers especially to the move, in western Europe, away from state-regulated broadcasting systems towards systems, which are more open to market forces.

description

provides details about an object, scene, person, process, etc., to help the listener create a visual image. The details are often sensory, appealing to sight, touch, hearing, smell or taste. A single, overall impression is usually created. Used to provide supportive/elaborative details for exposition, persuasion and narration.

desensitisation

some theorists argue that the constant media diet of violence desensitises audiences (makes them less sensitive) to real human suffering. It is hard to find proof for the theory, though the practice of systematic desensitisation in behaviour modification may lend incidental support to the theory.

A study of over 1500 teenage boys did not find any support at all for the desesitisation hypothesis. The effect of the 'distant violence' presented in the news was virtually nil and the effect of directly experienced violence was even slightly negative, which, if anything, suggests increased sensitisation to real-world violence.

design brief

a concise problem statement developed by a student or teacher that identifies what the student will do and what the successful solution will achieve.

■ **design portfolio**

a record of the development of a project from inception to completion.

■ **design principles**

qualities of balance, layout, measurement, colour, scale and projection.

■ **design process**

a planning and decision-making process that produces a solution.

■ **desktop video**

video editing and production using standard desktop computing platforms running with add-on video hardware and software.

■ **destination field**

location in a message header that contains the address of the station for which the message is destined.

■ **developmental journalism**

type of journalism, practiced by many Third World countries, that stresses national goals and economic development.

■ **developmental theory**

the assumption that government uses media to further national, economic and social goals.

■ **deviance**

deviance is a form of behaviour which is considered to violate society's norms and therefore to be unacceptable. Many critics of the media would argue that the apparent consensus as regards those norms is in part manufactured by the media by the process of labelling certain groups or individuals behaviour as deviant and then duly reacting to it with moral outrage on behalf of 'ordinary, decent people'. Thus the media serve to legitimate the dominant ideology, which in fact serves the interests of the powerful groups in society.

■ **deviance amplification**

the process whereby activity labelled as deviant is 'amplified' by a broad reaction in society which is co-ordinated mainly by the mass media. The development is seen more or less as a spiral: the initial behaviour is labelled 'devinat', information is relayed from primary definers to the media and thence to the wider society, there is a negative social reaction, consequently, the deviant groups become isolated and react by resisting the consensus view and possibly becoming more actively deviant, the increased 'deviance' leads to increased social control and at this point the whole spiral starts all over again.

■ **deviation**

the deviation of an FM radio is the maximum change or shift in the carrier frequency during modulation. It is usually expressed as peak deviation in kilohertz.

■ **diagnostics**

tests to check the correct operation of hardware and software.

■ **diddle**

a term used to describe the AFSK tone shifting in some nodes and TNC.

■ **die-cuts**

cuts between individual labels. Die-cuts are made by a machine in a predefined pattern.

■ **diffuse**

to soften contrasting edges and fill areas of an image or object via random patterns. Also used to simulate colours outside the colour pallet.

■ **diffusion**

1. a filter used on the camera to create a soft focus effect.
2. a white or pearlecent sheet of material used on a movie light to soften the shadows.

■ **digicom 64**

a software and modem package designed to emulate a TNC on a Commodore 64 computer.

■ **digipeater**

a store and forward 'digital repeater' which will receive and transmit a data packet on the same frequency. All amateur packet station are capable of digital repeating in a simplex environment.

■ **digital**

the storage and transmission of information by reducing it to digits and then reassembling it for an exact reproduction.

■ **Digital Audio Radio Service (DARS)**

direct home or automobile delivery of audio by satellite.

■ **Digital Audio Tape (DAT)**

introduced in the early 1970s, offers digital quality sound purity in a cassette tape format

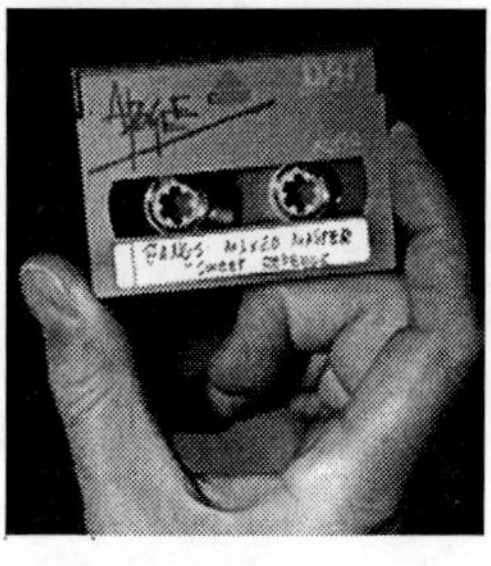

digital betacam

a development of the original analog Betacam which records digitally on a Betacam-style cassette.

digital comb filter

clear separation of the combined colour and black-and-white signals, preventing colour smudging, vibrating edges and ensuring precise details.

digital communication

a process that converts audio, video and text into computer-readable formats. Contrasted with *analog* communication, which uses continuously varying signals that correspond to variations in light and sound source.

Digital Constant Image (DCI)

in LCD projector sets DCI creates a completely flicker free screen image.

Digital Disk Recorder (DDR)

a video recording device that uses a hard disk drive or optical disk drive mechanism. Disk recorders offer nearly instantaneous access to recorded material.

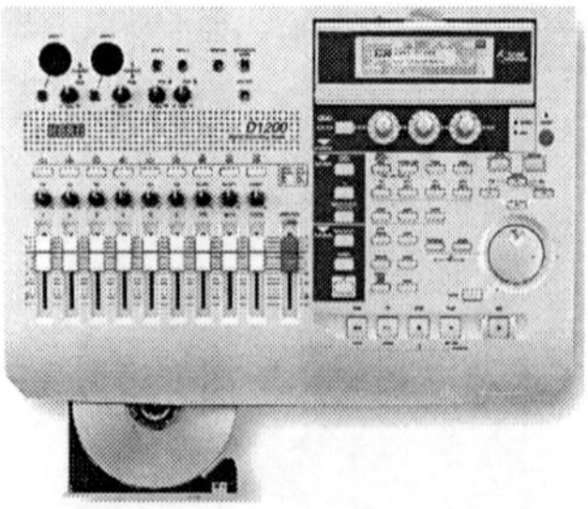

digital divide

the gap in Internet access and use between the 'e-haves' (rich) and the 'e-have-nots' (poor). This divide can reflect differences at the level of individuals or groups or at global levels.

digital recording

recording based on conversion of sound into 1s and 0s logged in millisecond intervals in a computerised translation process.

digital signal

an electrical signal that changes in discrete steps each representing a numerical data value or logic state.

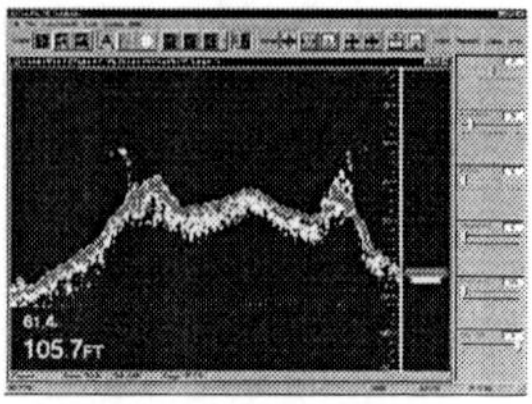

digital signalling

using techniques that transmit information as a series of discontinuous pulsed signals in a pattern representative of the inputted signals, requiring reconstitution at the receiver, capable of being regenerated to minimise noise contribution in transmission in contrast to Analog.

■ **Digital Sound Processing (DSP)**

DSP can alter the atmosphere of the sound reproduction to suit your wishes with effects such as 'cathedral', 'hall', 'stadium' or stereo simulation for mono recordings.

■ **digital switching**

establishing and maintaining a connection under stored program control, when information passed through the switching matrix is in the form of binary encoded information.

■ **digital technology**

a system that encodes information-sound, text, data, video-into a series of on and off pulses that are usually denoted as zeros and ones.

■ **Digital Television (DTV)**

1. television signals consisting of binary signals that allow for improved picture quality.
2. Transmitting a broadcast signal by encoding it as zeroes and ones-the digital code used in computers. DTV can be compressed to provide four, five or more channels in the same bandwidth required for one channel of the current standard television, sound and about five times more picture information (picture elements or pixels) than conventional television. Calculators, computers, compact discs and high definition television are examples of digital technology.

■ **Digital Videodisk (DVD)**

a disk that stores audio, movies, video and graphics in digital format that is compatible with DVD players and home computers.

■ **Digital-to-analog**

The process in which a series of discrete binary integers is converted to a continuous analog signal.

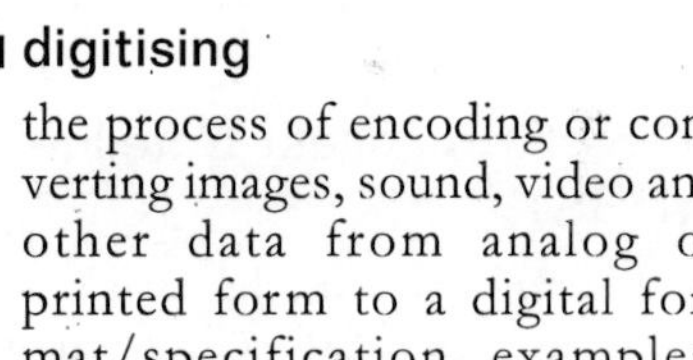

■ **digitising**

the process of encoding or converting images, sound, video and other data from analog or printed form to a digital format/specification. examples: Scanning= Printed image to Digital Image file, video capture=analog video signal to still or motion digital file.

■ **diode matrix**

the device used to interface several nodes to enable communications over their RS-232 ports. When more than two TNCs are used at a node site the diode matrix is required for cross-connection and internode linking.

■ **diopter**

the diopter is part of the view finding system of a camera that can be adjusted to compensate for your own particular eyesight, allowing you to see the groundglass clearly.

■ **DIP**

Dual In-line Package, as applied to sub-miniature switches and monolithic integrated circuits.

■ **direct action**

an ad that contains a direct response item (such as a toll-free number) that allows advertisers to see results quickly.

■ **Direct Broadcast Satellite (DBS)**

a system in which a home TV set receives a signal directly from an orbiting satellite.

■ **direct mail**

a marketing effort conducted exclusively by mail.

■ **direct marketing**

marketing via leaflets, brochures, letters, catalogues or print ads mailed or distributed directly to current and potential consumers. The direct marketing industry has grown enormously as a result of increasingly specialised mailing lists.

■ **direct response**

an advertising technique that urges the audience to respond in a particular manner, usually to buy a product and provides that audience with the means to do so. A business reply card (BRC) is a direct response tool.

■ **director**

the person responsible for the overall look of a video or film product and directs the action behind and in front of the camera. Sometimes directs the editing process.

■ **discourse**

a distinctive and coherent way of talking or thinking about social reality. Discourses about the world 'out there' are constructed in the same way as literary texts (i.e., they involve choices within contexts). These discourses are relative to a particular position rather than reflective of an inherent 'rightness' or 'goodness', imply the social constructedness of human realities, work on the principle that the totality is greater than the sum of its parts and possess their own internal logic and underlying assumptions about the audience. The term 'discourse' is frequently used by those postmodernists who argue that there is no reality outside of representations since the world out there can only be known through symbols, images or narratives.

■ discourses in defence of ideology

a way of describing media , not as neutral or disinterested reflections of reality that mechanically convey information passively created, but rather as ideological in reflecting and reinforcing the status quo. According to this perspective, media are ideological in two ways: first, they consist of ideas and ideals that reflect and reinforce unequal power relations in society, second, they convey ideas and ideals that legitimise those patterns of inequality that empower some, disempower others.

■ discriminator

in an FM radio the discriminator is the circuit that derives audio from the IF signal. After the discriminator the FM receiver will change the audio to remove white noise.

■ discussion forums

a listing of electronic discussion forums of or pertaining to communication, development and community building.

■ dish antenna

an antenna in the shape of a circular dish and parabolic form, used to receive satellite broadcasts. The lower the power of the satellite, the larger the diameter of dish required.

■ disintermediation

the process of delivering a product or service directly to the consumer.

■ disk drive

a disk drive is a computer accessory that stores data in the form of magnetic impulses on a flat media that is much like an extremely high quality magnetic recording tape. The media is on a spinning platter, like a phonograph. The media is of two basic qualities and is called floppy or hard disks. Floppy media is low tolerance, meaning that if the media is dented or dirty it should still work. Floppy media can store about 200,000 characters of data per square inch. Most floppies store less. The rate at which data can be read or written to a floppy drive usually less than 30,000 characters of data per second.

■ display ad

an illustrated advertisement in a newspaper or magazine.

■ dissolve

a transition between two shots, where one shot fades away and simultaneously another shot fades in. Dissolves are done at the lab in the printing phase, but prepared by the negative cutter, who cuts in an overlap of the two shots into the A&B rolls. Labs will only do dissolves in fixed amounts, such as 24 frames, 48 frames, etc.

■ distribution quality

the level of quality of a program feed from a network to its stations.

■ distribution system

the actual cables that deliver the signals to subscribers.

■ distributors

sector of media industry that takes products from manufacturers and delivers them to retailers.

■ dithering

the process of using patterns to simulate colours or gradients.

■ DMX

Digital Music Express. Home delivery of audio by cable.

■ DNG

Digital News Gathering. Electronic news gathering (ENG) using digital equipment.

■ docudrama

a filmed dramatisation based on fact that combines documentary and fictional elements. In the production process, 'based on' allows the creators of the text wide creative latitude and a docudrama is, at best, a skilful representation of a real person or event.

■ documentary

refers to film or video that explores a subject in a way the public expects to be factual and accurate. Documentaries may be balanced by including various viewpoints or they may be subjective, offering the viewpoint and impressions of one producer.

■ dolly shot

a dolly shot is one where the camera is placed on a dolly and is moved while filming. Also known as a tracking shot.

■ dominant

when a text is read by the audience in a way that is intended by the creators of the text.

■ dominant ideology

those ideas and ideals commonly used by the mainstream to justify and rationalise the prevailing patterns of power, privilege and property. See also **ideology**.

■ double exposure

a double exposure occurs when (prior to development) an exposed piece of film is re-shot with a second image on top of the first. Several exposures can be made, but it still valid to call it a 'double' exposure rather than a 'triple' or 'quadruple' exposure. It is perfectly alright to say 'five double exposures', as numerically incongruous as it may sound.

■ **double feature**

practice started by theatres in the 1930s of showing two feature films on the same bill.

■ **double perf**

16mm film with a row of perforations running along both edges. On the film can this will be indicated by 2R appearing on the label.

■ **double pumping**

the programming tactic of presenting the same program twice in one night or twice in one week.

■ **double reel**

in 35mm a double reel is 2 single reels joined together, the maximum size being 2,000 feet. Double reels are labelled 1 A/B, 2 A/B etc., to distinguish them from single reels.

■ **double system**

the term double system refers to sound and picture as two separate elements, recorded, edited or projected in sync. 16mm and 35mm use the double system format. A camera photographs the picture and a tape recorder records the sound. In the end, the final print is Single System, combining sound and picture onto the same piece of print stock.

■ **double system projector**

a projector designed to project a workprint and play a mag track in sync.

■ **DOVE**

an OSCAR satellite (OSCAR 17) whose full name is Digital Orbiting Voice Encoder.

■ **downconverting**

the process which changes the number of pixels and/or frame rate and/or scanning format used to represent an image, by removing pixels. (See **upconverting**)

■ **downlink**

a circuit from a node to a user, initiated by the node on command from a distant user.

■ **dramatic tension**

also known as rising action. In traditional narrative structure, dramatic tension marks the beginning of a story as conflict moves toward a climax.

■ **drive time**

the hours when the most commuters are in their cars. During 'drive time', radio advertising costs more because of increased listenership.

■ **dropout**

Brief signal loss caused by a tape head clog, defect in the tape, debris or other feature that causes an increase in the head-to-tape spacing. A dropout can also be caused by missing magnetic material. A video dropout generally appears as a white spot or streak on the video monitor. When several video dropouts occur per frame, the TV monitor will appear snowy. The frequent appearance of dropouts on playback is an indication that the tape or recorder is contaminated with debris and/ or that the tape binder is deteriorating.

■ drypoint

similar to etching, but the lines are simply scratched into the plate manually, without the use of acid. The hallmark of a drypoint is a soft and often rather thick or bushy line somewhat like that of an ink pen on moist paper.

■ DSP

Digital Signal Processing. A modern technique of analysing analog signals by converting the analog signal to a digital form and processing it with a specialised computer circuit.

■ DTC

'Direct-to-consumer' which is a term used to denote advertising that is targeted to consumers and not businesses.

■ DTE

Data Terminal Equipment. Usually refers to a terminal or computer or any equipment that generates data.

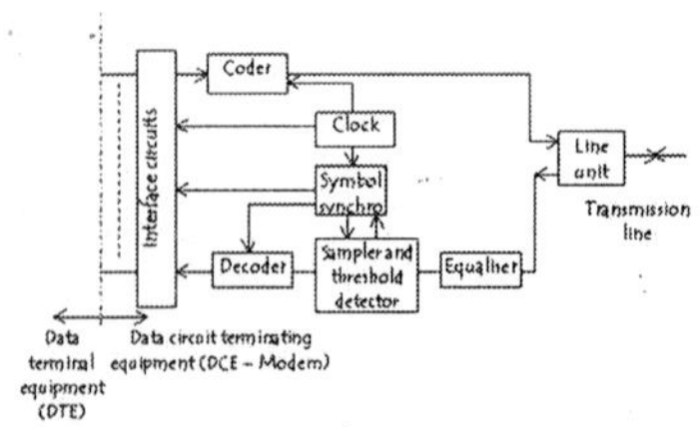

Block diagram of a baseband data modem

■ DTR

Data Terminal Ready. One of the RS-232 signals (pin 20 on DB-25) that indicates to the computer or terminal of the ready-state to send data. It is associated with the RTS (ready To Send) signal and is often used in conjunction with this signal to enable one form of 'hardware' handshaking.

■ DTV

Digital television. This comprises all the components of digital television including HDTV, SDTV, datacasting and multicasting.

■ DUAL Tone Multi-Frequency (DTMF)

also known as Touch-Tone. A type of signaling which emits two distinct frequencies for each indicated digit.

■ dub

most commonly, a copy of a film or tape. It can also mean making a completely new soundtrack, as in dubbing English for a foreign film. A dubbed tape is also called a dupe.

■ dubbing

the recording of dialogue in a sound studio, after the footage is shot, where the actors watch the film and match the lip movements.

■ dumb terminal

a data communications euphemism indicating a DTE with no processing capability. The data equivalent of a KSR teleprinter.

■ dummy

rough version of a magazine that's used for planning how final version will look.

■ duopoly

single ownership and management of multiple radio stations in one market

■ **duo-tone (2 colour) printing**

a printing process using two colours, printing one colour on top of the other. This is a screening process.

■ **dupe**

a dupe is a positive copy of a positive. A dupe can also be a negative copy of a negative. A dupe is a print made in the reversal process. It can sometimes be clearer to call something a dupe, because to simply say 'positive print' you could just mean a positive copy of a negative, which would not be a dupe.

■ **duplex**

two-way transmission. Duplex means two channels. A full duplex signal consists of two separate channels. Both ends of the radio circuit need to have a separate receiver and transmitter such that the receiver on each end can hear the other station's transmitter regardless of the state of the local transmitter.

■ **duplex digipeater**

similar to a simplex digipeater, except that different receive and transmit frequencies are used. Compare to: Full duplex realtime repeater which repeats received data at exactly the same time.

■ **dutch tilt**

a composition with the camera viewing the scene at a diagonal. Same as a canted angle.

■ **DVD**

Digital Versatile Disk. (Formerly Digital Video Disk.) Same size as a CD but stores seven times CD capacity on a single side. DVDs can also be double-sided or dual layer. Today most DVDs are used to display full-length commercial motion pictures, plus additional material such as outtakes, director's notes, movie trailers, etc.

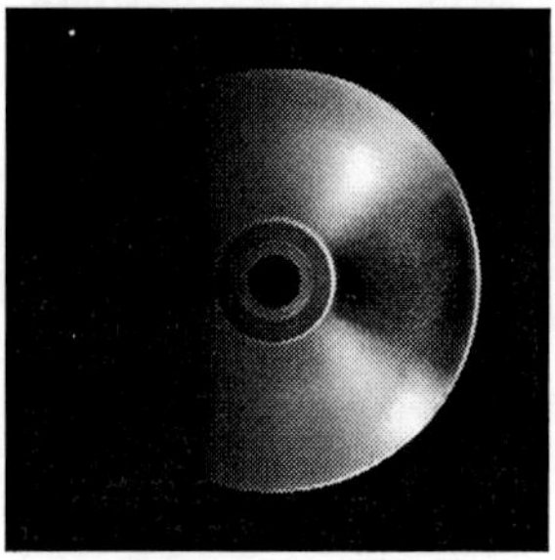

■ **DVI**

Digital Video Interactive. This is a compression format for recording digital video on a CD- ROM disk that provides up to 72 minutes of full motion video or four hours of one-quarter screen full-motion video.

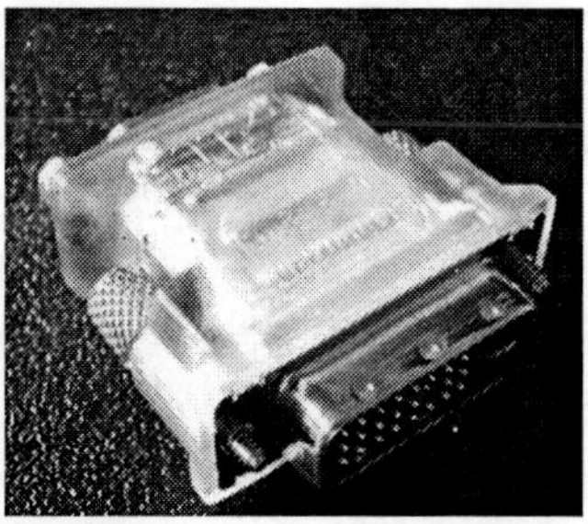

■ **DVTR**

Digital Videotape Recorder

■ **DWAIT**

Digipeat WAIT : A delay in sending a packet automatically inserted by a TNC when originating a packet. The delay starts when a packet is ready to be sent, after the channel becomes clear. A digipeated packet is sent without waiting this delay. Used as a collision avoidance system when digipeaters are in use.

■ **dynamic picture control**

using powerful algorithms the Dynamic Focus Circuit ensures a clean crisp image with sharp focus right to the very edge of the screen. Meanwhile, the Quad Pole Circuit adjusts the beam spot diameter to ensure the picture shape also remains true right to the corners and very edges of the screen.

■ **dynamic rerouting**

in a network where redundancy exists in the backbone from one city to another some types of network software allow for the network to recover automatically from backbone hardware failure by rerouting traffic through the redundant link. This is called 'dynamic rerouting' as it can adjust dynamically to a changing network.

■ **dysfunction**

consequence that is undesirable from the point of view of the welfare of society.

■ **E.C.N.**

stands for Eastman Colour Negative. It is simply your developed negative.

■ **E.D.L.**

stands for Edit Decision List. It is used by the negative cutter when you have cut digitally, in order to conform the original without the usual workprint.

■ **E.I.**

abbreviation for Exposure Index.

■ **E.S.**

abbreviation for Editorial Sync.

■ **earth station (ground station)**

a microwave radio transmitting and receiving station working with communications satellites.

■ **e-book**

digital version of a book, which can be read by using a computer or a special reader.

■ **echo**

a signal that has been reflected or otherwise returned with sufficient magnitude and delay to be perceived at the far end of the circuit.

■ **echo canceler**

an echo removal device that operates by generating an exact opposite of any echo signal and injecting it into the transmission path to cancel echoes. Used in both speech telephony and in some higher-speed data modems, notably those compliant with CCITT V.32.

■ **echo check**

one method of verifying accuracy of Packet transmissions, sometimes called 'pinging' by returning received data back to the sender as verification and to determine path throughput level.

edge fog

exposure along the edge of the film from raw light, in most cases from a lightleak, due to the camera door not being taped. Edge Fog can sometimes be visible in the frame or sometimes outside of the frame effecting the clarity of the latent edge numbers.

edge numbers or latent edge numbers

1. the edge numbers are small numbers running along the edge of the film, in between the perf in 16mm and just to the far side of them in 35mm. They are photographed onto the film in its manufacture and are there to aid the negative cutter in lining up shots in the process of conforming the negative. They are sometimes called latent edge numbers to distinguish them from inked-on code numbers.
2. code numbers are sometimes called edge numbers.

edit

1. the cutting and arranging of shots.
2. in the different stages or at the completion of editing the edited film itself can be referred to as 'the cut' or 'the edit.'

editing

the process of arranging, assembling or excluding images, text and sound to produce a completed media product.

editing bench

a workbench with rewinds attached and sometimes a built-in light table in the centre.

editing bin

see **trim bin**.

edition

an edition of a print includes all the impressions published at the same time or as part of the same publishing event. A first edition print is one, which was issued with the first published group of impressions. First edition prints are sometimes pre-dated by a proof edition. Editions of a print should be distinguished from states of a print. There can be several states of a print from the same edition and there can be several editions of a print all with the same state. For limited editions, cf. below.

editor

the person responsible for assembling the various parts of a media product. An editor can work in print or electronic media.

editorial

a statement of opinion from an editor or publisher about you and your business. Media coverage generated by news staff.

editorial association

the belief that product category ads will do better when placed in publications or positioned in certain sections which contain editorial material directly associated to the product. For example, advertising for scuba gear in a diving magazine.

editorial calendar

the listing of specific times a publication will focus on special sections or special news reporting.

■ editorial policies

guidelines the print media follow to persuade the public on certain issues or to achieve specific goals.

■ editorial sync

a set of sync marks on picture and sound that line up at the same frame, as opposed to Printer's Sync, where the picture and sound are displaced. Sometimes it is useful to label a sync mark E.S. to know that it is an Editorial Sync mark.

■ educational

describes programming which is part of an educational programme linked with a defined curriculum.

■ educative

describes programming which has educational value but which is not part of any educational programme linked with a defined curriculum.

■ effects research

a conventional approach to the study of media that focuses on the effects that media have on individual thought and behaviour, often based on a simplistic cause–effect model that ignores the complex and negotiated relationship between media texts and audience meanings.

■ EIA

Electronics Industries Association.

■ EIA RS-232

the most common DTE serial interface by far, in use for almost 30 years, with several revisions and additions, international equivalent: The suite of CCITT V.24 and V.28 combined with ISO 2110.

■ EIA STANDARD RS-232 and CCITT V.24 are similar

a major constituent of the International Telecommunications Union (ITU) that sets standards for the operation of telecommunications services across international boundaries. Some CCITT standards are adopted for use in the USA.

■ EISA

Extended Industry Standard Architecture. A 32-bit bus architecture standard designed for PC compatibles to take advantage of newer and faster microprocessors.

■ electrical properties

the electrical resistivity of the print media.

■ electricity

a form of energy that flows along a path and can produce heat, light, magnetism, motion or a chemical change.

■ electromagnetic spectrum

the entire range of wavelengths (the inverse of frequency) of electromagnetic waves extending from cosmic and Gamma rays down through visible light and heat to every form of radio communications signal.

electromechanical

a machine process or device that is controlled electrically.

electronic media

media that requires electricity in order to operate, function or communicate messages.

Electronic News Gathering (ENG)

producing and airing field reports using small, lightweight portable TV equipment.

Electronic Programming Guide (EPG)

an application that provides an on-screen listing of all programming and content that an interactive television service subscriber or digital television viewer has available to them.

e-magazines

a listing of electronic magazines and newsletters of or pertaining to communication and/or development issues.

e-mail

electronic messages sent from computer to computer.

emulate/emulation

imitating a system or device such that a connected device accepts the same information, executes the same computer programs and achieves the same results as if the emulator were one of its own kind. Most often, emulation is a downward step in capability of the device being used, as when a personal computer is used to emulate a mechanical teleprinter or a 'dumb' terminal on a computer network. While some degree of upward emulation is possible, it is less prevalent in the broad view of computer communications.

emulsion

the thin layer of silver attached to the base which, when exposed and developed, creates the film image through the areas of silver, which block light and the clear areas which allow light to pass through.

emulsion batch

the emulsion batch is the series of numbers on the film can the come after the Emulsion Type. When the film is made, each batch is given a number so that you can shoot a single sequence with one particular batch. Just as a suit where the pants and jacket were cut from different bolts of fabric might be a little off, a sequence shot with different emulsion batches might also be a little off. From one sequence to the next, of course, this doesn't matter. (And the batches themselves have become more consistent in recent years, so mixing them is less of a sin nowadays.)

emulsion leader

unlike plastic leader, emulsion leader can be cement spliced.

emulsion type

a film's emulsion type refers to the composition of its emulsion, whether it was manufactured to be fast, slow, grainy, fine-grained, colourful, pastel, black and white or colour, daylight balanced, tungsten balanced, etc. The emulsion type is represented by a number.

The '72' always stands for 16mm camera stock and the same emulsion type is found in 35mm as 5248, '52' being the designation of 35mm. When picking out a stock to use the film speed and in the case of colour film, whether the film is daylight or tungsten, are the primary reasons for choosing a certain emulsion type. Allowances might also be made to achieve a certain look. Several different emulsion types are usually used on a project, fast for night scenes, slow for daylight scenes, etc. However, unless you are trying something novel, it is a good idea to shoot a single unbroken sequence with one emulsion type.

■ encoding

the activity in the communication process by which thoughts and ideas from the source are translated into a form that may be perceived by the senses.

■ encryption

a mechanism for changing the broadcast signal in a systematic way so that the picture would be unintelligible without a suitable decoder. The procedure is highly mathematical and very secure. Encryption usually implies a higher degree of security than 'scrambling', which is a simple rearrangement of parts of the signal according to some simple formula and its therefore less secure.

■ engineering principles

the method of operation used to plan, build and manage engines, machines, roads and structures.

■ engraving

a form of intaglio printing in which lines are incised into a metal plate with a carving tool called a burin. The characteristics of burin engraving differ from that of etching in that engraving, requiring considerable force, is done from the strength of the arm and eliminates the quavering autographic qualities of etching, which is done more from the finger tips like fine drawing. The hallmarks of engraving are often elegantly swelling and tapering lines.

■ EOC

Emergency Operations Centre. This is a term used by state governments for a state or county government owned facility where emergency services and radio equipment is co-located. The EOC provides for rapid deployment and coordination related to emergency communications and associated drills.

■ EPP

Enhanced Parallel Port.

■ equal opportunities rule

part of the Communications Act of 1934, Section 315 allows bona fide candidates for public office to gain access to a broadcast medium during political campaigns.

■ equalisation

the procedure of compensating for fluctuation in circuit amplitude or envelope delay distortion.

■ error

in Packet Radio communications, any unwanted change in the contents of a transmission.

error control

in Packet Radio communications, methods used to detect and correct transmission channel errors.

error rate

in Packet Radio communications, the ratio of bits, characters, elements, blocks, messages or files incorrectly received to the total number transmitted during a specified time interval.

estimate

the proposed or expected budget for an advertising effort. Prior to the inception of any promotional project or ad campaign, advertising provides its clients with a detailed cost estimate.

etching

marks are made through an acid-resistant coating on the plate, after which the plate is bitten in a chemical bath to etch the image into the metal.

etchings

prints taken on paper from plates incised using an acid to corrode the plates' surface. The plate is first covered with an acid resistant ground through which the artist scratches a design with a stylus or needle, revealing the bare metal below. This plate is then immersed in an acid bath that cuts the incised lines into the plate. Etched lines often betray the subtle motions of the artist's fingertips.

evaluation

research done to measure the effectiveness of an advertising or a public relations campaign.

events calender

an international listing, by year, month and day, of events, courses, conferences and designated days that might be of interest to people and organisations working in communication and development.

exclusion

the opposite of selection. An editing technique to select desired areas of an image by ruling out all undesired areas. Particularly useful in selecting and removing an object from its background.

exclusive

news item or feature article that only one newspaper, magazine or television station may carry.

experiment

a research technique that stresses controlled conditions and manipulates variables.

exposure

the number of potential consumers reached through specific medium.

exposure index

this is the sensitivity to light of a particular type of film. It is the specific number used to measure Film Speed. Your film will list an E.I. number on the box or the film can as the film speed. It is the same as A.S.A. and I.S.O. on your light metre.

■ **extension tubes**

these are a handy way to turn any long lens into a macro lens for ultra-close shooting. They are hollow metal tubes that are mounted between the camera and the lens. Typically they come in a set of different lengths, which can be combined. It is a good idea to open up the lens a little when using an extension tube, as a little light is lost. It should be noted that they do not work when used with wide lenses.

■ **extrusion**

the process of converting resin pellets under extreme pressure to a liquid form. The first step in the 3-step process of manufacturing film.

■ **eye line**

eye line is the direction an actor should look off-screen to match a reverse angle or a P.O.V. shot. It is best to give the actor an actual thing or spot to look at rather than a blank spot on an empty wall or an empty space in mid air.

■ **e-zine**

online newsletter or magazine.

■ **F.E.M.A.**

Federal Emergency Management Agency.

■ **face sheet**

the face sheet is the printable surface on a sheet of adhesive labels and can be made from different materials, including paper, polyester and vinyl. It is common for a face sheet to be die-cut so that individual shapes can be removed after printing. Polyester and vinyl labels require a topcoat to provide the proper electrical and toner adhesion properties. It is important to purchase labels from a knowledgeable converter who is familiar with these processes and with laser printing.

■ **face-to-face communication**

the sender and receiver of information are in contact. The receiver may disagree, ask a question or repeat information. The sender and receiver can engage in a dialogue about the message. There is an opportunity for feedback.

■ **facsimile (fax)**

graphic transmission of pictures, maps or documents via communications circuits using terminal devices that scan documents, transforming scanned images into coded data-like signals and reproduce likenesses of original documents at a distant point.

■ **fact sheet**

a short (generally one-page) document that provides a 'snapshot' look at a company, product or service.

■ **fade**

a transition from a shot to black where the image gradually becomes darker is a Fade Out or from black where the image gradually becomes brighter is a Fade In. Fades are done at the lab in the printing phase, but prepared by the negative cutter, who cuts in an overlap of black into the A&B rolls. Labs will only do fades in fixed amounts, such as 24 frames, 48 frames, etc.

fair use

the legal guidelines which exempt educators from certain copyright restrictions. Fair use of educational materials allows some media products to be used to a limited degree in the classroom. Individual school districts interpret Fair Use policy differently.

fairness doctrine

now defunct FCC doctrine that required broadcast stations to provide various points of view on a controversial issue.

false light

that portion of privacy law that prohibits all publications or broadcasts that falsely portray an individual in an offensive manner.

family hour

The time slot, typically between 6 P.M. and 8 P.M., during which television and radio programs are free of violence and sex.

FAQ

(Frequently Asked Questions): a list of questions and answers for the media pertaining to a press release, often included in a press kit.

FCC (Federal Communications Commission)

a board of Presidentially-appointed commissioners empowered to regulate interstate and international communications and all uses of radio in the United States. It operates under the Communications Act of 1934 and several more recent laws. Disseminates its own regulations interpreting those laws, as Title 47 of the Code of Federal Regulations (CFR 47, 47CFR).

FCS

Frame Check Sequence. A 16 bit (2 byte) number included with each frame in the packet used for error checking.

feature

a longer, more probing article or story (as opposed to an 'objective' news item or account). Magazines and newspapers may have a features department or desk.

FEC

Forward Error Correction. A technique of error correction in which packets or AMTOR groups combine the data from two or more transmissions to yield less errors. AMTOR FEC mode, the data is sent twice and the receiving station(s) record all known characters without resorting to an ARQ ACK/NAK transmission.

Federal Communications Commission (FCC)

a regulatory agency, composed of five individuals appointed by the president, whose responsibilities include broadcast and wire regulation.

■ feed

to send a program or signal. For instance, feeding a program from one station via satellite to other stations.

■ feedback

the process of communication whereby a person can disagree, ask a question, repeat information for understanding or otherwise talk back in the communication process.

■ Fibre Optics (FO) 'light-pipe'

a technology using light as a digital information bearer. Fibre optic cables (light pipes) are a direct replacement for conventional wire, coaxial cable and many forms of radio, including microwave. The shortcoming of fibre optics is when a fade occurs in it, it is of long duration and may have been caused by a 'back-hoe' Thus the term 'Back-hoe fade'.

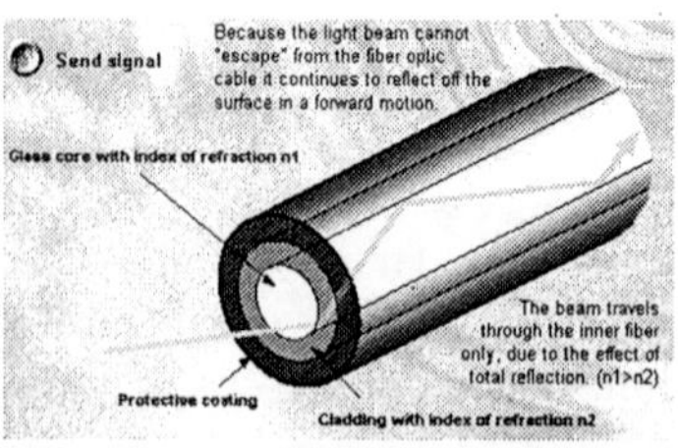

■ file server (server)

in LANs, a station, often microcomputer-based, that provides the mass storage and file access to users on the LAN. Server capabilities vary widely, some even include ability to ' gateway ' to other communications means or ' bridge' to a similar nearby LAN or even determine for users if those functions are needed and decide the route to the user's destination, in which case they are called ' routers'.

■ filler, fill or sound fill

filler is scrap film, most often used to keep a sound track running the same length as the picture, even though there is just silence. When used this in way can also be called sound fill. Filler is usually a print with the emulsion scraped off the centre all the way along, perhaps to prevent bootlegging, but also useful in that a mark can be seen on both sides through this wide scratch.

■ film

the medium whereby images are recorded on plastic through a photochemical process. As a verb, 'to film' means the production process used to record images and sound on film using film hardware.

■ film cement

a liquid that is actually not a glue, but a chemical that melts and fuses two pieces of film together.

■ film plane

the film plane is the plane of depth from the lens of the film, behind the gate, in the camera. It is also the point from where the distances on the focusing ring should be measured from and is indicated on the outside of the camera with a little symbol that looks like the planet Saturn turned on its side.

film recording

a service used to produce film transparencies from digital images. Recorder specs, vary from one manufacturer to another near 4000pixels for 35mm film @ 24bpp.

film scanning

scalable optical digitisation of photographic transparencies negatives and slides. High quality standards requirements for Pre-press Digitisation have resulted in capture specs exceeding 48bpp @ 6000pixels.

film speed

the sensitivity to light for proper exposure of a given film stock. This is primarily a result of the size of the silver halides in the emulsion, the larger the grain, the less light is needed for exposure. Film stocks are generally spoken of as being fast or slow, a fast film having large grains and needing less light, a slow film having smaller grain and needing more light.

filter

a tinted glass or small tinted plastic sheet placed in front of the lens or behind the lens in a filter holder, used to change the colour rendition of the entire shot. Filters are used to convert tungsten balanced film for use in daylight or vice versa. They can also be used for aesthetic reasons, such as a red filter to darken the sky when filming in black and white.

fine art & historical prints

prints can be separated into two general types, fine art prints and historical prints. These types can best be understood through a differentiation of their emphasis. The distinction between the two types of prints is not clear-cut nor is it understood by all experts in the same way, but generally a fine art print is one conceived and executed by an artist with as much or more concern for the manner of presentation of the print as for its content, whereas the concern of the maker of an historical print is focused more on the content of the image than on its presentation.

finish/smoothness

characterises a paper's finish. Textured paper causes inconsistent or blotchy print and can wrinkle. Glossy-smooth paper tends to highlight defects and might not hold toner. For best results, use smooth paper.

finishing

a production process by which the appearance or internal structure of a product or material is changed to improve its durability, strength, usefulness or aesthetics.

finishing precision

dimensions (length and width) of a piece of media, how closely it is cut to the stated size and how square it is. Use media that is accurately cut, so that it can be handled properly.

fin-syn regulations

the laws passed by the Federal

Communications Commission limiting the networks' ownership of the programming they broadcast. The laws prohibit networks from acquiring a financial interest in the program's producers and from distributing the programs in syndication, except overseas. The regulations were repealed because of increased competition from cable and other forms of home entertainment. The repeal has led to the phenomenon of one network producing programming that appears on another network.

■ first generation

the original film or tape. Dubs or dupes are made from it.

■ fixed data rate compression

techniques designed to produce a data stream with a constant data rate.

■ fixed focal length lens

See **prime lens**.

■ fixed position

a guaranteed position in a publication that will not be pre-empted.

■ flag

this has two meanings.

1. it can be a large black cloth on a frame used on a shoot to keep light out of part of the composition.

2. in the cutting room it is a small piece of tape attached to a shot in a roll and used exactly as you would use a bookmark. The flagsticks out the side of the roll, making it easy to find that shot again quickly.

■ flak

an organised attempt to influence media content, which can take the form of letters, phone calls, petitions, lawsuits and legislation.

■ flange pack

A condition where the tape pack is wound up against one of the flanges of the tape reel.

■ flare

this has two meanings:

1. when using film on a daylight spool, the erratic pattern of raw light that washes out the beginning and end of the roll are known as 'the flares'.

2. a flare of the other kind is a Lens Flare. It is caused when light strikes the lens and either causes the entire image to be fogged in appearance or for a little row of polygons (the silhouette of the iris) to appear from the light hitting the surfaces of the many elements in the lens. It is solved by flagging the lens.

■ flash frame

1. a flash frame is a single frame that is completely clear between two shots. It occurs when the camera is stopped with the gate open, allowing for a very long exposure on that single frame. Rather than a problem, a flash frame can actually be a very helpful thing in the editing room, making it very easy to see where one shot ends and another begins. This type of flash frame usually does not occur with spring wound cameras except when the spring winds all the way down, but the second type

is something with which to be more concerned.
2. a flash frame is also used to describe the first few overexposed, brighter frames at the beginning or the end of a shot, due to the camera needing time to reach speed. These can often be hard to see while editing, but are much more noticeable in a final print.

flash memory

flash memory is a non-volatile memory medium (it 'remembers' even when the power is turned off) that can easily be updated. This credit card-sized package will be used to replace floppy and hard disk drives in portable personal computers in the future. Flash memory cards substantially reduce the computer's power consumption (when compared with traditional mechanical disk-drive memories).

flat rate

rates that are not subject to discounts.

flatbed

an editing machine resembling a desk with a screen in the middle. The film sits flat on plates, which are threaded through the centre section that has transports for picture and sound.

flatbed scanning

document and image scanning utilising a level glass bed scanner. Device specifications range includes RGB @600dpi,single pass.

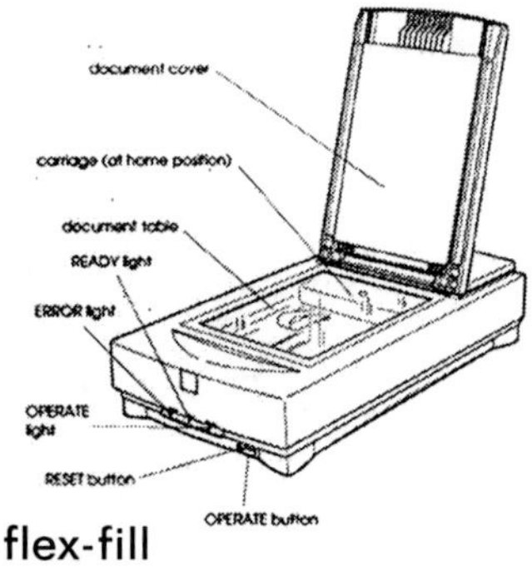

flex-fill

a round cloth bounce card mounted on a flexible ring that can be folded up when not in use.

flicks

common term for digital motion sequences.

flow chart

a pictorial representation of a sequence of events.

flow control

the process that starts and stops terminal output to prevent loss of characters or data by the receiving device. In packet and data communications, the use of buffering and other mechanisms that operate to avoid data loss in case the receiver cannot keep up with the transmitter. The ASCII control characters X-ON and X-OFF (Ctrl-Q & Ctrl-S) are frequently-used examples. They are sent in reverse direction as an instruction for the sender to hold or continue (software handshaking).

flyer

a handbill or loose sheet with a printed advertisement.

■ **FM**

1. 'Frequency Modulation' of radio waves.
2. this is a method of transferring data or voice information over a carrier signal. FM is achieved by changing the frequency of the carrier in proportion to the wave form of the superimposed audio signal be it voice or data. In most FM voice applications, the FM deviation is set to 5 kHz or less. In Packet or digital FM communications the deviation is set between 3 and 3.5 kHz. Never set Packet Radio deviation to more than 3.5 KHz.

■ **focal length**

simply put, how wide or narrow a view the lens will provide, smaller numbers being wider and larger numbers being narrower.

■ **focus group**

a group of potential consumers used in a market research effort, which is usually designed to determine the likely effectiveness of a product or advertising strategy.

■ **fog**

this is when stray raw light has found a chance to expose your film.

■ **foley**

the recording of custom sound effects during post production in the same way that dialogue is dubbed. The term comes from the name of its inventor.

■ **follow focus**

a shot where focus is changed while shooting to correspond with the moment of the subject (or the camera).

■ **follow-on**

a product, service or article, for instance, that results directly from a previous product, service or article.

■ **foot candle**

measurement of light. One foot candle is the light of one candle, one foot away. Many light metres will use foot-candles as a starting number, which then must be converted into an f-stop based on the sensitivity of the film you are using. (Because of the great variety of different film speeds it is sometimes ambiguous to talk too much about foot candles, since a given number of foot-candles will not yield the same f-stop from one film speed to another.)

■ **footage**

1. the amount of film one has shot.
2. the whole of the exposed film itself.

■ **footprint**

the area of the earth's surface in which a particular satellite signal can be received.

■ **format**

consistent programming designed to appeal to a certain segment of the audience.

■ **format conversion**

process of both encoding/decoding and re-sampling digital rates to change digital data from one format to another.

format wheel

visual aid that helps radio programmers plan what events happen during a given time period.

formative research

advertising research done before developing a campaign.

Forward Error Correction (FEC)

an error-correcting technique that avoids the need for any reverse channel by enabling self-correction of errors at the receiver. FEC operates by adding information that enables the receiver to determine what the error was and to substitute information that corrects the error.

forward file

this is the disk file on a packet bulletin board system (PBBS) that is responsible for directing the autoforward operation. By making entries in this file the PBBS system may select what packet paths are used to each PBBS that is forwarded to, when each operation is per formed and what traffic is sent during each piece of the forwarding operation. FOOTPRINT - In satellite communications, the area on the surface of the earth that a given satellite covers, this technology has reached a high state of development, with satellite coverages capable of being quite shaped and tailored to the purpose of the satellite.

forwarding

the transfer of files between BBSs.

four-colour process

a sophisticated process of reproducing a colour image onto a magazine page. This involves separating the image into four universal colours. They are always yellow, blue, red and black (shades may vary). The separation process is done by the production department of an agency. The publication combines the separated colour sheets and reconstructs the actual colour image onto the magazine page.

FRACK

Frame Acknowledge delay: This is the time after a packet is transmitted by a TNC before the TNC decides that a frame acknowledge is not going to occur. At that point the TNC performs backoff (some TNCs + TCP/IP) and a retry. FRACK is calculated based on the number of digipeaters that you specify in your connect command.

fragmentation

scattering of data over a hard disk caused by successive recording and deletion operations. Generally this will eventually result in slow data recall - a situation not suitable for video recording or replay.

frame

a process that involves imposing boundaries (or a 'framework') on a news story. A familiar frame of reference ('framework') is imposed that not only imparts a distinctive spin (interpretation) on the news item, but also encourages a distinctive reading of it by drawing reader/viewer attention toward some aspects of reality, but away from others. Frames operate as a filtering device that preselects relevant facts and arranges the elements into satisfying storylines with predictable plots and stock characters.

■ frame handles

frame handles are extra frames at the beginning and the end of every shot, the exact number will vary from one application to the next, which are used primarily when preparing original material for optical printing, such as the Zero Cut method of blow up or the creation of a superimposed title, etc. The purpose they serve, in the case of zero cut, is to make sure the registration pin of the printer is not grabbing a splice, which can cause the image to wobble. With opticals they are often used merely to avoid printed-in dirt, which is much more prevalent close to a splice where bits of film cement can flake off.

■ frame line

the small sliver of space between frames. This is where two shots are cut apart and joined.

■ frame of reference

perspective or point-of-view of individuals that serves as a lens through which they may analyse and interpret media. Life experiences (e.g., gender, family background, socio-economic status, education level, political leanings, career, regional/geographic affiliation, religious affiliation) contribute to the frame of reference.

■ Frames Per Second

the number of still frames (pictures) that gives the illusion of motion, which appear in a single second of time.

■ framing

the general way a news medium treats a topic.

■ free marketplace of ideas

press philosophy that endorses the free flow of information.

■ Freedom of Information Act (FOIA)

law stating that every federal executive-branch agency must publish instructions on what methods a member of the public should follow to get information.

■ freelancer

writer who sells writing services and is not under regular contract to any one publication.

■ free-link exchange

web advertising technique in which one company exchanges free ad space with another.

■ free-to-air

broadcasts which can be received without the necessity for any encrypting process.

■ freeze frame

display of a single (frozen) frame of video.

■ **french flag**

a small black metal flag attached to the camera with a positionable arm that is used to shade the lens from light in the case of a Flare (2).

■ **frequency**

the number of times a publication comes out in a given period of time, such as daily, weekly, quarterly, etc.

■ **Frequency Division Multiplexing (FDM)**

the analog method of deriving multiple transmission channels from a single physical facility, divides of an available frequency range (bandwidth) into various sub-channels. Widely used in many formats by virtually every kind of telecommunications technology, the ' carrier systems ' of telephony. Also called Frequency Division Multiplex , Frequency Division Mux.

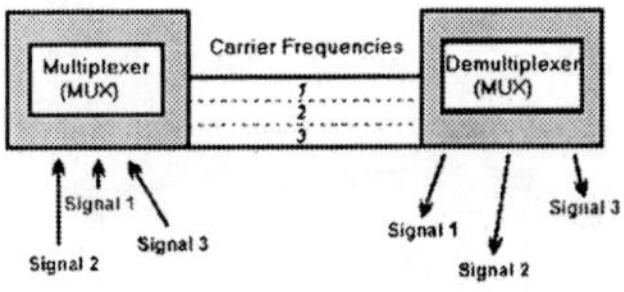

■ **frequency response**

the measurement of how well a transmission channel or device transports all the frequencies sent into it, a measure of how faithfully signals are transported or reproduced. In Bell terms, the arithmetic is reversed and the name 'amplitude response' or 'amplitude variation' is used for the same expression.

■ **Frequency Shift Keying (FSK)**

when associated with HF (300 baud) Packet, the shift is 200 Hz. One of the more basic and durable forms of transmitting binary information, in FSK, one of the binary states is represented by one known frequency and the other by another known frequency. The receiver produces outputs only when one of the two known frequencies is received in the absence of the other. Applications of FSK abound in every form of telecommunications.

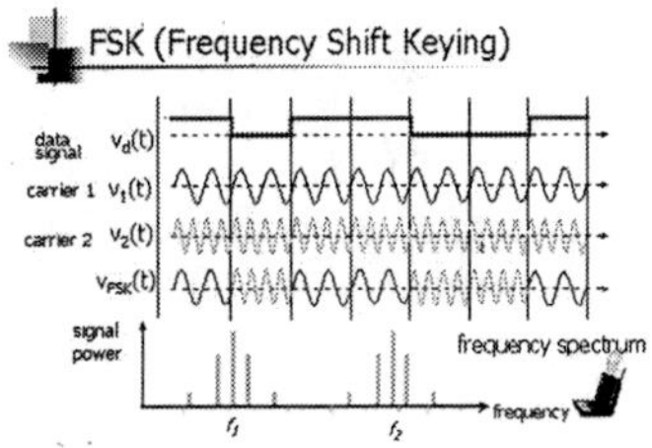

■ **fresnel zone**

the area in open space that must be practically free of obstructions for a microwave radio path to function properly, some degree of fresnel consideration is required in the immediate vicinity of the form of microwave radio used on satellite links.

■ **f-stop**

the scale used to measure the size of the opening of the iris on a lens. closing it down, smaller, lets opening the iris wider lets in more light and in less light. F-stops can be a little confusing, because the larger the number, the smaller the opening of the iris and conversely the smaller the number, the larger the opening. The typical f-stop scale is 1.4 - 2- 2.8 - 4 - 5.6 - 8 - 11 - 16 - 22. When the reading is between stops, this should be accounted for it setting the lens, however, it is much more clear, even if it sounds grammatically incorrect to the mathematically inclined, to say 'One third above 5.6' rather than '5.8' because it is very hard to judge the distance in decimals between numbers like 5.6 and 8, whereas 1/3rd above 5.6 is perfectly clear.

■ **FTP**

File Transport Protocol. This is a part of TCP/IP which allows a user of a TCP/IP host to request or send files from another TCP/IP station.

■ **FUD**

short for 'Fear, Uncertainty and Doubt'. FUD is using positioning of one's own products or services to cast fear, uncertainty and doubt on the competitors.

■ **Full Duplex (FDX)**

a circuit which allows independent transmission of information in both directions simultaneously. In wire telephony, 4 wire circuit.

■ **full-motion video**

display of a video sequence at the broadcast TV frame rate of 30 fps. Sometimes used to define motion video that is perceived to provide smooth motion regardless of frame rate applied.

■ **full-service agency**

an ad agency that handles all phases of advertising for its clients.

■ **functional approach**

a methodology that holds something is best understood by examining how it is used.

■ **furnish (composition)**

composition (furnish) is the mixture of various materials, such as fibre, filler, sizing materials and other additives, used to make the paper stock.

■ **fusing compatibility**

compatibility of print media used in the printer and how it reacts when exposed to the fuser's temperature of: 205° C (401° F) for 0.1 second (0.2 second for HP Colour LaserJet printers) for paper, labels and envelopes and 205° C (401° F) for 0.1 second (0.4 second for HP Colour LaserJet printers) for overhead transparency materials Print media should not discolour, melt, offset, release undesirable emissions or break down in any way.

■ **g3ruh modem**

a 9600 bps plug-in modem for TNC-2s and other amateur TNCs. Circuitry contains adaptable filters to adjust for bandwidth limitations in commercial radios and a 'randomiser' circuit to prevent DC offsets on modulated data. Similar to but may not be totally compatible with K9NG modem. Believed to be compatible with the most recent TAPR 9600 bps modem.

■ **gaffer's tape**

cloth tape specifically for use on film shoots, usually 2 inches wide in black or silver. The nice thing about gaffer's tape is that, unlike duct tape, it is designed not to leave a sticky residue behind.

■ **gag order(s)**

a restrictive court order that prohibits all or some participants in a trial from speaking about a case or that stops publications and broadcasting stations from reporting on certain aspects of a case.

■ **gag rules**

judicial orders that restrict trial participants from giving information to the media or that restrain media coverage of events that occur in court.

■ **gain**

denotes an increase in signal power in transmission from one point to another, usually expressed in decibels.

■ **game button**

selects the Front AV Input, switches 16:9 televisions into Wide Mode and optimises pre-sets for colour and brightness – ideal for the reproduction of game graphics.

■ **gate**

the opening on a camera or a projector just behind the lens, through which a single frame is exposed (in the camera) or projected (in the projector).

■ **gatefold**

a full-page or spread with an extended page or page of a page, that folds outward.

■ **gatekeepers**

those in control of the flow of information. The gatekeeper can choose to accept or reject a piece of information for public consumption. Newspaper publishers, editors and reporters, television producers, radio station owners and broadcasting executives have all been cited as examples of media gatekeepers.

■ **gatekeeping**

the selection or rejection of events in the 'real' world. For example, an editor decides on what's going to be covered, an organiser briefs the camera crews, the reporter decides what 'angle' the story will be covered from and so on. These people are all gatekeepers. The concept of gatekeeping tends to be related to rather mechanistic models of communication processes. Though it may serve to remind us of the operation of a selection process in the representation of news, it is essentially too simplistic to be a great deal of use.

■ **gateway**

with Packet radio, a gateway is a 'bridge' that provides a means to communicate digitally from one frequency into another or from one baud rate to another. A node-stack connection is between two different Packet networks, frequencies, baudrates or LAN. A configuration of nodes where connectivity is available by deliberate manipulation but where automatic end-to-end routing is not possible. This is useful for connecting two networks together such that users and servers on one network can access users and servers on the other network without compromising networking practices on either.

gauge

the size, specifically the width, of a film format: 16mm, 35mm, Super-8 are gauges.

gel

a large sheet of transparent tinted plastic used as a filter for a movie light or to cover a window. There are two basic types: ones that will covert one colour temperature to another (such as C.T.O. and C.T.B.) and others that come in a wide variety of colours.

gendered media

used in several ways. First, a belief that men and women have a different and unequal relationship to mainstream media in terms of how they are portrayed. Second, a belief that a male bias is so deeply entrenched within media structures, processes and outputs that its expression is systemic and structural rather than individual prejudice. Third, a tendency to see, interpret and frame media content from a male point of view as natural, normal and inevitable, while female perspectives are ignored or distorted.

generation loss

video degradation caused by successive recordings (dubs of other dubs) from the master source. This is overcome by digital recording.

genre

specific kinds of media content, e.g., entertainment, information, news, advertising, etc. Each category is defined with traditional conventions, but categories may overlap.

genre prints

prints depicting scenes from everyday life.

geosynchronous orbit

a position at an approximate altitude of 23,000 miles above the Equator, where a velocity of about 1,000 miles per hour in the same direction as Earth's rotation makes a satellite appear stationary over the Earth's surface. At such a point, ground-based microwave antennae can remain fixed and achieve linkage with transponders on board the satellite to produce a microwave relay between points as much as one-third of the way around the globe or about 8,000 miles.

ghostwriter

person writing articles or speeches for another person who claims authorship.

gillotage

a relief process made by transferring a lithographic image to a metal plate that is then etched to produce a relief plate. The term is also used inaccurately to indicate varieties of photomechanical relief printing.

■ **giveaway**

a novelty or gift used in a promotion. Banks frequently offer giveaways or prizes, to customers opening accounts.

■ **grain**

the orientation of paper fibres in paper.

■ **graphic design**

any form of visual artistic representation.

■ **graphic designer**

the person responsible for producing artistic representations, usually under the guidance of an art director or creative director.

■ **graphic equaliser**

the graphic equaliser influences the characteristics of a predefined range of different frequencies. Frequencies can be adjusted individually or by selecting set styles.

■ **graphics**

includes pictographs, typography and some types of text, as well as symbols, photographs and geometric designs. Graphics are visual elements used to point readers and viewers to particular information.

■ **greek**

the gibberish or nonsense text placed in a 'dummy' to signify where the copy will eventually be.

■ **green room**

a small room near a broadcast studio in which program guests wait before they are interviewed.

■ **grey background**

paper looks grey or appears dirty because small toner particles are transferred to non-printed areas (white space). This condition is a symptom of a print-quality problem.

■ **groundwood**

wood fibres that are extracted using a mechanical rather than a chemical process. Groundwood papers are generally weaker than chemical wood papers.

■ **group delay distortion**

also called envelope delay distortion. A distortion of the data signal produced when the different frequency spectral components of the digital signal are phase shifted by different amounts resulting in a distorted pulse shape. For best results, it is important that radio filters, amplifiers and other components in the communication system have a constant phase shift across their bandwidth. This is called 'flat group delay' characteristic.

■ **guillotine**

a type of tape splicer which uses unperforated splicing tape.

■ **gunning fog index**

system for measuring copy readability. It provides a close approximation of the educational grade level that a person of average intelligence would need to understand the material without difficulty.

■ gutter

the white space formed by the inner margins on two facing pages.

■ halation

halation is the effect that occurs when the bright areas of an image appear to softly bleed around the edges of dark areas. This is caused by light going through the emulsion layer, bouncing off the base of the film and exposing the adjacent emulsion. Some film is manufactured with a black anti-halation coating on the base side.

■ half duplex

a circuit capable of transmitting or receiving information in two directions, but only one direction at a time, a function of both computer protocols and transmission channels. Many computers operate only half duplex on transmission channels capable of full duplex operation.

■ halftone

an image formed by printing close-set dots of varying sizes on paper or other 'hard' media.

■ half-tone engraving

a photochemical process that uses a screen to break up the image into dots of varying sizes, which results in tone variations.

■ halogen

this is the gas contained in the lamp of a Quartz Light, which prolongs the life of the tungsten filament. Quartz Lights are sometimes called Halogen Lights for this reason.

■ hamming code

in data transmission, a code with added redundant bits for error detection purposes.

■ hammock

the programming slot between two hit shows, often used to launch a new program.

■ handbill

a small, printed advertising sheet or flyer distributed by hand.

■ handheld

shooting without a tripod, but with the camera held by the cameraperson.

■ hard news

timely stories with significance for many people.

■ hard sell

a general term to describe any aggressive advertising technique.

■ hardware

the technology used to create and communicate with media. The physical device, which enables messages stored on software to pass from a sender to a receiver. Television, radio, computers, movie projectors, telephones, etc., are hardware. Although pencils and printing presses are also technically hardware, the term is most often used to refer to electronic media.

■ harmonic

an exact multiple of a 'fundamental' frequency. Examples: Second harmonic = double the fundamental frequency, third harmonic = three times and 12th harmonic = one dozen times and so on. Sometimes an expression of the required bandwidth for transmission, as in the case of binary transmission where it is well established that a bandwidth equal to the tenth odd harmonic is needed for accurate reception of the pulses, this means the fundamental, third, fifth, seventh, ninth, eleventh, thirteenth, fifteenth, seventeenth, nineteenth and twenty-first harmonics must be passed. Thus a 50 bps binary pulse requires a bandwidth of 50 x 21 or 1050 Hertz for accurate capture of the pulses ... unless it is somehow encoded for transmission.

■ harmonic distortion

the ratio, expressed in decibels, of the power at the fundamental frequency, to the power of a harmonic of that fundamental. Odd harmonics, particularly third harmonics, are especially harmful to many forms of telecommunications by both wire and radio, as well, they are annoyingly difficult to design out of electronic circuitry.

■ hbaud

data speed between the TNC and the transceiver. Sometimes referred to as the 'station to station' baud rate.

■ HDLC

High Level Data Link Control. A bit-oriented international standard data link protocol used in CCITT X.25 packet network links and influencing many others. An example is the process employed in X.25 and AX.25 to format data into Packets. These packets of data have the destination address, checksum count and other necessary components added through HDLC to help make it an error-free mode. The ISO level 2 link level.

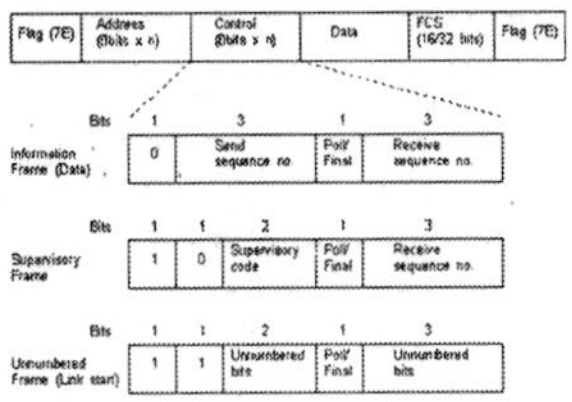

■ HDPE

acronym for High Density Polyethylene. Recyclable and chemical-resistant HDPE is found in printing films.

■ HDTV

High Definition Television. The broadcast standard that offers greater resolution by increasing the number of scan lines.

■ head

1. the beginning of a shot or a roll is called the head.
2. a small round clamp, usually used in conjunction with an arm on a C-Stand.
3. the Tripod Head

■ Head clog

Debris trapped in the playback head of a video recorder. Clogging of the playback head with debris causes dropouts.

■ head end

the antenna and related equipment of the cable system that receives and processes distant television signals so that they can be sent to subscribers' homes.

■ head room

the space between the top of a subject's head and the top of the frame. Headroom must be carefully apportioned so that there is not too much or too little, especially if shooting for transfer to video or for blow-up, where the frame will be cropped in a little on the top and sides.

■ head shot

a glossy 8 x 10-inch photo focussed on the face, usually of an actor or model.

■ header

that portion of a message containing information for routing, handling and delivering a message, such as address, size, priority, intermediate routing and synchronisation signals.

■ headline

the title of an article or press release.

■ heard or mheard list

Monitored & Heard: On several different packet devices, including user TNC BBSs, nodes etc., there exists a feature whereby a list of stations heard are recorded. This list is called a heard list. Access to the list is different depending on the application.

■ hegemony

dominance, in the realm of mass media, it involves a process of thought control in which dominant ideas and ideals are reproduced without people's awareness that their attitudes are being changed. This dominant consensus works in a concealed way that may have the effect of naturalising the social and constructed as normal and necessary. Media are prime players in winning rather than coercing consent: they promote values and practices that (1) are no longer questioned or challenged but taken for granted, (2) represent an article of faith to be defended at all costs or (3) become so deeply ingrained as to fall outside the realm of normal consciousness.

■ helical scan recording

The recording format in which a slow moving tape is helically wrapped 180° around a rapidly rotating drum with a small embedded record head. The tape is positioned at a slight angle to the equatorial plane of the drum. This results in a recording format in which recorded tracks run diagonally across the tape from one edge to the other. Recorded tracks are parallel to each other but are at an angle to the edge of the tape.

■ HF

High Frequency.

■ hi hat

this is a square of plywood with a bracket attached, to which a tripod head may be added (or is sometimes permanently affixed) used for filming with the camera very low to the ground. Its name is a bit of a contradiction, to its use nowadays, but it used to be that a Hi Hat was for shooting from very high up, with the plywood board being mounted up high somewhere.

■ hicklin rule

a long-standing obscenity standard based upon whether a book or other item contains isolated passages that might deprave or corrupt the mind of the most susceptible person.

■ hidden persuaders

a range of subtle or subliminal advertising messages.

■ hierarchy of access

the media rarely give first-hand accounts of 'deviants" behaviour. Their behaviour is explained for us by others. The behaviour of such groups is often reported in the press, but they have little or no control over what is said.

In any system of ranked groups, members of the highest group have the right to define the way things really are those at the top have access to a more complete picture of what is going on than anybody else. Members of lower groups will have incomplete information and their view of reality will be partial and distorted in consequence.

The 'accessed voices' speak from a limited range of social positions, usually those contained within the safe limits of parliamentary democracy. Voices that appear too radical are not allowed to speak directly, but are reported, that is, mediated, if their point of view is represented at all.

■ hit

a visit to a particular page on a web site by a web visitor.

■ hits

a hit is the sending of a single file whether text, image, audio or other file type. Since a single request can bring with it a number of individual files, the number of hits from a site is not a good indication of the actual visitors.

■ HMI

this is a type of light. HMI stands for Halogen Metal Incandescence. HMIs are very bright, power efficient lights. They are balanced for the Colour Temperature of Daylight, making them handy in mixed lighting situations. However, they are rather expensive, costing something in the few thousands of dollars and are not very portable due to the large and heavy ballast that is attached. This is vitally important to keep in mind, they must be used with a Crystal Sync camera, otherwise they will flicker and throb.

■ homophobia

the fear of homosexuality as expressed by demeaning images in media texts.

■ hook

a clever phrase or melody used to capture the consumer's attention and help make the advertising message more memorable.

■ horizontal publication

a publication having very broad editorial material. A vertical publication reaches a far more segmented audience.

horticultural tags

fade-resistant full colour weatherproof labels, tags and signs for outdoor use on potted plants, trees and shrubs. Commonly printed on weatherproof and outdoor durable printing film.

hot

usually in reference to a microphone meaning it's 'on'.

house drop

the section of the cable that connects the feeder cable to the subscriber's TV set.

house lights

you can request 'House Lights' for a print and the lab will not time your film, but print it without any exposure or colour correction. House lights are typically at the middle of the printing scale: 25-25 -25.

house organ

a newsletter produced by a company for the employees of that company.

HTML

HyperText Markup Language: a standard language used to make documents for the web. Most Web pages are coded using HTML, which defines such things as type size, position of graphics and all other features of the Web page.

HTS

Hidden Transmitter Syndrome. This describes a condition where throughput is drastically reduced to well below the specified baud rate because a single station is able to hear two or more stations that can't hear each other.

human interest

news value that emphasises the emotional, bizarre, offbeat or uplifting nature of a news story.

hygroscopic

The tendency of a material to absorb water. An effect related to changes in moisture content or relative humidity. The hygroscopic expansion coefficient of a tape refers to its change in length as it takes up water upon an increase in the ambient relative humidity.

hype/hyperbole

extreme promotion of a person, idea or product.

hyperband tuner

for picking up the extended range of special channels with cable TV facilities.

hyperfocal distance

the hyperfocal distance is a distance set on the focussing ring of the lens that will most efficiently use the Depth of Field present. A depth of field chart will list possible distances and graph out the area of focus at different f-stops. There does not necessarily have to be a subject to focus on at that distance.

hypermedia

a multimedia application that lets the user point to objects, images, video or text to navigate the application.

■ **hypertext**

digital navigational tool that links one electronic document to another.

■ **IF - intermediate frequency**

the function of a radio receiver is to convert a radio wave, which has audio on it, to audio information to be played into a speaker or into a packet modem. The process is often done in two steps. First the radio signal (RF or radio frequency) is converted from the tuned frequency to a known constant frequency. This is done by mixing the incoming signal with the VFO or synthesiser. This known constant frequency is the I F. Next the IF is converted into audio via a discriminator (in the case of FM). I F Bandwidth, Intermediate Frequency bandwidth. The width of the band of signals that can pass easily through the intermediate frequency stage of a superheterodyne receiver.

■ **IBOC**

In-Band, On-Channel. Digital radio broadcasting system that is also compatible with current analog radio.

■ **IDE**

Integrated Drive Electronics.

■ **identification**

as used in a libel suit, the requirement that the plaintiff prove that at least one person believes that the subject of the libellous remarks is the plaintiff and not some other person.

■ **ideology**

can be used in two senses. In its broadest sense, it refers to a complex of ideas and ideals that attempt to explain or justify a specific set of circumstances. Ideology can also be employed in the Marxist sense of false consciousness to refer to a complex of ideas that secures the status quo, justifies the prevailing distribution of power, privilege and resources in society and bolsters the dominant sector as natural or normal. According to this notion of ideology, subdominant patterns are dismissed as irrelevant or inferior.

■ **IEEE**

'Institute of Electrical & Electronic Engineers': A professional organisation that helps set transmission system standards.

■ **IMA**

Interactive Multimedia Association. An umbrella organisation grouping over 220 suppliers and end-users to deal with multimedia standards and data exchange issues. Endorses and supervises technical aspects of JPEG and MPEG compression standards and developing multimedia platform standards.

■ **impact**

the degree of success of a campaign, the reaching of consumers.

■ **impeachment**

a criminal proceeding against a public officer that is started by written 'articles of impeachment' and followed by a trial. The House of Representatives, for example, can issue articles of impeachment against the president, who is then tried by the Senate.

■ **importing**

a method of accessing or bringing in files created on other platforms or applications.

■ **impression**

an impression is a single piece of paper with an image printed on it from a matrix. The term as applied to prints is used in a manner similar to the term 'copy' as applied to a book.

■ **impromptu method of speaking**

involves speaking without specific preparation. This method is used when speakers are called upon without prior notice.

■ **in the can**

a show or portion of it that is complete and ready to broadcast. The tape or film literally is in a can.

■ **In-Band-On-Channel (IBOC)**

digital radio technology that uses digital compression to ìshrinkî digital and analog signals allowing both to occupy the same frequency.

■ **incident light reading**

an incident light reading measures the amount of light hitting the subject. You take an incident reading with a light meter equipped with a white half-sphere, which acts as a stand-in for the subject. The sphere is pointed at the camera, so that the same light hitting the subject is hitting the sphere. The other type of light reading is a Reflective Light Reading.

■ **independents**

radio or TV stations unaffiliated with any network.

■ **indirect action ad**

advertisement that works over the long run to build a company's image.

■ **industry**

the agencies and institutions involved with the production of media texts. The term is also used in a more restrictive sense to describe the commercial production of media texts for the purpose of making a profit.

■ **infinity**

the furthest distance on the focussing ring of a lens.

■ **information**

messages used as the basis for decision-making.

■ **information gathering**

phase of a public relations campaign where pertinent data are collected.

■ **information processing**

the conversion of data into information by sorting in useful ways.

■ **information/communication systems**

the use of a device or method to collect, process, store or deliver information using electronic, graphic, photographic or mechanical means.

infotainment

a television program that combines news and entertainment features, such as interviews, commentaries and reviews.

initialise

setting all counters, switches, addresses or pointer registers to zero or the beginning of or at prescribed points in the operation of a computer routine. As related to the 'reset' of a Packet node or 'rebooting' a computer.

injunction

a court order that requires an individual to do something or to stop doing something.

ink

space devoted to a company, its products or services in the print media.

input

data, materials, resources or instructions entered into (most often) a computer system.

insert

a printed sheet or sheets inserted into a publication or enclosed with a mailing.

insert shot

a close-up of some detail in the scene. (Sort of like a cutaway without the '-away' aspect.)

instrumental surveillance

a media function that occurs when the media transmit information that is useful and helpful in everyday life.

intaglio

any of the techniques in which an image or tonal area is printed from lines or textures scratched or etched into a metal plate (engraving, etching, dry point, aquatint, lift ground, soft ground). The plate is covered with ink, then wiped clean leaving ink in the incised lines or textures of the image. This plate is then printed in a press on moistened paper. The paper is forced down into the area of the plate holding ink and the image is transferred to the paper.

intaglio printing

printing from a plate into which an image has been cut. The ink is deposited in the depressions and then transferred to the paper.

intelligent terminal

a terminal containing a programmable processor capable of some degree of local processing, the range of functions and degree of capability is not standardised and subject to wide discussion of what constitutes 'intelligence'.

interactive

describes two-way process of communication in which feedback is used to modify subsequent messages between sender and receiver.

interactive television

TV programming with interactive content and enhancements, blending traditional TV viewing with the interactivity of a personal computer.

interactivity

the ability of a user to control the

presentation by a multimedia system, not only for material selection, but for the way in which material is presented.

■ **interchange file**

a family of file types whose specifications are standardised to facilitate use in a broad range of applications and in some cases platforms.

■ **interference**

any unwanted noise, cross-talk or spurious signals on a communications circuit that acts to reduce the intelligibility of the desired information signal or speech.

■ **interlaced**

the means by which traditional television picture tubes create images onscreen. An interlaced-scanning tube sends information to each pixel in the even-numbered rows of pixels on a screen, left to right and then top to bottom. Then it sends information to odd-numbered rows. The even and odd lines of each frame are referred to as fields. The 1080i (interlaced) high-definition standard, to be used for most high-definition broadcasts including those by NBC and CBS, is an interlaced-scanning standard.

■ **interleaving (interleave)**

in Packet or data communications, interleaving may be a character or bit interleaved, with optimum applications for each. A technique to minimise effects of error bursts on message throughput by interleaving groups of characters or blocks that approximate the burst length.

■ **interlocked**

two or more devices (most commonly dubbers in a mixing facility) with motors that run in sync are interlocked. It is not quite correct to say that a sync sound camera and tape recorder are interlocked, regardless of whether they use crystal of cable sync, since the tape recorder is recording pilottone and not really running with its motor interlocked with the camera motor.

■ **internegative**

an intermediate copy of a film, made on a very fine-grained stock and used to make a greater number of prints than it is practical to make from the A&B Rolls.

■ **internet**

a global network of interconnected computers that freely communicate (transmit information) according to some accepted protocols. Millions of computers are connected globally, creating a network in which any computer can communicate with any other on the network.

■ **internet addiction**

condition in which a person spends too much time on the Internet, cannot control his or her Internet use and neglects social responsibilities to spend time online.

■ **interpersonal communication**

a method of communication in which one person (or group) interacts with another person (or group) without the aid of a mechanical device.

■ **interpositive**

an intermediate copy of a film, made on a very fine-grained stock, usually required as an intermediate step to making an internegative.

■ **interrupt**

data processing term for a processing stoppage made in such a way as to be resumable. Compare to a 'halt' typically meaning a stoppage that requires initialising the machine to restart processing.

■ **interstitial**

an ad that opens in a separate browser window while waiting for a web page to load.

■ **intertextuality**

when a media text makes reference to another text that, on the surface, appears to be unique and distinct.

■ **intervalometer**

a device that attaches to the camera for filming single exposures, much like an animation motor, except that an intervalometer is capable of exposing single frames automatically, as in the technique of Time Lapse photography.

■ **interviews**

transcripts of discussions between The Communication Initiative and a range of people involved in various aspects of communication, change and development work.

■ **intrusion**

an invasion of privacy committed when one individual intrudes upon or invades the solitude of another individual.

■ **invasion of privacy**

a civil tort that emerged in the early 20th century and contains four distinct categories of legal wrongs: appropriation, intrusion, publication of private facts and false light.

■ **inverted pyramid**

journalistic style of writing where the most important information is written first, followed by information of decreasing importance (this allows the reader to stop reading having gained the most important information, it also allows editors to cut or edit the story from the bottom up without omitting vital information)

■ **investigative reports**

news reporting that requires extraordinary efforts to gather information about matters of public importance.

■ **IP**

Internet Protocol. The core protocol of the ARPA suite IP is a simple protocol that handles addressing, fragmentation and type-of-service routing in the heterogeneous internet environment

■ **iris**

like the iris of the eye, a valve within a lens to control the amount of light that passes through. Opening the iris permits more light to pass through the lens and closing the iris less. The degree to which the iris is open or closed is measured in F-Stops and on some lenses supplemented by T-Stops.

■ **IS**

Intermediate System. ISO's term for a packet switch. ISO standards apply to physical aspects of the '25-pin connector' of CCITT V.24/28 data interfaces (RS-232), definitions of several layers of data networks for which different hardware units may be required and such diverse things as the exposure speeds of photographic film and definitions of units of measurement.

■ **ISA**

Industry Standard Architecture.

■ **ISDN**

Integrated Services Digital Network. Telecommunications networks based on fibre optics with greatly enhanced transmission capacity for handling video images and applications such as video conferencing.

■ **island position**

an ad positioned in the middle of a page (floating), surrounded by editorial material.

■ **ISO**

International Standards Organisation. A world organisation which serves to promote establishment of standards in facilitating international exchange of goods and services and develop mutual cooperation in scientific, technical, intellectual and economic areas of activity. The American National Standards Institute (ANSI) is the current U.S. voice in the ISO.

■ **ISO 9660**

the designated specification number for the file structure standard of CD-ROM adopted by the International Standards Organisation.

■ **ITU**

International Telecommunication Union based in Geneva, Switzerland. Assigns frequency spectrum to different parts of the world through the International Frequency Registration Board (IFRB).

■ **jargon**

language known only to members of a specific group, company or industry.

■ **jazz**

a form of popular music that emerged during the Roaring Twenties and was noted for its spontaneity and disdain of convention.

■ **jazz journalism**

journalism of the Roaring Twenties that was characterised by a lively style and a richly illustrated tabloid format.

■ **JBIG**

Joint Bi-level Imaging Group. A working group established to develop a standard for compressing bi-level images such as black-and-white photographs or pages of text. JBIG is a loss less compression technique.

■ **jingle**

a catchy musical refrain delivering an advertising message, frequently used on radio or television.

jitter

Short term instability of the amplitude and/or phase of a signal. The latter condition is commonly called PHASE JITTER. Variations in the phase or amplitude of a data modulated signal having no relationship to the data. In amateur packet signals, phase jitter may cause error in decoding the data.

joint venture

method of movie financing in which several companies pool resources to finance films.

Joint-Operating Agreement (JOA)

an agreement, intended to preserve editorial competition, in which two newspapers merge their business and printing operations but maintain separate newsrooms.

jolts

moments in a media text that are generated by a broad comedy, a violent act, movement within a frame, a loud noise, rapid editing, a profanity or a sexually explicit representation, all of which are calculated to engage an audience's excitement.

JPEG

Joint Photographic Experts Group. A standard for compression algorithms for digitising still photographic images. JPEG compression ratios may range from 10:1 to 80:1, but it is a continuous trade-off between image quality and speed of delivery and storage capacity. Multimedia platforms are being equipped with special boards or chips implementing JPEG compression standard based on the DCT algorithm. There are also software solutions available to accomplish JPEG compression.

jump cut

basically, two similar shots cut together with a jump in continuity, camera position or time.

jump scrolling

characteristic of a terminal with vertical motions of a whole line of characters at a time in discrete steps of one line, much as a teleprinter terminal might do in contrast with 'smooth scrolling' as done by graphics terminals.

junior page

unit of measurement indicated a standard full-page, 7 x 10 inches, placed in a tabloid publication 9 7/8 x 12 inches.

k

'K' has two different meanings and both apply to movie lights, so one should be careful to differentiate one from the other.

1. an abbreviation for Kilowatts. There are 1,000 Watts in 1 Kilowatt. It is used when talking about quartz lights or HMIs, as a way to measure their brightness based on their power consumption. A '1K' is a 1,000 Watt light, a '2K' a 2,000 Watt light, etc.

2. an abbreviation for Kelvin, such as 3,200K for tungsten balance, 5,400K for daylight, etc.

ka band

microwave radio frequencies in the region of 20 to 30 gigahertz, portions of which are used for local microwave ' bypass' notably the region near 23 gigahertz , while future satellite applications have allocations reserved as well.

kantronics

kantronics designs, manufactures and markets a range of amateur packet products including the popular KPC TNCs and KAM multimode controller.

KBPS

Kilobits Per Second. A measure of transmission rate in thousands of bits per second commonly referred to as baud rate. Communication channels using telephone modems are established at set bit rates, 300, 1200, 2400, 4800, 9600, 14400 respectively. (example 14.4kbps)

kelvin

this is the Colour Temperature scale that takes its name from the scientist Lord Kelvin.

key

the special effects technique which allows one picture to be inserted within another. The video 'box' over the newscaster's shoulder on television is an example of a key.

key influencers

individuals, groups or publications whose opinion or coverage of a product, service or company can significantly affect public perception within a specific market

keyboard-to-keyboard

communications between two packet user stations in real time. A fun part of Packet radio that is again being experienced by many Packet users. Emergency digital communications are a few ways that keyboard-to-keyboard is useful.

kidvid

children's television programs or videotapes.

kinescope

a film of a transmitted television program.

kinetic energy

the energy of a mass in motion (e.g., pendulum swinging, spring unwinding).

kinetoscope

the first practical motion picture camera and viewing device, developed by William Dickson in 1889.

KISS

Keep It Simple & Short: the TNC operating mode where the TNC merely translates packets between half duplex, synchronous HDLC on the radio port and full duplex asynchronous SLIP framing on the host port, the host computer must implement all higher level protocols, including AX25 if it is used. The KISS TNC is only responsible for TX delay and DCD hold-off. Kiss is used with TCP/IP hosts and also often used with BPQ and other such PC based packet switches.

■ **knowledge gap**

the knowledge gap hypothesis states that 'as the infusion of mass media information into a social system increases, segments of the population with higher socio-economic status tend to acquire this information at a faster rate than the lower status segments, so that the gap in knowledge between these segments tends to increase rather than decrease'.

■ **ku band**

Microwave radio frequencies in the region of 10 to 20 gigahertz, portions of which are used for satellite (notably VSAT) operations at 12 to 14 gigahertz and local terrestrial 'bypass' at 10 and 18 gigahertz.

■ **L.F.O.A.**

this stands for Last Frame of Action and basically it is just what it sounds like: the last frame of image and sound on a reel. It is important to the people who mix your film (it should be written on the cue sheet), especially if you need to do Pull Ups.

■ **lab roll**

a large roll (usually up to 1,000 feet) made up of camera rolls joined together by the lab for printing.

■ **latency**

used by some to describe the time delay from the point when a Packet network station seeks access to a channel and the time access is granted by the network, an evolving term unique to certain LANs.

■ **latitude**

the degree to which a certain film stock can tolerate under- or over-exposure. Reversal film, for all practical purposes, has a very little latitude. Colour negative has a higher latitude and particular of its latitude it is tolerant of much more overexposure than underexposure.

■ **launch**

the introduction of a new product or service.

■ **layout**

a design for graphic advertising production, roughly depicting the look of the finished advertisement.

■ **lead or lede (pronounced leed)**

the opening sentence or paragraph of a news story.

■ **lead time**

period of time that reporters and producers need to prepare stories and information for publication or broadcast.

■ **leader or leader blank**

the blank film or tape used at the 'head' or start of a program. Can be used to thread a projector or tape machine so the show can go on the air as soon as the machine starts running.

■ **learning log**

a record of activities completed during an assignment.

■ **lens flare**

it is caused when light strikes the

lens and either causes the entire image to be fogged in appearance or for a little row of polygons (the silhouette of the iris) to appear from the light hitting the surfaces of the many elements in the lens. It is solved by flagging the lens.

letterbox

a technique for showing wide-screen movies on television that preserves the original aspect ratio by filling the top and bottom parts of the screen with black bars.

lettering

the lettering of a print refers to the information, usually given below the image, concerning the title, artist, publisher, engraver and other such data.

letterpress

typographic printing from movable type.

letterpress printing

oldest form of printing in which the printing plate has raised surfaces and the ink is spread onto the plate and then transferred directly to the paper.

letters to the editor

your opportunity to congratulate, discuss or criticise an article you have read.

level

an expression of the relative signal strength at a point in a communications circuit compared to a standard, the standard is most often 1 milliwatt of power at a frequency of 1000 Hertz in a 600 Ohm load. The output impedance of most terminal node controllers is 600 ohms.

libel

written defamation that tends to injure a person's reputation or good name or that diminishes the esteem, respect or goodwill due a person.

libel per quod

written material that becomes libellous under certain circumstances.

libel per se

falsely written accusations (such as labeling a person a 'thief' or a 'swindler') that automatically constitute libel.

liberal pluralism

a philosophy and political principle that argues for the universality ('sameness') of humanity. According to liberal pluralism, what people have in common as rights-bearing and equality-seeking individuals is much more important than what divides them as members of a group, that the content of our characters is more important than the colour of our skin and that what we do and accomplish is more important than who we are because of birth or biology. A commitment to this principle makes it difficult to take differences seriously.

■ **libertarian theory**

the assumption that all human beings are rational decision makers and that governments exist to serve the individual.

■ **licensed characters**

characters, usually cartoons, licensed by their creators for use by mass marketers. Each time an item bearing that image is sold, a royalty is paid to the licensed owner.

■ **licensing process**

the process by which a government gives a publisher or a broadcaster prior permission to print a newspaper or operate a broadcasting station. Revocation of a license can be used as punishment for failing to comply with the law or the wishes of the government. Licensing of the printed press in the United States ended in the 1720s.

■ **lift-ground aquatint**

a form of intaglio printing in which the artists draw with a specially formulated ink on a metal plate. The plate is then covered with an acid resistant ground and immersed in water. The characteristics of the drawing medium (which may be applied with a pen or brush) allow it to dissolve and work through the acid resistant ground. When bitten in acid, the final result resembles pen or brushwork.

■ **lightleak**

stray light that penetrates into a camera giving the film little patches of fog. Also the term for the access point itself. Typically light leaks occur around the camera door or where the magazine is joined to the camera body. Often they can be easily prevented with camera tape around the door.

■ **lights**

see **timing lights**.

■ **limited edition**

a limited edition print is one in which a limit is placed on the number of impressions pulled in order to create a scarcity of the print. Limited editions are usually numbered and are often signed. Limited editions are a relatively recent development, dating from the late nineteenth century. Earlier prints were limited in the number of their impressions solely by market demand or by the maximum number that could be printed by the medium used. The inherent physical limitations of the print media and the relatively small size of the pre-twentieth century print market meant that non-limited edition prints before the late nineteenth century were in fact quite limited in number even though not intentionally so. German printmaker Adam von Bartsch, in his 1821 Anleitung zur Kupferstichkunde, estimated the maximum number of quality impressions it was possible to pull using different print media. Engraving: 500 (and about the same number of weaker images). Stipple: 500 (and about the same number of weaker im-

[illegible] mezzotint: 300 to 400, [illegible] quality suffers after [illegible]. Aquatint: Less than 200. Wood block: Up to 10,000. The development of lithography and of steel facing of metal plates in the nineteenth century permited tens of thousands of impressions could be pulled without a loss of quality. These technological developments led to the idea of making limited edition prints, by which printmakers created an appearance of rarity and individuality for multiple-impression art.

■ **limited partnership**

method of movie financing in which a number of investors put up a specified amount of money for a film.

■ **line printer**

descriptive of computer printers that set and print an entire line of data at a time. - e.g., Line-printer or LPT1, often indicative of a high-speed, high volume printer. Line side - descriptive of observing from or sending into the transmission path.

■ **lineage**

a newspaper term denoting the number of agate lines or amount of space in an ad. An agate line measures one column wide and 1/14 inches deep. Therefore, 14 lines equal one column inch.

■ **link**

a portal to another web site or to another area within a web site.

■ **link layer**

the logical second layer of the OSI Reference Model for Open Systems Interconnection, located between the Physical and Network layers. Level 2 in the 7 layer OSI computer communications protocol set. AX.25 is the amateur packet level 2 protocol.

■ **linkage**

the ability of the mass media to join different elements of society that are not directly connected by interpersonal channels.

■ **links**

website resources - summary links to organisations and projects that are addressing aspects of communication and change.

■ **linocut**

the relief image is carved from a linoleum surface.

■ **linoleum cut**

a relief print carved into linoleum rather than wood.

■ **lip sync**

another way of saying Sync Sound.

■ **liquid barretter**

first audio device permitting the reception of wireless voices.

listening strategies (techniques for effective listening)

these include: concentrate (have an open attitude and an interest), understand what to listen for (determine the speaker's purpose, main ideas, support), listen critically (relate the message to own experience, analyse the message, evaluate the message) and use graphic organisers (note taking, webbing, charting, etc.) when appropriate.

lithograph

a printing technique in which the image is drawn on a very flat slab of limestone (or a specially treated metal plate). This stone is treated chemically so that ink, when rolled on to the stone, adheres only where the drawing was done. This inked image can then be transferred to a piece of paper with the help of a high-pressure press.

lithography

marks made on a prepared stone are printed by means of certain inks' varying affinity for oily and watery surfaces (very loosely speaking).
'State' is a key term related to all of these processes. Two prints are of different states if they were made from a matrix, which was altered (for example, by etching more lines into it) after the making of the earlier impression and before the making of the later one.

lithotint

a tonal lithograph printed from a single stone or plate.

live tag

the voice-over at the end of a pre-recorded commercial that provides current or local information, dealer addresses, etc.

live-streaming

feeding (streaming) video/audio or other data to end-users at a specific time (that is, live). Today the term is most often used for on-line services.

LNA

Leading National Advertisers. A service available to advertisers for the purpose of researching competitive advertising expenditures on a quarterly basis.

loading booth

a small darkroom sometimes found on a sound stage for loading film into magazines as a roomier alternative to a Changing Bag.

Local Area Network (LAN)

when associated with amateur radio Packet, the term defines an area or locale where a group of Packeteers use the same frequency to converse or receive messages into their personal Packet mailbox.

location sound

this is the sync sound or any other sort of wild track or room tone that was recorded at the shoot. Same as Production Sound.

locked cut

the so-called final cut of a film when there are to be no more changes to picture.

■ **locked down shot**

a shot taken [illegible] pan and tilt releases on the [illegible] ened so that the camera [illegible] move. Often done for [illegible] effects where camera [illegible] would ruin the illusion [illegible] a cut that causes [illegible] magically disappear from a [illegible].

■ **locked route**

The NET nodes [illegible] capacity to generate rout[illegible] automatically based on [illegible]ers set in the node's RAM. [illegible]ameters specify default [illegible] values to be assigned to [illegible] each neighbor, separat[illegible] and for radio port neighb[illegible] RS-232 [illegible]ble us- [illegible] command [illegible] speci- [illegible] Port [illegible] CALL/SSID + VALUE] EXAMPLE: [illegible] ABT-7 + 192 [illegible]

[illegible] used to [illegible] company [illegible]

■ **logotype**

the stylised lettering [illegible] employed in a logo.

■ **long lens**

a lens with [illegible] length greater than 25mm in 16mm or 50mm in 35mm which, like binoculars, will provide a view [illegible] magnifies a small area.

■ **longitudinal recording**

a recording format in which a slow or fast moving tape is passed by a stationary recording head. The recorded tracks are parallel to the edge of the tape and run the full length of the tape.

■ **loop**

1. slack film above and below the gate to allow a transition from the constant motion of the supply and take up rollers to the intermittent motion that takes place at the gate. 2. a small magnifier useful in the editing room.

■ **loopback**

a test in which the output of a modem modulator or other full-duplex digital device is looped back to the input of the demodulator or device. The looped back signal may be either analog or digital. LOOP BACK (pinging) - A transmission testing method of simply having the distant node (end) on a network send back the signals it receives for evaluation at the transmitting end.

■ **looping**

see **dubbing**. Called looping because the film is on a loop to give the actor several tries at a line. Also called A.D.R.

■ **LOS**

Line of Sight. Descriptive of the use of free-space communications technologies requiring an unobstructed path between transmitter and receiver, as in microwave radio, satellite communications and infrared optical communications links.

■ **low con print**

a low contrast print specifically for transfer to video, which favours less contrast in the transfer process.

■ **lubricant**

a component added to the magnetic layer of a tape to decrease the friction between the head and the tape.

■ **luminance**

refers to the brightness value of all the points in an image.

■ **M&E**

M&E stands for Music and Effects. After a mix a big production will have an M&E track made, which is used when the film is dubbed into other languages so that all the Music and Effects do not also have to be redone. An M&E track is only essential if you plan on dubbing your film into a different language.

■ **M.O.S.**

a shot, a sequence or a film that is shot without sound, which is added later. M.O.S. stands for 'Mit Out Sound' and derives from an old Hollywood story about a German director asking for a shot to be filmed 'mit out sound' and the camera assistant complying with this request by writing 'M.O.S.' on the slate.

■ **MAB**

Magazine Advertising Bureau. An organisation, which sponsors studies, generates and distributes me-

dia and ... and ... dium.

■ **machin...**

an ... change ... rection ... purp...

■ **ma...**

a ... a me... with ...

■ **ma...**

a len... ... again. ... on th... apply

■ **mac...**

a soci... siders th... a system ... entire ...

■ **mag**

short f...

■ **mag st... magn...**

mag tr... coated ... lides. ... ing t...

Iron oxide, chromium dioxide, barium ferrite and metal particulate are various examples of magnetic pigment used in commercial tapes. The term pigment is a carry over of terminology from paint and coating technology - the magnetic coating on a tape is analogous to a coat of paint in which the magnetic particle is the paint pigment.

■ **Magnetic pigment**

See **magnetic particles.**

■ **magnetic remanence**

The strength of the magnetic field that remains in a tape or magnetic particle after it is (1) exposed to a strong, external magnetic field and (2) the external field is removed. The property of a tape that determines its ability to record and store a magnetic signal. Mr is the common abbreviation for magnetic remanence. Magnetic remanence, Mr and magnetic retentivity, Br, both refer to the ability of the tape to retain a magnetic field, however the latter is expressed in units of magnetic flux density.

■ **magnetic retentivity**

See **magnetic remanence.**

■ **magneto-optical**

see **CD-WREM**.

■ **mail box**

a personal BBS in a TNC. Sometimes also refers to any personal BBS system handling personal mail. (Also called Mail Drop, PMS, Personal BBS, PBBS)

■ **mail drop**

a part of a TNC program that allows messages to be loaded into the TNC and then retrieved from over the air or from the terminal at the TNC.

■ **mail order**

retail sales conducted by mail.

■ **mailer**

a mailed advertisement.

■ **mailing list**

a list of prospective customers organised by defined factors such as location, income or other consumer profile aspect.

■ **mainstreaming**

in cultivation analysis, the tendency of differences to disappear among heavy-TV-viewing people, apparently because of cultural and social factors.

■ **manufactured materials**

materials that do not exist in nature (e.g., steel, fabric).

■ **manuscript method of speaking**

involves writing out the speech and reading it. This method is commonplace among heads of state and business officials, for example, when precise wording is essential and there could be serious consequences for any word 'misspoken'. For novice speakers, this method may be the easiest and safest, training in planned/extemporaneous speaking may be more valuable.

■ **mapping**

in network operations, the logical associa[illegible] such as [illegible] with [illegible] other [illegible] ond [illegible] address[illegible] work-re[illegible]

■ **MARC**[illegible]

Marketing [illegible]

■ **mark**

1. the clapp[illegible] create a [illegible] shot.
2. a piece [illegible] indicates [illegible] stand.

■ **mark**

one of two [illegible] in data com[illegible] mark is the [illegible] chronous ser[illegible] tive voltage [illegible] is called [illegible] tone in an [illegible] mark. (See [illegible] state). M[illegible] on a b[illegible] a '1.' C[illegible] hole in [illegible] negative [illegible] 232.

■ **market**[illegible]

the pr[illegible] given pro[illegible]

■ **market**[illegible]

the charac[illegible] area targe[illegible]

■ **market re**[illegible]

a study of [illegible] business connecti[illegible]

[illegible] market.

■ marketing

[illegible] packaging, advertising, [illegible] distributing your [illegible] and the pub- [illegible] support this [illegible]

■ [illegible]

[illegible] often adver- [illegible] performance.

■ mass

[illegible] amorphous category [illegible] the media per- [illegible] distinct iden- [illegible] organise or act in [illegible] power.

■ [illegible]

[illegible] which a com- [illegible] the aid of [illegible] produces [illegible] messages that [illegible] large, heteroge- [illegible] scattered audiences.

[illegible] driven process [illegible] one-way flow [illegible] content from a [illegible] audience, with [illegible] for feedback. [illegible] technology is [illegible] the mass [illegible] communication. This [illegible] creates the pos- [illegible] customised to [illegible] specific and tar- [illegible]

[illegible] and the institutions [illegible] communication.

[illegible] transmission in- [illegible] communication of one [illegible] the top down, by way of electronic or mechanical channel.

3. any form of communication produced by a few for consumption by many people. Mass media are channels of communication through which messages flow. As the messages go through the channels, they are distorted. When people receive media messages they have no opportunity for immediate feedback with the producers of the messages.

■ **mass media appeals**

these are techniques used in mass media to persuade listeners or viewers to develop a particular attitude or to purchase a product or service. Some of the techniques are ethical, others are questionable and involve fallacious reasoning. Some mass media appeals may be referred to as propaganda techniques. Selected examples include bandwagon appeals, testimonial appeals and glittering generalisation appeals. These techniques may be found in the print medium as well as in the visual and aural media.

■ **mass media communication**

see **mass media**.

■ **mass society**

a society whose members are dominated by a small number of interlinked elites with controlling powers over persuasion and manipulation. Also implies the idea that media are a corrupting influence that homogenises the social order and personal integrity.

mass society theory

the view that the mass media address a mass audience who are doped by the media. This view of the media audience (in the singular) as a passive, undifferentiated mass informs the hypodermic needle model media effects, as well as some aspects of the concern with cultural effects.

master shot

a single shot, usually a wide shot, that incorporates the whole scene from beginning to end. Typically a master shot will be filmed first and then all the close-ups and other shots afterwards.

mastering

a real time process in which videotaped materials are used to create a master optical disk that can be replicated into final videodiscs or CD-ROM disks for operation with desktop computers. Usually performed by an outside specialty shop.

masthead

1. used in print media to identify the location, ownership and management of newspapers and magazines. Analogous to Station ID in electronic media.
2. list of editors, publishers and senior reporters in each publication's issue. It includes an address and telephone number.

materials

a listing with summary information on materials that focus on communication, development and change themes or have significant coverage of communication strategies and programmes in relation to a specific development issue.

matrix

a matrix is an object upon which a design has been formed and which is then used to make an impression on a piece of paper, thus creating a print. A {wood} block, {metal} plate or {lithographic} stone can be used as a matrix.

matte box

a square shade that goes in front of the lens, usually supported by a pair of rods that attach to the camera. A matte box often has filter holders for square glass filters. (Often helpful for doing a Matte Shot.)

matte shot

a double exposure that does not meld two images on top of each other, but masks off part of the frame for one exposure and the opposite area for another exposure. This is also known as a split screen. Matte shots can also be done as Opticals.

meaning

the interpretation an audience makes of text.

media *(pl.)*

the concept has proven difficult to define. Generally speaking, media may be defined as those institutional structures that foster the rapid transmission of 'standardised' information to a relatively large audience through some mechanised channel ('medium'). See also **ideology**.

■ media agencies

producers of media. Also media institutions and industries that buy and sell media products.

■ media buying service

an organisation that specialises in buying media time to resell to advertisers.

■ media centre

in schools, the place where media hardware and software are stored, checked out by teachers or procured. Often the school library.

■ media content

messages which are produced by the few for the many and delivered to large audiences simultaneously.

■ media coverage

mention in the media of a company, its products or services.

■ media education

traditionally, it's the process by which one learns the technical production skills associated with creating media texts. More recently, it has also included the intellectual processes of critical consumption or deconstruction of texts.

■ media languages

media conventions, formats, symbols and narrative structures which cue the audience to meaning. The symbolic language of electronic media works much the same way as grammar works in print media.

■ media literacy

the characteristic of persons who grasp the distinction between what the media are designed to do and what they really do. One who is media-literate has the skills to decode or deconstruct the media by reading between the lines or digging beneath the superficial. The process of inculcating media literacy is sometimes called mediaproofing.

■ media log

a record of media use, often used to assess and control personal media use.

■ media messages

see **media content**.

■ media outlet

a publication or broadcast program that transmits news and feature stories to the public through any distribution channel.

■ media pack

a folder of information issued by a particular publication concerning the publication and the process of placing ads in the publication. Regular elements of the standard media pack include contract rates, column sizes, deadlines, editorial calendars, special features, media circulation, geographic coverage, audience demographics, etc.

■ media planner

an employee of an advertiser or agency who coordinates media aspects of a campaign and selects the most effective media to use. Important factors in media planning include: the campaign, the budget, size and character of the market profile and the positioning opportunities in the media.

■ **media policy**

organisational directive as to how company representatives will communicate with the media.

■ **media relations**

the function of gaining positive media attention and coverage.

■ **media research**

a study of radio, television and print media for the purpose of reaching the optimal consumer audience.

■ **media specialist**

in schools, the term covers a broad spectrum of educational roles. It can mean the person who operates audio-visual equipment, the librarian, a teacher with broad knowledge of media resources and the communication process or one who helps other teachers locate an array of resources.

■ **media targets**

audiences are media targets. Audiences are targeted, sold and delivered to advertisers by media agencies. Groups are targeted on the basis of demographics, media use patterns, zip codes and polling by those who wish to sell or persuade.

■ **media technology**

the hardware used to create information and communicate it, such as radio, computers, telephones, satellites, printing presses, pencils, etc.

■ **media text**

any example of communication in a medium. A photograph is a text and so is print on a T-shirt. A campaign button worn on a lapel is just as much a text as a newspaper editorial. A billboard on the highway is a text and so is a video clip. The use of the word text is not restricted to the printed word.

■ **media use**

the way people interact with media. Media use varies from person to person, group to group and at various times during an individual's life.

■ **media vehicle**

a single component of a mass medium, for example, a newspaper or TV network.

■ **mediacentrism**

derived from the concept of androcentrism or Eurocentrism , both of which concepts acknowledge the fact that reality is never interpreted objectively but tends to be routinely and automatically defined as natural and normal according to a particular set of beliefs and values. Other perspectives are dismissed accordingly. Mediacentrism refers to the process of interpreting social reality through creation of media '*frames*' that impose boundaries or a preferred reading.

■ Mediamark Research Inc. (MRI)

a syndicated study of magazine readership and product usage.

■ medium

any singular, physical object used to communicate messages. Television is a mass medium, but there are many other kinds of mass media.

■ megabyte

one million bytes (actually 1,048,576), one thousand kilobytes.

■ megahertz (mhz)

a unit of a million Hertz, meaning millions of cycles per second of AC current.

■ memorandum order

the announcement by an appellate court of a decision in a case that does not include a written opinion containing the rationale or reasons for the ruling.

■ mention

a brief item in the press or broadcast media referring to a person, product or service.

■ menu system

menu systems are on-screen display systems enhancing ease of use. Either the user is guided through all the levels by means of coloured items on the menus or the Advanced Menu offers screen prompts. Access via the remote control unit.

■ message

the actual physical product in the communication process that the source encodes.

■ message research

pretesting messages in an ad campaign.

■ metadata

informational data about the data, included in a signal's data stream.

■ metal cut

a form of relief printing from an intaglio plate. In the fifteenth century metal cuts often employed drill holes that printed as white dots. Engraved lines will print white rather than black in metal cut since the surface, rather than the marks in the plate, is inked.

■ mezzotint

an intaglio process invented around 1650 that allows the printing of rich tonal areas of black and grey. The mezzotint process begins by texturing a metal plate in such a way that it will hold a great deal of ink and print a solid black field. This is done with a tool called a 'rocker'. A rocker is essentially a large curved blade with very fine teeth along its edge. This blade is rocked back and forth, putting courses of fine dots into the metal plate. After this has been done repeatedly the plate will be covered with fine stipples that can hold ink. The next step is to scrape away the stippled texture where lighter passages are needed. The more vigorously the plate is scraped the less ink it will hold and the whiter it will print. Mezzotint differs conceptually from other intaglio methods because the artist works from black to white rather than white to black. For this reason mezzotint lends itself to scenes with many dark passages.

■ **microanalysis**

a sociological perspective that considers the functions performed by a system (e.g., mass media) for the individual.

■ **microbroadcasters**

low-power, community radio stations

■ **microwave (m/w)**

radio transmission using very short wave-lengths, corresponding to a frequency of 1,000 megahertz or greater and not subject to 'backhoe fades.'

■ **mind share**

amount of thinking an individual or group does about a particular product, service or company.

■ **mir**

Russian (Soviet) space station whose cosmonauts regularly use packet radio to communicate with amateurs around the world.

■ **misaligned**

an address is unaligned or misaligned if it does not comply with some alignment constraint on it.

■ **misappropriation**

taking what belongs to someone else and using it unfairly for one's own gain, for example, attempting to pass off a novel as part of a popular series of novels written and published by someone else. It is often called unfair competition.

■ **miss**

a miss is a lookup failure in any form of cache, most commonly at some level of a storage hierarchy, such as a cache or virtual memory system.
The cost of a miss in a virtual memory system is considerable — it may be five orders of magnitude more costly than a hit. In some systems, such as multi-process operating systems, other work may be done while a miss is serviced. Opposites hit.

■ **mistracking**

the phenomenon that occurs when the path followed by the read head of the recorder does not correspond to the location of the recorded track on the magnetic tape. Mistracking can occur in both longitudinal and helical scan recording systems. The read head must capture a given percentage of the track in order to produce a playback signal. If the head is too far off the track, recorded information will not be played back.

■ **mix**

this is the process of combining all your soundtracks into one, with all the sounds blended together at their correct volumes, together with any equalisation, filtering and effecting of the sound to give you the desired end result.

■ **mix master**

this is a copy of your sound mix on mag stock or on DAT, which you sometimes have to request in addition to the optical track. It is always a good idea to get a copy of the mix on tape, which will be of much better quality than the optical track for transfer to video or to save some mixing time in the event you have to remix.

■ mixed method

a mixed method print is one whose design is created on a single matrix using a variety of printmaking techniques, for example: line engraving, stipple and etching.

■ mixer

1. a device for blending together sounds from multiple sources with a volume control for each.
2. the person who sits at the mixing console during the mix, who decides initially on how the sounds are to be combined (you are the one with final say) and operates the faders and other audio controls.

■ mixing house

a sound studio specifically for mixing sound for film.

■ M-NET

Electronic Media Network: an encoded subscription television service in South Africa owned by a company listed on the Johannesburg Stock Exchange, founded by a consortium of six newspaper groups.

■ mobile unit

TV equipment used outside the studio, as at a football game.

■ mock-up

a scale-dimensional display model used in planning.

■ modem

device that allows computers to communicate via phone lines.

■ modem header

the connector inside a TNC used to connect an external modem to the TNC for higher speed or a different mode of communication. All the data and control lines from the CPU to the modem pass through this connector.

■ modulation

alterations in the characteristics of analog carrier waves, impressed on the amplitude, phase and/or the frequency of the wave.

■ moisture content

how much moisture print media will absorb or give up depending on the humidity in the air around it.

■ monitor

the part of the feedback loop that has to do with observing the output of a system.

■ monopoly

any commercial process in which one seller controls prices and supply of a product.

■ monotype

a form of printmaking in which the artist draws or paints on some material, such as glass and then prints the image onto paper, usually with a press. The remaining pigment can then be reworked, but the subsequent print will not be an exact version of the previous print. Monotypes may be unique prints or variations on a theme.

■ **moral panic**

a sudden increase in public perception of the possible threat to societal values and interests because of exposure to media texts.

■ **morph**

the special effect merging object attributes from multiple images into composite views.

■ **mostly-copying garbage collection**

a type of semi-conservative tracing garbage collection which permits objects to move if no ambiguous references point to them. The techniques used are a hybrid of copying garbage collection and mark-sweep. Mostly-copying garbage collectors share many of the benefits of copying collectors, including compaction. Since they support ambiguous references they are additionally suitable for use with uncooperative compilers and may be an efficient choice for multi-threaded systems.

■ **Mostly-exact garbage collection**

a variant of conservative garbage collection which deals with exact references as well as ambiguous references.

■ **Motion Picture Patents Company (MPPC)**

an organisation formed by the nine leading film and film equipment manufacturers in 1908 for the purpose of controlling the motion picture industry.

■ **MOTION-JPEG**

uses JPEG (computer) compressed images as individual still frames for motion. For example, 30 Motion-JPEG frames viewed in one second would approximate 30-fps video.

■ **moving garbage collector**

(also known as moving memory manager)

A memory manager (often a garbage collector) is said to be moving if allocated objects can move during their lifetimes.

In the garbage-collecting world this will apply to copying collectors and to mark compact collectors. It may also refer to replicating collectors.

■ **moviscop**

spelled Moviscop but pronounced 'movie-scope.' This is a small, 16mm tabletop viewer, often used on an editing bench.

■ **mp3**

digital method of encoding sound files on the Internet.

■ **MPEG 2**

compression standards for moving images and audio are set by the Motion Pictures Expert Group (MPEG), an international committee of industry experts. MPEG-2 is the basis for ATSC digital television transmission in the U.S.

■ **MRI**

Media Records Inc. An

organisation that publishes summaries of the lineage by various categories that are run in daily and Sunday newspapers. It provides competitive data to advertisers and newspapers in a market.

■ MSYS

an amateur packet BBS software written by WA8BXN. Latest Versions also contain DxCluster and conference modes. MSYS has support for TheNET routing and emulates a TheNET node. Note that MSYS's simulation of TheNET is limited by the performance of the PC and may be very poor when the PC is doing BBS operations. The MSYS TheNET emulation features are best utilised as a way to pipe user traffic in and out of the board via the TheNET style node mnemonic.

■ MTBF

Mean Time Between Failure. A statistical method developed for purposes of estimating maintenance levels required by various devices and systems.

■ muckrakers

term coined by Theodore Roosevelt to describe the reform movement undertaken by leading magazines in the 1890s, corrupt practices of business and government were exposed to the general public by crusading members of the press.

■ mult, mult box or multiplexer

a device, connected to the main microphone at a news event, which individual broadcast journalists or crews can plug or 'patch' into, eliminating the need for a forest of mikes at the podium. Each mult unit usually handles 12-24 separate lines.

■ multi pip

divides the screen into 9 small screen for a variety of different uses.

■ multi tier

paying commission on more than 2 tiers of affiliates - this is MLM not affiliate marketing and subject to strict legislation.

■ multicasting

the ability to send out more than one channel of programming within the broadcasters allotted channel spectrum. Whereas analog channels have traditionally used a standard amount of spectrum (represented by each click on your tuner dial), digital channels can squeeze up to four or more channels into their spectrum by reducing the quality of the signal. All digital set-tops will be capable of interpreting 18 different compression algorithms, resulting in a video/audio resolution that ranges from sub-VHS quality to near-35mm-film quality.

■ multimedia

any media that combine text, graphics, sound and video. For example, video games.

■ multiple access

in Packet Radio communications, the capability to function as part of the communications link between more than a single station.

When accomplished with analog methods, FDMA is the term, if digital, TDMA.

■ multiplex/multiplexing

transmitting more than a single message simultaneously on a physical transmission path, if analog, the technique is FDM, but if digital it is TDM.

■ mutable

any object which may be changed by a program is mutable. Opposite of immutable.

■ mutator

in a garbage-collected system, the part that executes the user code, which allocates objects and modifies or mutates them. For purposes of describing incremental garbage collection, the system is divided into the mutator and the collector. These can be separate threads of computation or interleaved within the same thread.

■ MW

Medium Wave (band): radio frequencies between 300 and 3000 kHz.

■ NACK/NAK

'Negative Acknowledge' character in many data codes, typically used to indicate receipt of a corrupted message ordering retransmission, compare to 'REJECT' character in Packet Radio nodes. Negative AcKnowledgement- a Packet or AMTOR ACK response that indicates that the data was NOT received correctly.

■ narrative

relates/narrates/tells a story to stimulate interest, persuade or explain a point or concept. The story can be real (from life), fictional (from literature) or hypothetical (created by the speaker). A narrative can be brief or elaborated.

■ narrowcasting

aiming media messages at specific segments of the public defined by values, preferences or demographic attributes. Also called niche or target marketing. Narrowcasting is based on the idea that mass audiences do not exist.

■ national

a commercial running throughout the country.

■ national advertiser

advertiser who sells a product all across the country.

■ National Public Radio (NPR)

a non-commercial U.S. radio network.

■ negative

the original film that is used in the camera, from which a positive print is made for editing. The negative is assembled to match the edited workprint and an answer print, for projection of the completed film, is struck from the negative.

■ negotiate

the process of give and take by which members of the audience interpret, deconstruct and find meaning within a media text.

■ neighbour

in a network of nodes the neighbour of a node is any node that is talked to directly, via the RS-232 port or via the radio port.

■ net

the amount paid to the advertising medium by the advertising agency after deducting the agency commission.

■ network

1. an organisation composed of interconnecting broadcasting stations that cuts costs by airing the same programs.
2. a collection of terminals, computers, peripheral devices and Packet Radio nodes connected to one another for a defined purpose of Packet Radio networking. A network is a system of nodes interconnected in such a way that any node can communicate with any other node in the system in an efficient and speedy manner. An example would be a network of user ports wire-linked to backbone nodes that are in turn connected to each other by UHF point-to-point links.
3. chain of broadcast or radio stations controlled and operated as a unit, often using the same editorial material

■ network interface

the point of interconnection between one Packet Radio network and another. In most applications it is called a 'Gateway'.

■ network layer

generically, any of several functions in a Packet Radio communications network, such as Terminal, Switching and Transmission. Specifically in the OSI Reference Model, the third layer, servicing the Transport Layer, ensuring that information is properly routed throughout the network. Level 3 of the seven layer OSI communications protocol set. The network layer specifies the communication between adjacent nodes or networks and interfaces with the user at the level 2 link layer and with distant nodes at the level 4 transport layer protocol.

NeST

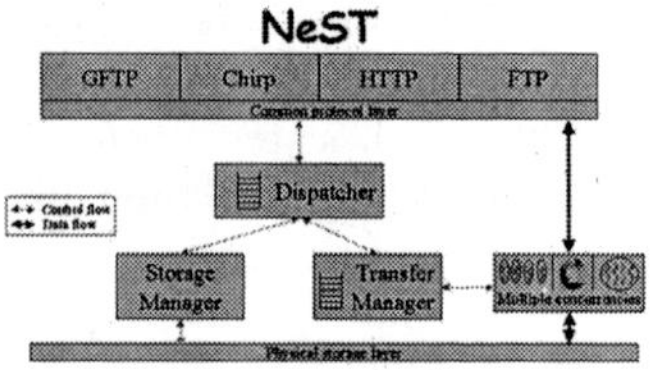

■ network virtual terminal

a Packet Radio communications concept in which a variety of DTE's with different data rates, codes, speeds, formats and protocols are accommodated on a single network. In such networks, Network Processors convert all into a common format for exchange between processors, then reconvert as needed to output data elsewhere.

■ neutral reportage

an emerging libel defence or privilege that states that it is permissible to publish or broadcast an accurate account of information about a public figure from a reliable source even when the reporter doubts the truth of the libellous assertion. The defence is not widely accepted.

■ new media

the different kinds of communication that combine text, graphics and video with computer technology to create a distinctive product.

■ news

any information deemed suitable for newscasting. The lack of a widely agreed upon definition suggests that news is whatever the news media define as news. Certain attributes pertaining to newsworthiness are usually involved, including references to negativity, magnitude, novelty, celebrity and conflict. Print and broadcast news differ because they rely on different logics for information processing.

■ news conference

a scheduled presentation to a group of media representatives.

■ news feature

special story or article in a print publication or broadcast program that goes in detail about concepts and ideas of specific market interest.

■ news feed

electronically transmitted broadcast information.

■ news management

this term is normally used to describe the way that individuals or organisations attempt to control the flow of news to the media and to 'set the agenda' for the media. This might involve issuing a press release, which is embargoed, holding press conferences times to make the lunchtime and early-evening news or staging an event which is big enough or unusual enough to grab the media's attention.

■ news peg

a device for making a story topical or relevant by providing it with a 'spin' or 'angle'. For example, protest groups are usually portrayed by mainstream media as a threat to the social order. Assigning a news peg to a story is also known as spiking it. See frame.

■ news values

the criteria which journalists and editors use to determine whether or not an event is 'newsworthy'.

■ newsgroups

section of the Internet devoted to message boards that are organised according to topic.

■ newshole

the amount of space available each day in a newspaper for news.

■ newsmagazine

the genre of television programming that covers current events and topical issues.

■ newsworthiness

are usually involved, including references to negativity, magnitude, novelty, celebrity and conflict. Print and broadcast news differ because they rely on different logics for information processing.

■ niche marketing

focus on certain segments of the population as targets of advertising messages. See **narrowcasting**.

■ nickelodeon

a popular name for the many penny arcades and amusement centres that emerged around the beginning of the 20th century and specialised in recordings and film.

■ node broadcasts

each node transmits a message out at quarter or half-hour intervals, depending on the settings the SNO has installed. This message tells the neighbour nodes what nodes are contained in the nodes table. The neighbour nodes interpret this information based on the 'quality' setting in the node parameters.

■ node knocking

or Node hopping is denoted as a user who constantly DXes the network by the process of connecting from one node to the next along a path and checking the routes available by reading the nodes table, nodes list and INFO response. One of the features of TheNET X-1J4 is that a user may hunt through a network and take advantage of local Routes commands to determine what all of the neighbours of a particular node are. With this knowledge the user may then connect to a neighbour node and repeat the process.

■ node stack

two or more nodes on one site interconnected by a diode matrix.

■ node/network node

a termination point for Packet Radio communications links, in the sense of Packet Radio communications, a node equipped with an X-1J4 EPROM. An active element in a network, this means any connect, from a user station to a bulletin board. A node in Packet radio is an intelligent router of real time data, somewhat more intelligent than a digipeater but faster than a store and forward BBS.

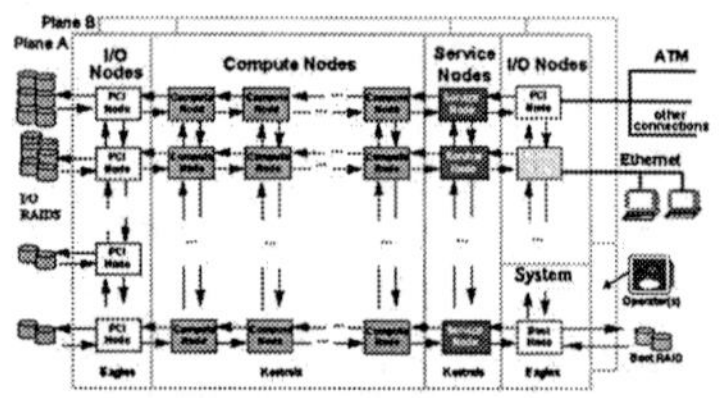

Logical System Block Diagram for the ASCI Option Red Supercomputer. This system uses a split-plane mesh topology and has 4 partitions: System, Service, I/O and Compute. Two different kinds of node boards are used and described in the text: the Eagle node and the Kestrel node. The operator console (the SPS station) is connected to an independent ethernet network that ties together patch support boards on each card cage.

■ noise

1. in communication, anything that interferes with the delivery of a message.
2. unplanned energy introduced into a communications channel, resulting in transmission errors.
3. confusion caused by too many messages trying to be delivered at one time.

■ non-commercial television

television programs broadcast by those stations whose income is derived from sources other than the sale of advertising time.

■ Non-duplication rule

FCC rule passed in 1965, stating that an AM-FM combination may not duplicate its AM content on its FM channel for more than 50 per cent of the time.

non-linear

a term used for editing and storage of audio, video and other data. Information (footage, for example) is retrievable and processed almost immediately without having to locate it in a traditional timeline format.

non-reflex

a camera that does not have a 'through the lens' viewfinding system, but gives you an image in the viewfinder through a separate lens.

non-verbal cues

purposeful or involuntary communication made with one's body. Examples include stance, gestures, eye movement, hand and/or arm placement, facial expression, etc.

normal lens

in 16mm this is the 25mm lens. In 35mm it is the 50mm lens. It is the point between the widening of the image by the wide-angle lens and the magnifying of the image by the telephoto lens.

nose grease

just what it sounds like. Used in the old trick among camerapersons to lubricate the pressure plate by wiping it along the side of the nose.

nose room

when a subject is in profile, nose room is the space between their face and the edge of the frame, similar to Head Room. In a profile shot, nose room is considered 'good' when a little extra room in front of the person's face, rather than behind their head. The general rule is that the space around the subject should be apportioned to 2/3rds in front of the subject's head and 1/3rd behind.

novelties

free items, such as calendars, letter openers, mugs or buttons, bearing an advertiser's logo - also referred to as advertising specialties. The purpose of such novelties is to keep the advertiser's name in front of its audience over time.

NRZ

Non Return to Zero. A binary code format in which binary ones and zeros are represented by two discrete voltage levels and the voltage remains at the indicated level for the duration of the code bit. Compare with bipolar pulse modulation in which the signal would return to an average level between bits. NRZ is the form that most binary signals take within computer circuitry.

NRZI

Non Return to Zero Inverted. A binary code format in which a data 0 (zero) produces a transition (either from 0 to 1 or from 1 to 0) in the code. It does not mean that the NRZI code is merely inverted. The main advantage of NRZI is that it does not matter at what point in the transmission that one starts to decode, the subsequent data will be the same. The code signal actually sent to the modem and transmitted by an amateur packet TNC, is in NRZI format. At the receive end the TNC converts it back to NRZ format for the CPU to process.

■ NTSC

National Television Systems Committee and the name of the current analog transmission standard used in the U.S., which the committee created many decades ago.

■ NTSC Video In

TVs with NTSC Video In can be connected to NTSC Camcorders, Video Disc Players and home video recorders.

■ null modem

an interconnect device or data cable used to connect together two DCE or two DTE digital devices. The RS-232 TXData/RXData and RTS/CTS lines are swapped.

■ numbered print

a numbered print is one which is part of a limited edition and which has been numbered by hand. The numbering is usually in the form of x/y, where y stands for the total number of impressions in this edition and x represents the specific number of the print. The number of a print always indicates the order in which the prints were numbered, not necessarily the order in which the impressions were pulled. This, together with the fact that later impressions are sometime superior to earlier pulls, means that lower numbers do not generally indicate better quality impressions. As with signed prints, the numbering of prints is a development of the late nineteenth century.

■ o&o

a broadcasting station that is owned and operated by a network.

■ O.C.N.

O.C.N. stands for Original Colour Negative. It is simply your developed negative.

■ objective

the ideal that the media producer is representing a balanced viewpoint on issues. The ideal that media producers are fair, accurate and conduits for information. Opposite of subjective.

■ objectivity

a commitment to news values that embraces a commitment to factual accuracy, lack of explicit bias, separation of fact from comment, transparency about sources and balanced coverage. True objectivity, as in 'value-free', does not exist and it is misleading to pretend that news is anything but ideological (a 'value judgement').

■ observational learning

a form of education in which individuals learn by observing the actions of others.

■ ODB

Object Database. A database that can handle diverse and complex data including video images, audio, bit maps, graphics and unstructured text.

■ offset

a printing process in which ink or toner is transferred from a preprinted form or a printed page onto rollers in the printer.

■ offset lithographs

lithographs printed by transferring an images from a stone or plate to an intermediate surface and then to the print paper.

■ offset printing

a form of printing where the image is transferred from the rotary plate to a rubber blanket and then pressed on printing.

■ oleographs

chromolithographs printed on a textured surface. Popularly used to produced inexpensive reproductions of oil paintings in the late nineteenth century.

■ ombudsperson

an individual in a media organisation assigned to handle complaints from audience members.

■ on timer

using 'On Timer' the TV can be set to switch on (from standby) in a period of time within 12 hours of setting. If there is no command to the TV after it has been switched on for 1 hour, it will switch back to standby.

■ on-demand streaming

sending video/audio or other data that is transmitted to the end-user upon request (widely used on news and sports-oriented Web sites, for example).

■ one button tuning

with the touch of a button, you can automatically tune your TV without having to access the menu.

■ one light

the alternative to a Timed Print, a one light is a print that has not been corrected shot by shot, but shows what all the shots look like with the same printing lights in contrast to each other. Sometimes this can be helpful to know the range of fluctuation in exposure and colour. (But it is curiously common for a lab to do some timing, even on a one light print, at the change of locations, at the change of rolls or if one shot is so drastically off from the rest and it would be practically unseeable otherwise.)

one-stops

individuals who sell records to retail stores and jukebox operators who are not in a position to buy directly from the record company.

online research

electronic and web-based surveys.

opacity

determines degree to which printed matter shows through a sheet of paper (either from the backside of a duplexed page or from an adjacent sheet).

op-ed

article written by an expert that is positioned on the page opposite the editorial page. Not to be confused with Letters to the Editor.

open-meetings laws

state and federal statutes that require that certain meetings of public agencies - normally in the executive branch of government - be open to the public and the press.

open-mike

a microphone in use.

open-records laws

state and federal statutes that require that certain records of public agencies-normally in the executive branch of government - be open for inspection and copying by the public and the press.

operating policies

guidelines that cover the everyday problems and situations that crop up during the operation of a media organisation.

Operating System (OS)

software that allows a computer to function by controlling all its application programs (e.g., DOS, OS2, Macintosh OS, UNIX).

oppositional

a critical position that is in opposition to the values and ideology intended by the creators of a media text, usually the dominant reading of a text.

optical printing

basically, rephotographying film frame by frame. This is a way to make a copy of a film with many more possibilities than contact printing, but at least with 16mm, resulting in a little added contrast and a little loss of clarity.

optical sound

optical sound is the system used by a projector to play back sound from a film print. The sound is exposed onto the film as a clear modulating line against black. It corresponds to the modulations of the sound. The projector reads the track by passing it between the exciter lamp a light-sensitive photoelectric cell which generates a voltage that is amplified and fed into a speaker.

optical track

an intermediate step from going from your mix master to your final print is to have an optical track struck. An optical track is photographed onto a blank piece of special high contract stock by the facility where the mix is done or by the lab. The optical track is a separate roll of film from the original negative and is combined with picture when a print is struck. (The track itself still remains a separate element from the A&B Rolls, it is printed in a separate pass through the contract printer.)

■ **opticals**

effects produced through Optical Printing, including transitions, superimposed titles, etc. Sometimes called Optical Effects. However, anything optically printed can be called an optical, so even blowing film up from 16mm to 35mm, though it does not involve an effect, is an optical.

■ **original**

any film, negative or reversal, that was shot by a camera, as opposed to a print or intermediate copy. The term original can be used interchangeably with negative, but is as especially handy term when taking about reversal film, where it is the clearest way indicating whether something is a dupe or the original.

■ **original jurisdiction**

jurisdiction in the first instance, as distinguished from appellate jurisdiction. A court exercising original jurisdiction determines both the facts and the law in the case, courts exercising appellate jurisdiction may only rule on the law and the sufficiency of the facts as determined by a trial court.

■ **original print**

an original print is one printed from a matrix on which the design was created by hand and issued as part of the original publishing venture or as part of a connected, subsequent publishing venture. For fine art prints the criteria used is stricter. A fine art print is original only if the artist both conceived and had a direct hand in the production of the print. An original print should be distinguished from a reproduction, which is produced photomechanically and from a restrike, which is produced as part of a later, unconnected publishing venture.

■ **OSI**

Open Systems Interconnect. The OSI is a project of the International Standards Organisation to develop a set of computer communication protocols. The OSI is a framework with which communications protocols are described.

■ **othering/otherising**

the process by which minority women and men are portrayed as removed in time, remote in space, marginal to society and undeserving of equal treatment because of their inferiority or irrelevance.

■ **outdated stock**

film is perishable. When it starts getting stale the dyes will shift colour and the grain will build up, giving you a generally fogged, muddy and desaturated effect. It is only after about 2 or 3 years that this will start to happen, provided the film is refrigerated. Faster films tend to become outdated slightly faster than slow films. Likewise, colour film will become outdated a little sooner than black and white. The flip side is that outdated stock can be gotten quite cheaply and often for free.

■ output

the actual results of a system, desired or undesired, expected or unexpected.

■ outtakes

the footage from your workprint that is not used in your edited version. Very small bits, a few frames or as little as one frame, are known as Trims.

■ overcrank

to run the camera faster, producing slow motion. The term has survived from the time when you would crank a camera.

■ overexposure

filming a scene with more light than the emulsion of the film can easily tolerate. The image will be too light and there will be less depth of field than if the lens had been set correctly. If compensated for in printing, the image will appear contrasty.

■ overhead

that part of a Packet frame that contains the address, routing and error-correcting components that support the message delivery to the target station or node. Some node protocols have less overhead than others.

■ P.O.V. Shot

Point of View Shot. A shot from the perspective of one of the characters, as if the audience were seeing the scene from their eyes. It is often important to get a Reaction Shot to establish that any given shot really is a P.O.V.

■ p2p

person-to-person software that permits direct Internet-based communication or collaboration between two or more personal computers while bypassing centralised servers.

■ paccomm

packet Radio Systems Inc. PacComm designs, manufactures and markets a range of packet radio products, both amateur and commercial.

■ pack slip

A lateral slip of selected tape windings causing high or low spots (when viewed with tape reel laying flat on one side) in an otherwise smooth tape pack. Pack slip can cause subsequent edge damage when the tape is played, as it will unwind unevenly and may make contact with the tape reel flange.

■ packaging

packaging is an important consideration when using paper in an HP LaserJet printer, because adequate packaging maintains the correct level of moisture and protects paper from damage during transport and storage.

■ packet

Amateur AX.25 communications, a structured group of binary digits in a prearranged sequence containing synchronisation, address, control an error-checking data. A packet is a block of many characters (or bytes) which are sent together along with a few extra characters (overhear/checksum) used to guarantee that the data is completely error free. The packet includes addressing information so that the receiving station knows the source and destination of the Packet.

■ packet network

a network dedicated to the routing and delivery of data throughput in the form of standardised 'packets'. Example is the SouthEastern Digital Association Networks (SEDAN), an AX.25/X1/X2 network.

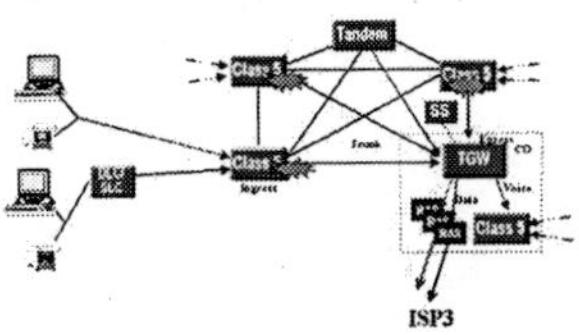

■ packet switching

the technique in which a stream of data is broken into standardised units called 'packets' each of which contains address, sequence, control, size and error checking information in addition to the user data.

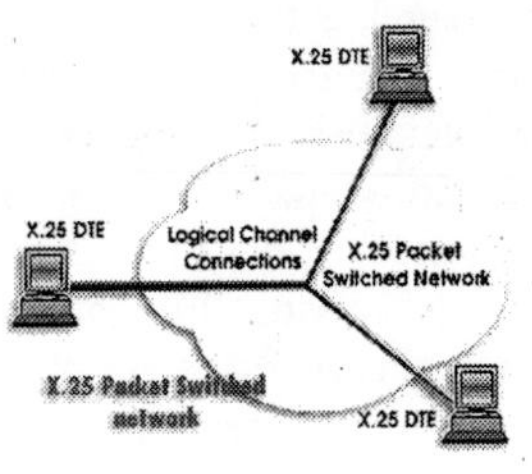

■ packetcluster

a proprietary software from Pavilion Software. It creates a specialised system for DXers and operates with all users connected in such a way that DX information can be distributed in 'real time'.

■ pacsat

an amateur radio satellite carrying a packet store-and-forward node. When launched became OSCAR 16.

■ PACTOR

PACket Teleprinting On Radio. An HF digital communications protocol developed in Germany. PACTOR combines the best features of both AMTOR and Packet for improved and more efficient HF data communications.

■ PAD

contraction of the term Packet Assembler/Disassembler in Packet Switched networks, the instrument that converts data between steady streams and packets. A device that interfaces our computer or 'dumb' terminal to an X.25 packet network. It gathers typed characters into outgoing packets and translates incoming packets back into serial asynchronous data streams. Also provides a simple command interpreter for setting up and tearing down connections, controlling parameters, etc. The amateur packet radio

TNC was called a 'PAD' in the early days of Packet Radio.

■ page unit

most magazine advertisements are sold in page units rather than in columns and inches. There are rates for a full page, half page, one-third page, one-sixth page, etc.

■ page views

the number of times a page is requested by a user, often measure by a function of time (page views per month).

■ paid circulation

a type of circulation in which the reader must purchase a magazine through a subscription or at a newsstand.

■ paint

to apply colour or gradient to an area of an image.

■ palette

a group of selected colours used by a graphics board. The EGA board uses a palette of 16 colours. VGA boards in some resolutions provide a palette of 256 colours.

■ pan

a horizontal camera move on an axis, from right to left or left to right. In a pan the camera is turning on an axis rather than across space, as in a dolly shot. Not to be confused with Tilt, technically it is not correct to say 'pan up' or 'pan down', when you really mean tilt.

■ panel study

a research method in which data are collected from the same individuals at different points in time.

■ paper

laid paper is made by hand in a mould, where the wires used to support the paper pulp emboss their pattern into the paper. This pattern of closely spaced, crossing lines can be seen when the paper is held up to light. Laid paper often has a watermark. Wove paper is made by machine on a belt and lacks the laid lines. False laid lines can be added to machine-made paper. Though wove paper was invented in the eighteenth century and laid paper is still produced, the majority of prints made prior to 1800 are on laid paper and the majority of prints made subsequently are on wove paper. China paper is a very thin paper originally made in China, which is used for chine appliqué prints.

■ paper tape

a skinny roll of tape used to tape down the ends of film when editing, called paper tape to distinguish it from splicing tape. (It should not be used for raw stock.)

■ paper weight

paper weight is measured on a metric scale (called basis weight or grammage) as the weight in grams of one square metre of paper. Basis weight is an important characteristic of paper. Paper that is too light or too heavy can cause misfeeds, misstacking, jams, poor print quality or excessive mechanical wear to the printer.

■ paradigm

a model used for analysis.

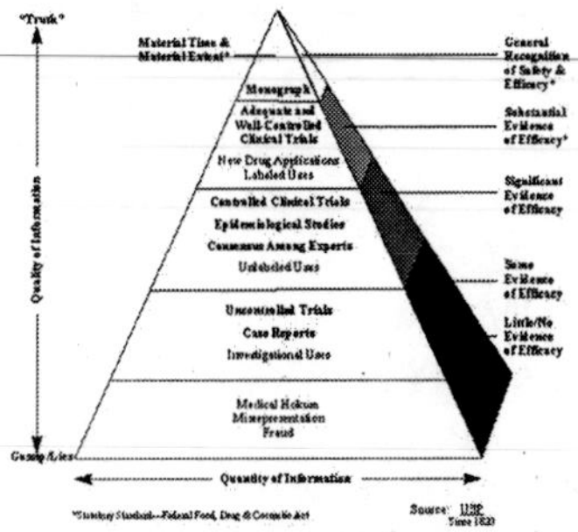

Paradigm of "Significant Evidence of Efficacy" vs. Standards

■ parallel editing

the technique of intercutting between two simultaneous stories or scenes.

■ parallel transmission

simultaneous transmission of all parts of a signal at one time, in data transmission, requiring a separate signal path for each of the bits of a character, internal to computers, this is called a 'parallel bus'.

■ parameters

restrictions affecting the design of a product or system (e.g., size, cost, materials).

■ parasocial relationship

a situation whereby audience members develop a sense of kinship or friendship with media personalities.

■ parity

a constant state of equality, one of the oldest and simplest methods of error checking data transmission. Characters are forced into parity (total number of marking bits odd or even as selected by choice) by adding a one or zero bit as appropriate when transmitted, parity is then checked as odd or even at the receiver. For odd parity, a 1 or 0 bit is added to 7 data bits so that the total bit count is an odd number. For even parity, the total bit count is made even with the parity bit. Parity words can similarly used with groups of binary words.

■ parity bit

a check bit appended to an array of binary digits to make the sum of all the digits always odd or always even.

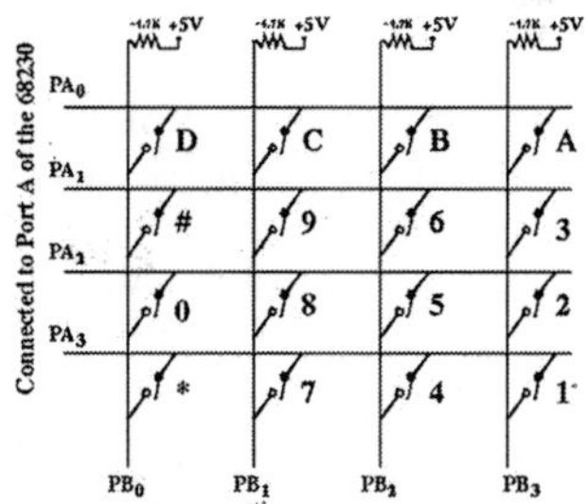

Connected to Port B of the 68230 PIA/T Chip

■ parity check

a checking method that determines if the sum of all the digits in an array is odd or even.

■ participation

a television program sponsorship pattern in which a number of advertisers are rotated through segments of the program. A 'participating' sponsor has no program content or station line-up control. Usually, their sponsorship commitment is limited to a relatively short period.

■ **pass-along audience**

that portion of a magazine's total audience composed of individuals who pick up copies of a magazine while at the doctor's office, at work, while travelling and so on.

■ **pass-along rate**

the number of times a received document (article, newsletter, brochure, report, etc.) is shared with other individuals.

■ **pass-along reader**

a person who reads a publication that he or a member of his family did not purchase. Also referred to as 'secondary' readers.

■ **paste up**

arranging articles, graphics and photos in print on the page to produce the final product. Can be done by hand or on a computer.

■ **payoff**

the results of an advertising campaign.

■ **payola**

bribes of gifts and money paid to DJs by record companies in order to gain favourable airplay for their releases.

■ **Pay-Per-View (PPV)**

a system that allows cable TV subscribers to pay a one-time fee to view one specific program or movie.

■ **PCI local bus**

the Peripheral Component Interconnect (PCI) local bus.

■ **PCMCIA**

Personal Computer Memory Card International Association. PCMCIA is becoming the link between desktop and notebook computing for data transfer and storage. PCMCIA slots perform the same functions as expansion slots on PC compatibles.

■ **peg**

a strong, memorable element of a press release or campaign, the hook.

■ **penetration**

the number of individuals who are actually exposed to the advertising medium.

■ **penny press**

the mass-appeal press of the early 19th century.

■ **percentage**

as used in connection with quotas is a minimum percentage.

■ **perf**

perforations. A hole or series of holes punched through the paper to aid in the separation of one piece of paper from another.

■ **periodical**

publication circulated at regular intervals, such as a weekly or monthly.

■ **persistence of vision**

a visual phenomenon where an image is retained in the eye for a short period of time, creating an illusion of continuous motion in film and video.

■ **persuasive speech**

the purpose of a persuasive speech is to gain assent, change attitudes or move listeners to action. It may include the use of narrative or descriptive elements as support. In a persuasive speech, supporting material serves to prove the main point and sub-points.

■ **PET**

Abbreviation for Polyethylene Terephthalate. The polymeric substrate material used for most magnetic tapes.

■ **ph**

refers to the acidity/alkalinity of paper as determined by the TAPPI (Technical Association of the Pulp and Paper Industry) cold-extraction method.

■ **Phase Alternation Line (PAL)**

a signal format used in video equipment in Europe and parts of Asia. PAL signals give you 25 frames per second and so are incompatible with NTSC, the American video signal format.

■ **phi phenomenon**

tendency of the human perceptual system to perceive continuous motion between two stationary points of light that blink on and off, basis for the illusion of motion in motion pictures.

■ **phi phenomenon**

tendency of the human perceptual system to perceive continuous motion between two stationary points of light that blink on and off, basis for the illusion of motion in motion pictures.

■ **phonograph**

a 'talking machine' developed by Thomas Edison in the late 1870s-the hand-cranked device preserved sound on a tinfoil-wrapped cylinder.

■ **photo CD**

generic term used to refer to Digital images on compact disc.

■ **photo flood**

a photo flood is a high power screw-in light bulb that is often used in with a clamp light fixture. Photofloods are usually anywhere from 250 watts to 500 watts.

■ **photo opportunity**

an event, sometimes staged, having visual appeal or interest for photographers and used as an opportunity to generate publicity.

Political strategists spend long hours devising and arranging 'photo ops' for their candidates.

■ photocopy paper

a grade of paper suitable for printing by the electrophotographic process. This paper is characterised by a smooth finish, heat stability, non-curling qualities and good aesthetic properties (such as colour, brightness and cleanliness).

■ photograph

a product produced by printing film negatives on paper through a photochemical process.

■ photogravure

a means of printing a photographic image by the intaglio process. The photographic negative (which may be of an artist's drawing) is projected onto a sensitised gelatin emulsion or carbon tissue that is transferred to a copper plate. After washing the plate areas that correspond to the image on the negative are dissolved and the plate can be bitten by acid as in routine etching. In hand photogravure, which is most commonly used in printmaking, the copper plate is first prepared for aquatint etching. The end result can closely resemble a traditional linear etching or soft ground etching.

■ photojournalism

journalism in which written text is secondary to photographs in news stories.

■ photomechanical relief print

there were many means available by the 1880s that allowed a black line drawing to be transferred to a relief printing block by photographic means. These are generically known as line blocks and the images printed from them typically share many of the qualities of woodcut. The means of transferring the image are often complex and can involve such techniques as etching photosensitised plates or electrotyping light sensitive gelatin plates.

■ photomechanical reproduction

this term is used to describe a variety of processes involving the transfer of a photographic image to a printing matrix, such as an etching plate, relief block or a lithographic stone. The term is used here whenever it is not certain exactly what photomechanical process is involved.

■ PIB

Publishers Information Bureau. A service that provides competitive information about magazine advertisers by clients and by magazine. It provides units of space, volume and cost.

■ pickup

a technique of financing a motion picture.

■ **picture**

the workprint, to distinguish it from the mag tracks.

■ **Picture In Picture (PIP)**

displays a small picture from another source, e.g. a VCR. Enables you to check another video source while watching one channel or a video- tape.

■ **PID**

Protocol ID : the first byte of the packet frame that identifies which protocol is used for the packet frame.

■ **pigeon**

this is a heavy round disc with a lighting stud, used to position a light on the floor, much lower than a stand will go. Basically, it is a Hi Hat for lights.

■ **pilot**

1. the first episode of a projected television series.
2. a television program produced as a prototype of a series being considered a network. The success or failure of the pilot usually determines if the network picks up the series.

■ **pilot testing**

a process that involves showing a sample audience an entire episode of a show and recording their reactions.

■ **pilottone**

a 60 Hz reference signal recorded onto the audio tape to allow transfer to mag precisely at sound speed, used for Sync Sound filming. (In Europe in it is 50Hz.)

■ **pitch**

1. the presentation of an advertising message to a prospective or existing client.
2. this is the distance between perforations along a roll of film. Print Stock has a slightly longer pitch than camera stock.

■ **pitch letter**

letter written to introduce a source and story idea to a member of the media.

■ **pix**

an abbreviation for picture used on the leader.

■ **pixel**

picture element. The smallest element of a screen represented as a point of specific colour and intensity level.

■ **plaintiff**

an individual who initiates a civil lawsuit.

■ **planned (or extemporaneous) method of speaking**

involves speaking from a prepared outline, but with the speaker choosing the wording and phrasing as she or he is talking. The message is prepared in advance, with predetermined purpose, main and sub points, explanation and reasoning and supporting material. Extemporaneous speaking, despite the Latin derivation of the term, does not mean speaking without preparation. Usage has changed the meaning. Speaking without preparation is termed impromptu.

planning models

summaries of frameworks and models for guidance in communication planning and review exercises.

planographic

the image on the matrix is flat, generally created by chemical means.

plastic leader

this is leader for putting at the head and tail of a print. It is, as one would guess, made out of plastic and is more durable than Emulsion Leader and much less expensive and so it is the better choice for a print. However, it cannot be Cement Spliced, so it should not be used for your negative.

platemark

a platemark is the rectangular ridge created in the paper of a print by the edge of an intaglio plate. Unlike a relief or planographic print, an intaglio print is printed under considerable pressure, thus creating the platemark when the paper is forced together with the plate. Some reproductions have a false platemark.

PLL

Phase-Locked Loop: a circuit using feedback methods to control the frequency of an oscillator. Usually used as frequency control in synthesised radios.

plot

the beginning, middle and end in narrative structure and all the devices that move the story from one scene to another.

plug

a favourable mention or a picture of a product in the non-advertising portion of a media presentation.

pluralism

in media studies a view of the mass media as enjoying a considerable degree of independence from the state, political parties and pressure groups. They are seen as being in the control of autonomous managers who allow media professionals a great deal of freedom. In this view, audiences are not seen as manipulated by the media as the audiences are considered to enter into the relationship with the media on equal terms. Broadly speaking the media are seen as offering a wide selection of the views of various groups in society. This view should be contrasted with those of radical researchers.

PM

Phase Modulation : a modulation technique in which the phase of the carrier is changed in relation to the modulating signal.

PMS

1. Personal Message System
2. PMS is the acronym given to colour codes associated with a specific ink colour library. Print shops often refer to a PMS colour such as 'PMS 328' a nice teal colour. PMS stands for Pantone Matching System.

■ Point-of-Purchase advertising (P-O-P)

signs, displays and other techniques of attracting attention and promoting products at their location of sale.

■ point-to-point

a Packet Radio communications circuit between two terminals only. No intervening node.

■ policy

a formal set of specific initiatives (including laws, rules and practices) designed to solve an articulated problem. Can also be defined as a broader framework that justifies the creation and implementation of specific initiatives to solve problems.

■ policy book

at radio and TV stations, a book that spells out philosophy and standards of operation and identifies practices that are encouraged or discouraged.

■ political economy

the study of power in shaping media structures, processes and outputs. Applied to media, it refers to the dominating role played by economic (material) forces in influencing the political dimensions of media-society relations. Politics are primarily about economic power and vice versa.

■ political press

newspapers and magazines of the 1790-1820 era that specialised in publishing partisan political articles.

■ politicisation

the process by which issues are taken out of the personal or private domain and situated instead within the public domain where they can compete for scarce resources.

■ polling

in packet terms, polling is a collision avoidance method in which one master station queries each of the users on the channel if they have a packet to transmit. The slave stations will not transmit until they have been 'polled' by the master station. In this way no two stations will transmit at the same time thus avoiding collisions.

■ polyester base

polyester base is a very durable type of film, that is virtually unrippable. Some people claim that it is harder to splice, but that is more a matter of getting used to the technique. Significantly, it cannot be Cement Spliced, making it impractical as original material (also, its durability could spell disaster for the delicate mechanism of a camera in the event of a jam). However, its durability makes it very advantageous for release prints.

■ polysemic

having many meanings.

■ polysemy

all signs are polysemic, i.e. capable of having a range of possible meanings. The range of meanings is narrowed down by the context. A photographic image is inherently polysemic. It's meaning is anchored by accompanying text.

■ pool

a camera crew and reporter(s) assigned to cover a story or event on behalf of all media and to share materials with them. Often used when tight space and security are considerations or when it is unlikely that any 'news' will be made.

■ popped strand

A strand of tape protruding from the edge of a wound tape pack. Print through the condition where low frequency signals on one tape winding imprint themselves on the immediately adjacent tape windings. It is most noticeable on audiotapes where a ghost of the recording can be heard slightly before the playback of the actual recording.

■ port

entrance or access point to a computer, multiplexor device or Packet Radio network where signals may be supplied, extracted or observed. An input/output channel or connector on a node or TNC. A TNC normally has one or more radio ports hooked to a radio transceiver(s) and a RS-232 or serial port that may be connected to the users terminal (computer) or another node serial port in the case of a (or other type of higher level node) node stack. A port may also refer to a special purpose node such as a user-port, IP port, backbone port, etc.

■ portal

the first page a person sees when opening an Internet browser.

■ positioning

in advertising, stressing the unique selling point of a product or service to differentiate it from the competition.

■ post-consumer waste

paper that the customer has used. Post-consumer waste can be office paper, mail, used boxes, old newspapers or magazines.

■ poster

a graphic advertisement attached to a flat surface or standing up with a clip backing.

■ practical

a practical is any photo flood-type of bulb, used within the shot, in a household lamp or otherwise visible. The term practical is sometimes used interchangeably with photo flood, even though it specifically refers to a light used in the shot.

■ precedent

an established rule of law set by a previous case. Courts should follow precedent when it is advisable and possible.

■ pre-consumer waste

paper that never reaches the customer after it has been manufactured. Pre-consumer waste can be unused paper stock, bindery trimmings, envelope cuttings, business forms or unsold books or magazines.

■ preferred reading (or dominant reading)

semiologists have sometimes made a distinction between open and closed texts. All texts are open to a variety of possible readings, but in a 'closed' text one particular reading is clearly preferred to others. Closed texts are associated with mass culture and thus include most mass media texts. The preferred reading of the text (also referred to as 'dominant reading') is the reading intended by the text.

■ premastering

in CD-ROM distribution, the process of preparing the data to be placed on the CD-ROM so that is optimally fits the CD-ROM format and limitations.

■ preroll

preroll is extra time at the beginning of a sound take to accommodate the slow lock-up time of some post production time code devices.

■ presentation

a pitch or a description of a proposed advertising campaign.

■ presentation layer

the presentation layer is where Packet Radio messages that are to be transmitted are grouped, formed, converted to and undergo conversion between computer and the terminal node controller.

■ press

members or vehicles of the media.

■ press agent

a publicist also known as a press officer.

■ press kit

a collection of editorial and promotional materials distributed to the media about a person, product or company. Journalists use these materials to learn about the subject. Michael J. Motto Public Relations has found that a concise, well-written press kit is an invaluable aid in generating print media publicity. Increasingly, audio and videotaped press kits are used to solicit radio and TV journalists' attention.

■ press release

a paper or electronic document submitted to the media with the intent of gaining media coverage.

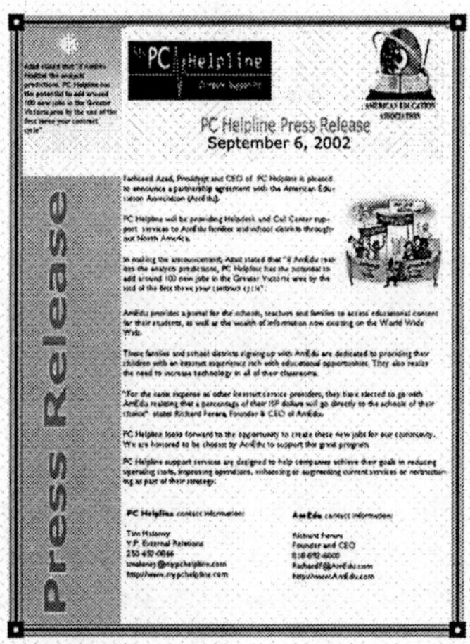

■ pressure plate

part of the internal workings of a camera, the pressure plate is located on the other side of the film from the gate. It is a smooth, spring-loaded plate that holds the film on the film plane and acts as a brake, helping to hold the film steady while it is exposed.

■ **presumed damages**

damages a plaintiff can get without proof of injury or harm.

■ **primary audience**

that portion of a magazine's total audience made up of subscribers or those who buy it at the newsstand.

■ **primary colour**

in a tri-stimulus colour video system, one of the three colours mixed to produce an image. In additive colour systems, the primary colours are red, green and blue. In subtractive colour systems, the primaries are cyan, magenta and yellow.

■ **primary definers**

the powerful groups in society who have greater access to the media and therefore a greater influence over the media's definition of 'reality'. For comment on crime, for example, the media will consult police and Home Office spokespersons, for comment on economic policy, they will consult politicians and 'independent City analysts'. Such people are 'primary definers'.

■ **primary demand ad**

advertisement that promotes a specific product category, such as milk.

■ **prime lens**

a prime lens is one with a single focal length, wide, normal or telephoto, as opposed to a Zoom Lens, which has a variable focal length. They often come in a set of different focal lengths. Prime lenses tend to be sharper, faster and will often focus closer than zoom lenses.

■ **prime time**

that part of a radio or television schedule expected to attract the largest audience.

■ **prime-time access rule**

rule adopted in 1970 intended to expand program diversity by barring network programs from the 7:30-8:00 P.M. (E.S.T.) time slot.

■ **principal**

a performer in a commercial who can be recognised or identified, including but not limited to those performing speaking parts.

■ **print**

a replica of an image made from an inked surface. Broadly considered, the two stages of making a print are the creation of a matrix and the pulling of an impression by inking the matrix and pressing a piece of paper against it.

■ **print advertising**

advertising in newspapers, magazines, catalogues or mailers. Usually, print ads use some combination of photographs, illustrations and copy.

■ print media

media consisting of paper and ink, reproduced in a printing process that is traditionally mechanical and photochemical.

■ print stock

film used by the lab for making copies (prints). It is usually of a longer pitch than camera stock so as to be smoothly sandwiched against the camera stock on the printing machine. It is also much slower (with an A.S.A. of about 12) than camera stock, as light is less of a problem in printing than it is when it is being focussed through a lens in a camera.

■ printer's sync

this is the offsetting of sound 26 frames earlier than picture, corresponding to the distance between the sound reader and the gate of the projector. To be in sync on a projector all prints are lined up in printer's sync. Usually the lab lines up the sound and picture in printer's sync, putting the beep on the track 26 frames earlier than the '2' in the Academy Leader. This is known as pulling up the sound. If there was some reason for you to line up the sound yourself, it is very important to label the sync mark 'printer's sync' so that the sound is not accidentally pulled up twice.

■ printers' ink statute

a model law drafted in 1911 to control false or misleading advertising. Most states adopted some version of this model in the early 20th century. Such laws are largely ineffective because they are not normally enforced.

■ printing on demand

one-at-a-time printing of books that exist in a digital database.

■ prior restraint

an attempt by the government to censor the press by restraining it from publishing or broadcasting material.

■ prior restraint

pre-publication censorship that forbids publication or broadcast of certain objectionable material, as opposed to punishment of a perpetrator after the material has been published or broadcast.

■ privacy act

a federal statute that forbids the disclosure of specific material held by federal agencies on the grounds that its release could invade the privacy of the subject of the report or document.

■ problematising

a process that makes transparent which is concealed by habit or conspiracy. The socially constructed nature of reality is thus exposed. Problematising can also involve a process by which the conventional and taken-for-granted are exposed for purposes of criticism and challenge.

■ processing delay

in Packet Radio communications, the time taken by a computer to operate on an inbound message and return a response, frequently not accounted for in complaints of telecommunications response time problems.

■ producer

the final authority in the electronic media production process. Sometimes the producer is the person who raises the money to produce media products.

■ product demo

a physical run-through of a product or service by company representative (usually to analysts or members of the press).

■ product placement

the process by which manufacturers or advertisers pay a fee in order for branded products to be prominently displayed in a movie, TV show or other media production.

■ production

the working process of putting together media content to make a finished media product. Production techniques include editing transitions, design, style, colour, placement in the frame or on a page, scripting, printing, broadcast engineering, etc.

■ production manager

the person responsible for overseeing details in the creation of a television or print advertisement.

■ production sound

this is the sync sound or any other sort of wild track or room tone that was recorded at the shoot. The term is used in sound editing to distinguish between added backgrounds and effects and those from the shoot.

■ production values

the elements that make up the complete media product. In electronic media, production values include cuts, dissolves, colour, placement in the frame, editing, etc. In print, paper quality, ink colour, placement on the page, size, shape, etc.

■ program

a clearly defined and labelled fragment of television output that is distinctive and distinguishable from non-programs such as advertising .

■ programme descriptions

summaries of programming activities using communication for development purposes.

■ progressive

refers to 'progressive scanning' as in DTV formats 480p or 720p. A system of video scanning whereby lines of a picture are transmitted consecutively (unlike interlaced), as on computer screens.

■ projection sync

same as printer's sync.

■ prominence

news value that stresses the importance of the person involved in the event.

■ promotion

a method of increasing sales of merchandise through advertising, any activity designed to enhance sales.

■ proof

a proof is an impression of a print pulled prior to the regular, published edition of the print. A trial or working proof is one taken before the design on the matrix is finished. These proofs are pulled so that the artist can see what work still needs to be done to the matrix. Once a printed image meets the artist's expectations, this becomes a bon tirer ('good to pull') proof. This proof is often signed by the artist to indicate his approval and is used for comparison purposes by the printer. An artist's proof is an impression issued extra to the regular numbered edition and reserved for the artist's own use. Artist's proofs are usually signed and are sometimes marked 'A.P.', 'E.A.' or 'H.C.' (Cf. glossary of abbreviations) Commercial publishers found that there was a financial advantage to offering so-called 'proofs' for sale and so developed other types of proofs to offer to collectors, generally at higher prices. Proof before letters (Avant les lettres): An impression pulled before the title is added below the image. Scratched letter proof: An impression in which the title is lightly etched below the image. Remarque proof: An impression pulled before the remarque is removed.

■ proofread

carefully reading a document to weed out errors.

■ propaganda

any media text whose primary purpose is to openly persuade an audience of the validity of a particular point of view.

■ propagation delay/propagation time

the time period between injecting a signal into a communications frequency and its exit at the target end. While not significant to speech, propagation delay can be restrictive to data and Packet.

■ protocol

a communications protocol is the set of rules and procedures used to implement a technique or method of communications. The rules for maintaining communications between similar devices. As with AX.25 maintaining orderly error-free data flow and data link control. A set of procedures for establishing and controlling the transmission of information. There are many different protocols for many different purposes. AX.25 is a protocol which describes how small computers can talk to each other. e.g., SDLC, Bisync.

■ protocol conversion/ protocol converter

generic name and name of the devices that perform a widely variable set of conversions of code, speed, electrical interface and/or block formatting and error checking/correction in data circuits. Example: a packet network TNC operating between an ASCII terminal and a packet network is a form of protocol converter. When the function is to make the line signals of a particular terminal appear like another, the protocol converter is a type called a Terminal Emulator.

■ prototype

a model used to test and evaluate a design before final production.

■ proximity

news value based on the location of a news event.

■ PSIP

Pronounced 'P-SIP'(Program and system information protocol)- a part of the ATSC digital television specification that enables a DTV receiver to identify program information contributed by content providers and use it to create sophisticated electronic program guides.

■ PSK

Phase Shift Keying. A data modulation method in which binary data is encoded as discrete changes in the phase of the carrier signal. In amateur packet, PSK is used mainly on OSCAR satellite data communications.

■ psychographics

a more sophisticated form of demographics that includes information about the psychological and sociological characteristics of media consumers such as attitudes, values, emotional responses and ideological beliefs.

■ pub

publication

■ public affairs

the public policy aspect of public relations.

■ public affairs programming

television and radio programming based on information of interest to the general public. Usually about government, public safety or health issues.

■ Public Broadcasting Act of 1967

Congressional act that established the Public Broadcasting Service.

■ public interest

matters are defined by the Press Complaints Commission as being in the public interest (and therefore an exception to the prohibitions of the PCC's Code) if they are a matter of i) detecting or exposing crime or a serious misdemeanour ii) protecting public health and safety iii) preventing the public from being misled by some statement or action of an individual or organisation. In any matters raising issues beyond these definitions, the PCC requires a full explanation by the editor of the publication concerned.

■ **public journalism**

the philosophy that newspapers should try to solve civic problems as well as report the news.

■ **Public Relations (P.R.)**

a variety of skills and tactics developed to create favourable opinion for a person, event or product that ultimately supports the firm's bottom line. You turn to a public relations firm to help you achieve media coverage.

■ **public relations advisor**

a person who provides public relations guidance (may work inside or outside a PR firm)

■ **public relations firm**

a company made up of public relations advisors and their support staff.

■ **public relations plan**

a document that details specific actions to achieve a public relations result.

■ **Public Service Announcement (P.S.A.)**

announcement on television or radio serving the public interest and run by the media at no charge. For example, a utility company might do a series of PSA's on the subject of saving energy in the home. Each one would feature the company's name.

■ **public service broadcasting**

a term which is not easy to define. The essential notion here is that broadcasting's function is not simply to satisfy commercial interests by giving the public what they want in an attempt to maximise audience figures, but, rather, to inform, educate and entertain the public, the notion of 'quality' being central. Examples are: that broadcasters are legally required to be impartial in their coverage of news and current affairs, that broadcasters must carry a certain proportion of educational programmes, that broadcasters must broadcast a certain proportion of current affairs during prime time and so on.

■ **publication**

newspaper, magazine or newsletter with information, news and feature stories, usually produced to be sold or as a service to members of associations or organisations.

■ **publication of private information**

in privacy law, publicising embarrassing private information about an individual that is not of legitimate public concern.

■ **publicist**

a person hired to promote a cause, individual or product by generating free advertising, a press agent.

■ **publicity**

the placing of stories in the mass media.

■ **publics**

the various audience served by public relations.

■ **publisher**

the publisher is the final authority for decisions in the print industry and is usually the owner of the magazine, newspaper or publishing company.

■ **publisher's statement**

a semi-annual sworn statement of circulation data given to the ABC by a publisher, who is a member of the Bureau and issued unaudited (but subject to audit).

■ **pull down**

a transfer of sound slowed down from film speed, 24 film frames per second, to video speed, 29.97 video frames per second, which is the equivalent of 23.98 film frames per second. This must be done to line it up with a video transfer of picture when transferring sync sound to video.

■ **pull processing**

pull processing is a special type of processing where the film is developed for a shorter time than normal, usually to make up for intended overexposure.

■ **pull up**

this term can be a little confusing since it has three meanings that both apply to sound.
1. The process of offsetting the sound 26 frames ahead of picture when making a print
2. Pull Ups, as a noun, are transfers of the first 26 frames of sound from a reel that are spliced onto the outgoing sound of the previous reel so that sound is not lost when the film is printed with the sound pulled up, since 26 frames of sound are cut off when reels are joined.
3. A transfer of the sound from a video, sped up from video speed, 29.97 video frames per second, which is the equivalent of 23.98 film frames per second, to film speed, 24 film frames per second. This must be done when the optical track is made after having mixed in video.

■ **pull down claw**

the pull down claw is part of the camera movement, which advances the film from the exposed frame to the next unexposed frame while the camera's shutter is closed.

■ **pulse**

in communications typically a signal characterised by a constant amplitude and duration, the line signal representation of a binary digit.

■ **Pulse Code Modulation (PCM)**

the form of digital transmission in which information for transmission is sampled at regular intervals and a series of pulses in coded form are transmitted representing the amplitude of the information signal at that time. The most common form of PCM in North America is one in which analog signals of less than 4 kilohertz are sampled 8,000 times per second and converted into an 8-bit code, resulting in 64 kilobits per second for transmission. Twenty-four of these streams are Time Division

Multiplexed into a 1.544 megabit stream for T-1 transmission. The European equivalent is 30 channels in a 2.048 megabit stream.

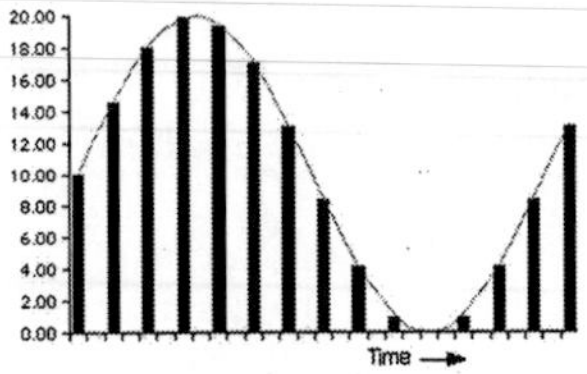

■ pulse modulation

the modulation of a series of pulses to represent information-bearing signals. Typical methods involve modifying the amplitude (PAM), width (PWM), duration (PDM) or position (PPM). Pulse Code Modulation (PCM) is the most common modulation technique involved in telephone work.

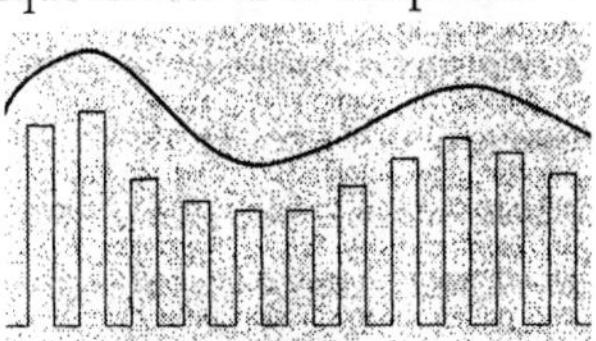

Pulse amplitude modulation

■ pulse opinions

opinion polls designed by the Communication Initiative to 'take the pulse of the social and economic international development community on major development issues'.

■ pulse-link repeater

connects two E&M signalling circuits back to back, changing the E of one circuit to the M of the other and vice versa.

■ punitive damages

money damages awarded to a plaintiff in a lawsuit aimed not to compensate for harm to the injured party but to punish the defendant for his or her illegal conduct.

■ push processing

push processing is a special type of processing where the film is developed for a longer time than normal, usually to make up for intended underexposure. It should be noted that only entire rolls can be pushed, not individual scenes. Pushing film will add some contrast and graininess.

■ push pull sound

using complementary speaker drive units in a single chamber an improved bass response is achieved, providing a crisp clear sound with excellent mid range frequencies.

■ pyramid structure

the typical structure of a news report whereby facts are written in order of importance. Called the 'inverted pyramid', the least important facts are last so that editors can easily cut them for space or time constraints.

■ QPSK

Quadrature Phase-Shift keying.

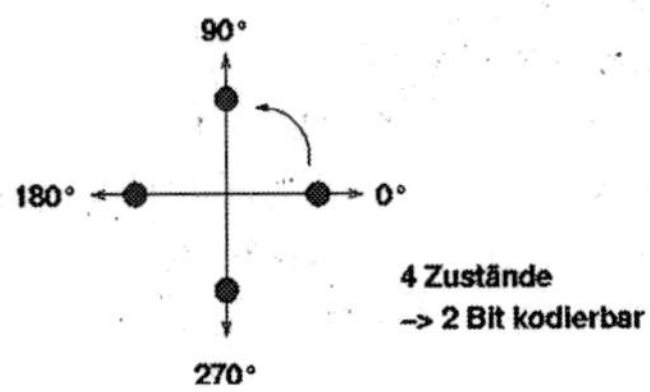

■ QRM

man-made interference on a radio frequency, intentional or not.

QRN Natural interference on a radio frequency. Lightning, solar noise (very week signal work) are examples of natural interference.

■ **qualified privilege**

in libel law, the privilege of the reporter (or any person) to publish a fair and accurate report of the proceedings of a public meeting or public document and be immune from lawsuit for the publication of libel uttered at the meeting or contained in the document.

■ **quartz light**

can also be called halogen light or tungsten light. A quartz light is a very bright type of light that uses a tungsten filament that is contained in a quartz envelope. The colour temperature will be a fairly consistent 3,200K. They can get very hot when in use. It is also very important never to touch the bulb with your bare hands at any time. Oil from your hands will cause the bulb to blister and explode.

■ **query letter**

a letter sent to a publication asking whether the publication would be interested in receiving a bylined article.

■ **queue**

a delay in forwarding data or traffic caused by the inability of the system or network to handle the quantity of data being attempted.

■ **quick release**

a latching device for quickly mounting and removing the camera from the tripod.

■ **quick release shoe**

the part of the quick release that attaches to the camera is called the quick release shoe and is inevitably worth double-checking, as they frequently stray away the tripod when left behind on the camera.

■ **rack focus**

a shot where focus is changed while shooting. Unlike a follow focus shot, a rack focus shot is usually done not from the necessity of keeping someone in focus but to shift attention from one thing to another.

■ **rack jobbers**

individuals who service record racks located in variety and large department stores by choosing the records to be sold in each location.

■ **radiation system**

wireless communication system allowing reliable sending and receiving of signals through the air.

■ **radical**

in media studies, the 'radical' tradition is that which is more or less Marxist in its approach, seeing the media as playing an important role in the transmission of the dominant ideology.

■ **radio frequency**

a broad part of the electromagnetic spectrum ranging from above audio frequencies to beneath infrared, characterised by the use of antennas to couple signals to the Earth's magnetic field.

RAM

Random Access Memory: that part of a computer or TNC that is holding data or memory during the power 'ON' period. If the RAM has 'battery backup' the memory is remains in the RAM until it is changed. If the RAM has no battery backup, no memory remains when power is removed. An IC in a computer that holds data only so long as power is applied. The RAM is usually used only for storage during the execution of a program. TNCs use RAM for temporary storage of messages and parameters. Normally TNC RAM is powered (batttery - backed) all the time using a lithium battery in the TNC.

raster/raster scanning

providing a means to place information on a screen by sweeping it completely from side to side an top to bottom in a regular fashion. Both CRT tube displays and fax machines utilise forms of raster scanning.

rate

a cost-per-space-unit of print advertising or cost-per-time-unit in radio and TV advertising. Newspapers usually publish rates per column inch or line. The electronic media sell 15, 30 or 60 second time units.

rate base

number of buyers guaranteed by a magazine and used to compute advertising rates.

rate card

document listing space or rates of an advertisement, technical specifications and closing dates issued by the seller of the advertisement space.

rate holder

a small classified ad run in every issue of a print publication for the duration of an advertising contract. The total linage entitles the advertiser to the lowest possible rate on all classified advertisements, both display and in-column.

rating

the ratio of listeners to a particular radio station to all people in the market, the ratio of viewers of a particular TV program to the number of households in the market equipped with TV.

raw stock

unexposed film.

RDP

Reconstruction and Development Programme.

reach

geographic area of the audience and the number of readers, listeners or viewers who can access the media in any region.

■ **reach (%)**

the number of unique individuals who visit a site within a specific period time expressed as a percentage of the web using population.

■ **reaction shot**

1. a shot of someone looking off screen. Used either to lead into a P.O.V. Shot (and let the viewer know that it is a P.O.V. shot) or to show a reaction right after a P.O.V. shot.

2. a reaction shot can also be a shot of someone in a conversation where they are not given a line of dialogue but are just listening to the other person speak.

■ **readership**

a term used to express readership of a particular advertisement and not of a particular publication.

■ **realtime**

processes that occur instantly as they occur, closely related to 'online'. When a signal is sent and a result is expected back with a short enough time to fall within a person's attention span the operation is said to be in real time. Keyboard to keyboard operation is real time. Keyboard to server is real time. Sending a message to a friend via a pack BBS is not real time because the sender doesn't know how long it will be before the receiver answers back.

■ **recans**

leftover film that was loaded into a magazine but (unlike a Shortend) not even partially shot and then loaded back in the film can. Basically, it is a roll a film that has been opened, but not used.

■ **receiver**

the target of the message in the communication process.

■ **recent catalogue albums**

albums that have been out for 15 months to three years.

■ **reception-analysis**

research which focuses on the way that individuals make meanings for media messages. Reception analysis has some similarity with uses and gratifications research, but is much more likely to use an ethnographic approach involving in-depth interviews, participant observation etc. Reception analysis has developed particularly since the early to mid-1980s. It tends generally to be associated with the view that audiences are active and is generally associated with the notion of resistive readings of media texts.

■ **recitation or memory method of speaking**

involves writing out a speech in full, committing it to memory and delivering it. This method is less common today than during earlier periods in history.

■ **record**

in data processing, one complete group of logically related information, closely related to 'block' and 'packet' in communications technology.

reduction print

an optical reduction of a film from one gauge to another, such as 35mm to 16mm.

reel

1. a metal or plastic spool for holding film, either for projection or editing.
2. in 35mm a reel is 1,000 feet of film (or usually a little less). Also known as a Single Reel.

reflective light reading

a reflective light reading measures the amount of light bouncing off the subject. You take a reflective reading with a light meter equipped with a honey-comb or lensed grid. The meter is pointed at the subject, so as to read only the light bouncing off the subject. The other type of light reading is an Incident Light Reading.

reflex

a viewfinding system in a camera where the image you see in the viewfinder is viewed through the same lens that is used to photograph the image on film.

reflexivity

a term used to refer to foregrounding by a text of its own madeness or constructedness. For those of you who study drama, this will be familiar as Brecht's 'alienation effect'. Brecht was concerned to avoid the 'swindle' involved in naturalistic theatre's pretence that the play 'happened' rather than 'was made'. It may be seen as a method of undermining the pretensions of bourgeois theatre, whose realism, by concealing its own workings, draws the spectator into the bourgeois ideology which is inscribed in its claims to represent common-sense reality itself. It is no doubt because of its anti-bourgeois intentions that we find it being frequently used in.

refreshing

This term can refer to periodic retensioning of tape or the rerecording of recorded information onto the same tape (or different tape) to refresh the magnetic signal. In the audio/video tape community, refreshing generally refers to retensioning of the tape, but it can also refer to the copying of one tape to another.

refusal

the right of the first actor or model cast in an advertisement to refuse or accept the assignment.

regional edition

a geographical portion of a national magazine's circulation which can be purchased by an advertiser.

registration

the degree to which one frame lines up with the next is registration. A camera with poor registration will create an image that will gently bobble when projected. Projectors too can have good or poor registration (sometimes making it difficult to tell if it was the camera). Good registration is most important for certain types of special effects shots where images are layered and will call attention to themselves if they are gently bobbling out of sync with each other.

■ **registration pin**

a registration pin is found in the movement of certain cameras and acts to steady the image during exposure.

■ **regulation**

agencies regulate media through laws and guidelines. Advertising regulation takes place through the Federal Trade Commission. Broadcasting is regulated through the Federal Communications Commission. Media messages are also regulated through laws governing libel and self-regulated by business and professional organisations such as the National Association of Broadcasters. Deregulation trends in the 1980s swept away many government regulations intended to constrain media industries in the United States.

■ **reinforcement**

support of existing attitudes and opinions by certain messages.

■ **release**

the signed permission given by a person to use his or her photo, voice, name or testimonial statement commercially.

■ **release print**

this is a print made after the answer print has been approved. It is not retimed, but struck using the same timing as the final answer print. Because it is not retimed it is generally much cheaper than an answer print. On a big production, these are the prints released to movie theatres, hence the name.

■ **relief**

a relief print is one whose image is printed from a design raised on the surface of a block. In this type of print the ink lies on the top of the block and is transferred to the paper under light pressure.

■ **relief print**

any print in which the image is printed from the raised portions of a carved, etched or cast block. A simple example would be a rubber stamp. The most common relief prints are woodcuts. The term 'relief print' is used when it is not clear which kind of relief printing has been used (photomechanical or hand carved, for example).

■ **remarque**

a remarque is a small vignette image in the margin of a print, often related thematically to the main image. Originally remarques were scribbled sketches made in the margins of etchings so that the artist could test the plate, his needles or the strength of the etching acid prior to working on the main image. These remarques were usually removed prior to the first publication of the print. During the etching revival, in the late nineteenth century, remarques became popular as an additional design element in prints and were also used in the creation of remarque proofs.

■ **remnant space**

print advertising space that is left over and sold at a discount at the last minute.

■ **remote**

a broadcast coming from outside the studio.

■ **reporter**

professional who gathers information and writes reports for newspapers, magazines, newsletters or television and radio broadcasts.

■ **representation**

the construction of an image or message in mass media communication. Some aspect of reality is represented through words or visuals into a media message by way of conventions that often say more about those producing them than about the objects being projected. According to postmodernism, there is no reality of representations, hence, reality can only be known through representations such as images or narratives that themselves are constructions created by conventions.

■ **reprint**

copy of an article that mentions you or your company.

■ **reproduction**

a reproduction is a copy of an original print or other art work whose matrix design is transferred from the original by a photomechanical process. A facsimile is a reproduction done to the same scale and appearance as the original.

■ **resampling**

the practice of interpolating an image of one specification and producing an image of another specification from that interpolation.

■ **residual**

a payment made to a model, actor or singer each time an advertisement is played, shown or run.

■ **residual error rate/undetected error rate/latent error rate**

the error rate at higher levels of Packet Radio communications system resulting from inability of the error detection/correction methods to trap all errors.

■ **resolution**

defines image quality of a display. It refers to the number of pixels available on a display. Resolution controls the level of detail that can be presented on a screen.

■ **resolver**

a device that governs the speed of a tape recorder during the transfer to mag, insuring the sound will be in sync with picture. The resolver uses the pilottone as a reference for adjusting the playback speed, hence something can only be resolved if it has been recorded with a properly equipped tape recorder.

■ **resonance**

in cultivation analysis, the situation in which a respondent's life experiences are reinforced by what is seen on TV, thus reinforcing the effect of TV content.

■ **resources**

components necessary to design, build and maintain technology (e.g., people, information, materials, tools and machines, energy, capital, time).

■ **respondent**

the person who responds to a petition placed before a court by another person, the opposite of the petitioner. At the appellate level, the respondent is often called the appellee.

■ **response time**

a measure of time from entering a data field on a remote terminal until the response is delivered to the remote by a central computer, a frequent measure of the overall performance of a Packet Radio Node Network (PRNN). The time between sending data to a remote device before an expected response returns to the originating station.

■ **restoration**

the process where a tape degraded by age is temporarily or permanently restored to a playable condition. The tape backing procedure is an example of a tape restoration procedure.

■ **restrike**

a restrike is a print produced from the matrix of an original print, but which was not printed as part of the original publishing venture or as part of a connected, subsequent publishing venture. A restrike is a later impression from an unrelated publishing project.

■ **retail (local) advertiser**

business that has customers in only one trading area.

■ **retailers**

segment of the media industry responsible for selling media products to the consumer.

■ **retensioning**

the process where a tape is unspooled onto a take-up reel and then rewound at a controlled tension and speed. In performing this procedure, tape pack stresses are redistributed and, thus, the tape is retensioned. This has sometimes been referred to as refreshing (or exercising the tape).

■ **retouch**

digital image editing processes used to restore damaged photographs for reproduction

■ **retraction**

in libel law, a statement published or broadcast that attempts to retract or correct previously published or broadcast libellous matter. A timely retraction will usually mitigate damages and in some states that have retraction laws, plaintiffs must seek a retraction before beginning a lawsuit or they lose the opportunity to collect anything but special damages.

■ **retry**

retry is the process by which a packet that is sent and not acknowledged will be resent by the sending station. This retry is repeated until the acknowledgment is received or until a 'retry counter' reaches its limit and the circuit is terminated.

■ revenue sharing

process by which video stores share movie rental fees with movie companies.

■ reversal

a type of film and method of processing that yields a positive original. This is the movie-film equivalent of slide film and processing, in still photography.

■ reverses

so called because the shot is taken from the reverse angle, for example, from over the shoulder or behind the interview subject, with the reporter in the frame. Used to splice together different parts of an interview. Related to 'cover' shots, of an audience at a press conference, for example.

■ rewinds

a simple device for winding film, consisting of a crank and a spindle for mounting one or more reels, typically found mounted on either side of an editing bench.

■ RGB

abbreviation for Red, Green and Blue signals, the primary colours of light — and television.

■ right of publicity

an offshoot of privacy law that protects the right of persons to capitalise on their fame or notoriety for commercial or advertising purposes.

■ right of reply

a little-used libel defence that declares as immune from a lawsuit a libellous remark made against an individual in reply to a previously published libellous remark made by that individual.

■ rivas

a type of tape splicer which uses perforated splicing tape. Two models exist: One for straight cuts used for picture and one for slanted cuts used for sound.

■ RLE

Run-Length Encoding. A data compression technique that records repeated data elements with the same value, which is coded once along with a count of the number of times it occurs.

■ ROI

Return on Investment. Generally refers to the advertiser's desire to have a return on the advertising funds invested in media.

■ rollout (informal)

geographic expansion of a campaign from a single test market outward, as to a regional or national market.

■ ROM image

the set of binary data that is programmed into an EPROM.

■ room tone

a recording of the 'silence' of a room or any location, to be used to fill in gaps when editing the sound. The silence of a location is really not very silent at all and the room tone of one location is not a substitute for another, so a sync sound shoot will usually end with the sound recordist asking everyone to be quiet for the recording of 30 seconds of room tone.

■ ROP

Run of Paper. A term used in newspaper advertising to indicate that the positioning of an advertisement is at the option of the publisher.

■ roto (roto-gravure)

a form of Intaglio printing where the image is chemically etched upon a copper cylinder. Many Sunday magazine supplements are printed in this process on various grates of coated paper.

■ rough cut

the edited film, between the stages of being an assembly and a fine cut.

■ rough layout

early version of a print advertisement.

■ round-up story

story geared to look back at what has happened over a specific period of time, such as the previous year or quarter. A story in which a reporter wants five or ten opinions on a subject

■ route diversity

two (or more) packet channels that assume two physically separate routes. A TheNET type node will substitutes an alternate path if the main path is lost thus preventing total loss of service.

■ routing

the process of determining or prescribing the path a connection will take through a network of nodes.

■ routing table

a matrix associated with a Packet Radio network control protocol giving the preferred network link directions beyond that point.

■ rs-232

a set of signals accepted as a 'standard' by the Electronics Industries Association (EIA), designed to make the interfacing of computers and networks, easier. RS-232-C is the current Electronics Industry Association (EIA) standard for the most common signals used between computers. A signal which uses the RS-232 standard is often said to be RS-232. The computer to TNC connection uses RS-232 signals. Normal computer internal data signals use ground and +5 volts to indicate a zero or a one.

■ RTS

Ready to Send. A control on a RS-232 port that indicated that the device has data ready to send. On some devices the DTR line is used instead of RTS. RTS is often used in conjunction with the CTS signal to engage 'hardware handshaking'.

■ RTTY

Radio Teletypewriting. An early mechanical based method of data communication on radio using the baudot code. In 1980 ASCII was also permitted on RTTY in the US. TELEX and TWX are commercial telephone systems using the same techniques.

■ rube goldberg device

a complex device that does a simple task.

■ RUDAK

Regenerativer Umsetzer fur Digitale Amateurfunk Kommunikation: meaning Regenerating Transponder for Digital Amateur Communications. A packet transponder project flown on board OSCAR 13 satellite. Developed by AMSAT-DL group in Germany.

■ running columns

regularly appearing articles of a specific theme or topic in a publication.

■ running time

how long it takes a show to go from start to finish. Often abbreviated TRT (Total Running Time).

■ rushes

the workprint, when it is just back from the lab, unedited, called the rushes because of the rush to see that everything came out alright. Also known as Dailies, in honour of the minority of labs that will have it later that day.

■ RXDATA

Received Data stream produced by a modem demodulator.

■ safety

an additional take, done after a successful one, as a backup.

■ sampling

digital process by which analog information is measured, often millions of times per second, in order to convert analog to digital.

■ sandwich board

two hinged boards, adorned with advertising messages, that are placed at an advantageous location or hung over someone's shoulders.

■ sans serif/serif

these terms apply to typeface and whether a particular typeface has 'tails' on it or not. Serif typefaces have 'tails' on them — Times Roman is an example of a serif typeface. Sans serif typefaces have no tails, Arial and Helvetica are examples of sans serif typefaces.

■ SAREX

Shuttle Amateur Radio Experiment : an educational program in which U.S. Shuttle astronauts communicate with classroom students using voice and packet.

■ Satellite News Gathering (SNG)

using specially equipped vans and trucks to transmit live stories from any location via satellite.

■ satellite tour

a feed from one point of origination to various downlink sites. An example is when an author is plugging a new book and is connected in series with several different interviewers in their newsrooms.

saturation

(sometimes called 'Grid-Lock')- when related to Packet Radio this definition refers to the absolute limit of traffic handling that a network of nodes will accept or handle.

SBE

Society of Broadcast Engineers.

scale

the relative size of a plan, drawing or model.

scanning

the most common practice of encoding real images into digital form. Accomplished by use of a scanner which passes an image sensor across the original.

scatter package

an arrangement to air television commercials at various times or intervals.

scattering

diffusion of an electromagnetic signal as it passes through a transmission medium, the ultimate cause of signal loss with distance in fibre-optic light-pipes.

scene

a scene is really just a single shot. But often scene is used to mean several shots, which is more to do with the word's origin in theatre. It is sometimes clearer to say 'sequence' for several shots, so as not to confuse the filmic and theatrical meanings of the word.

scienter

guilty knowledge. In many criminal prosecutions, the state must prove that the accused was aware of the nature of his or her behaviour. In an obscenity case, for example, the state must normally show that the defendant was aware of the contents of the book he or she sold.

scratch

damage to a film in the form of a long gouge of either the emulsion or the base. A scratch on the emulsion is pretty much unfixable, since part of the image itself is missing. Scratches on your workprint don't really matter at all, since you will go back to the pristine camera original for your final print.

scratch mix

a mix with little correction of the sound, that is usually done before the final mix in order to screen the film with all the sounds in place, to determine if there are any changes to be made. Typically this is not done on lower budget productions, as the added cost would be self-defeating.

scratch test

a scratch test is done before shooting, by running either a foot or two of the beginning of a roll of film or a dummy roll of film and checking for scratches, to insure that neither the camera nor the magazines are scratching the film.

scratch track

a sync recording made under conditions that make the sound useless, except for reference to the sound editor or to the actors for dubbing.

■ screen grabs

common term for the capturing screen rasterisation images and video stills to digital files. Can be preformed with software or hardware, but quality may vary between method used.

■ screen print

a form of stencil printing in which the stencil is adhered to a fine screen for support. Ink can be squeezed through the screen onto paper. Screen printing can have a hard edged quality caused by the crisp edges of the stencil. Also referred to as 'silk screen' and 'serigraphy'.

■ script

a blueprint for the action, narrative and dialogue in a media product.

■ SDTV

Standard Definition Television. Digital formats that do not achieve the video quality of HDTV, but are at least equal or superior to, NTSC pictures. SDTV may have either 4:3 or 16:9 aspect ratios and it includes surround sound. Variations of fps (frames per second), lines of resolution and other factors of 480p and 480i make up the 12 SDTV formats in the ATSC standard.

■ SECAM

a signal format used in video equipment in France and the former Soviet Union. SECAM (Système Electronique Couleur Avec Mémoire) is incompatible with PAL and NTSC formats.

■ second sticks!

if the clapper on the slate was not visible when the shot was being marked the camera person might call out 'second sticks!' to tell the person with the slate to mark it a second time.

■ secondary service

a radio station's second or non-primary, format.

■ seditious libel

libelling the government, criticising the government or government officers. It is sometimes called sedition.

■ segue

a gradual transition between two audio sources. The sources overlap as they go from one to another. Analogous to the dissolve transition in video and film.

■ select

using a menu system the viewer is able to select from one of the three pre-set modes the most appropriate picture and sound settings for the style of programme being watched. The modes have pre-set values for eight pictures and two sound parameters.

■ selection

the term for indicating the desired area to be a effected by editing.

■ selective demand advertisement

advertisement that stresses a particular brand.

■ **selects**

sometimes it is useful to separate out all the shots you are going to use before beginning to edit. These are known as selects.

■ **self-determination**

ethical principle that states that human beings deserve respect for their decisions.

■ **semiosis**

whereby one signifier refers only to another signifier, meaning constantly deferred in an infinite chain. This latter term tends to be associated with post-structuralism, one of the characteristics of which is the shift of emphasis from signified to signifier.

■ **sensing**

detecting, interpreting and monitoring energy with electric, electronic, fluid and mechanical devices.

■ **sensor**

a subsystem used to obtain information or data (e.g. light, temperature, number, movement).

■ **separating**

a production process in which a shape is changed by removing something (e.g. etching a printed circuit board, cutting wood).

■ **sequential pictorials plans**

a series of images representing steps used to complete a task.

■ **sequestration of the jury**

separating the jury from the community during a trial. Usually a jury is lodged at a hotel and members are required to eat together. In general, sequestration means to keep jurors away from other persons. Exposure to news reports is also screened to shield jurors from information about the trial.

■ **server**

in telecommunications traffic engineering, the generic term for a register or outgoing line that would provide the connection a subscriber demands. In LANs, a processor providing specific services to network users, as a file server to manage orders for file access, a gateway server to manage exit and entry of information to LAN users and similar LAN operations. This may include BBSs, DxClusters, DOSgates, TheNET nodes, TCP/IP hosts etc.

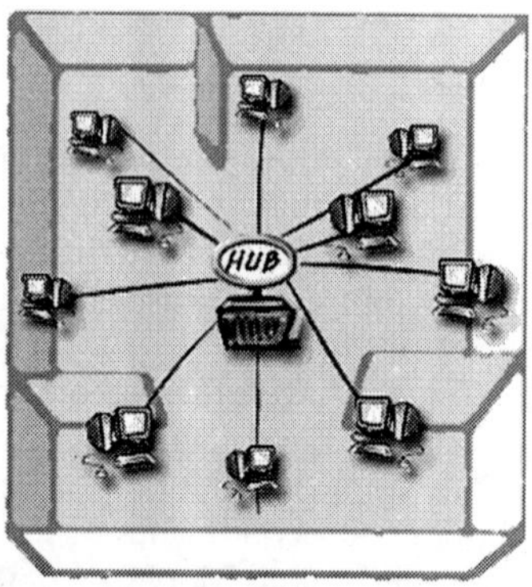

■ **server (video)**

system that provides large-capacity audio and video storage for video-on-demand retrieval, transmission, post production, news, etc. Most professional servers use digital disk storage.

■ session

recording session for a radio or TV commercial, also, a photo session.

■ session fee

the amount paid to talent or artist for a day's work in a single session.

■ Set-Top Box (STB)

device that converts and displays data from analog cable, digital cable or digital broadcast television to a standard frequency (channel number) for display on a standard analog television set or a box that receives off-air DTV signal for display on a DTV monitor.

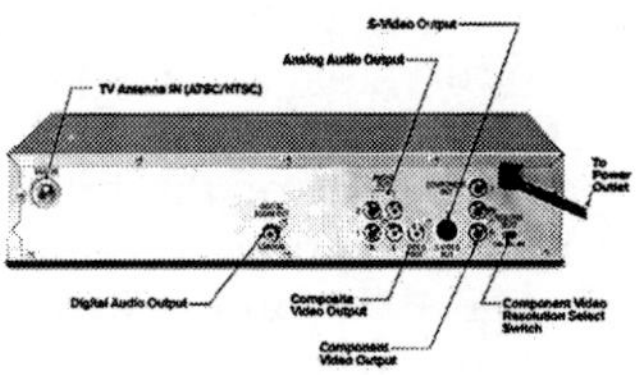

■ share

the percentage of televisions actually in use that are tuned to a specific program.

■ share of the audience

the ratio of listeners to a particular radio station to the total number of listeners in the market, the ratio of the number of households watching a particular TV program to the number of households watching TV at that time.

■ sharpen

to increase contrast along object edges to improve image appearance.

■ sharpie

a permanent felt-tipped marker useful for labelling the cans of exposed rolls out on a shoot and in the editing room for labelling your leader.

■ shield laws

state statutes that permit reporters in some circumstances to shield the name of a confidential news source when questioned by a grand jury or in another legal forum.

■ shoot

the taping or filming of a commercial, in a studio or on location.

■ shooting ratio

the ratio of how much film shot compared to running time of the finished film. For instance a 5 minute film for which you shot 30 minutes of footage would have a shooting ratio of 6 to 1.

■ short rate

an additional charge an advertiser must pay at the end of a full year if he has not fulfilled his contract.

■ shortends

the unexposed remainder of a roll of film in a magazine that is clipped and placed back into a can for use later. Unlike recans a shortend is something less than 400 feet.

■ shot

a shot is the film exposed from the time the camera is started to the time it is stopped. Shot and Scene are interchangeable terms.

side panels

used with imaging a standard 4:3 picture on a wide-screen 16:9 aspect ratio television screen, typically with black bars (side panels) on each side. Used to maintain the original aspect ratio of the source material.

sideband

the resultant added signals above and below a carrier frequency resulting from the modulation process placing information on the carrier. Telephony has in most systems for years filtered out one of the sidebands to save transmission space in AM analog systems. The resulting sideband is called 'single sideband'. In recent years this same technique has been applied to FM microwave radio as well, resulting in twice the transmission capacity.

sidebar

legal term that the media adopted to describe a portion of a story that is relevant but not necessary to the body of the story, such as data, a glossary or a deeper explanation of a concept mentioned in the story. Usually it is set apart from the body of the article by a box or screen to make it stand out

sig file

a signature block consistently used that includes a tag line about the company.

signal

energy intentionally introduced into a transmission path for the purpose of transmitting information.

signal to noise ratio

ratio of the signal power to the noise power in a specified bandwidth, usually expressed in decibels, the smaller the ratio, the poorer the channel. Generally speaking, a ratio of 20 db or more is a channel subjectively 'excellent' for voice, while broadcast television video requires 30 db or more, but 1200 bps can function with only 12 db, requiring greater S/N as the baudrate increases.

signed

a signed print is one signed, in pencil or ink, by the artist and/or engraver of the print. A print is said to be signed in the plate if the artist's signature is incorporated into the matrix and so appears as part of the printed image. Proof prints were originally signed as 'proof' that the impression met the artist's expectation. Later proof prints were signed in order to add commercial value to these impressions. In the late nineteenth century, in response to the development of photomechanical reproduction techniques, fine arts prints were signed by the artists in order to distinguish between original prints and reproductions.

silent camera

this term is often a little confusing because it does not mean a camera that is itself silent and therefore usable for sync sound, but it means a noisy, unsilent camera, usable only for shooting silent, M.O.S. scenes.

■ silent speed

18 frames per second. A slightly archaic notion left over from the time when 16m.m. was used exclusively for home movies. It is not always that easy to find a projector that will project at 18 frames per second and so films shot at silent speed will often be speeded up slightly, whether the filmmaker intended this of not.

■ silver print

a photographic print utilising paper impregnated with silver nitrate (distinct from a platinum print, for example).

■ SIMM

Single In-line Memory Module. A small narrow circuit board containing Random Access Memory Chips (the electronic devices that store data while your computer works with it). SIMMs plug into special slots inside the computer to give the computer extra memory.

■ simmons (smrb)

a syndicated magazine readership survey organisation which reports on reader demographics, product usage and other media usage.

■ simple machines

basic devices or mechanical powers on which other machines are based (e.g. lever, wedge, pulley, wheel, axle, inclined plane and screw).

■ simplex

a communication method in which communication between two stations takes place one direction at a time regardless of whether the receiving and transmitting on the same frequency or on split frequency. Amateur radio, simplex usually means receiving and transmitting on the same frequency. Most Packet communications are conducted in 'simplex.'

■ simplex digipeater

a digital store-and-forward node or digipeater is a regenerative digital repeater that receives a packet, verifies that it was received correctly and if the Packet is correct, retransmits it on the same frequency it was received on. The node retransmits the signal only after confirming that the frequency or channel is clear.

■ simulcast

the broadcast of the same program simultaneously over two or more different systems or channels. An accelerated amount of simulcasting of both analog and digital programming will be required by FCC rules, during the DTV transition period.

■ simultaneous submission

sending a by-lined article to more than one publication at the same time (often frowned upon).

■ single mistake rule

in libel law, a rule that states that it is not libellous to accuse a professional person or business person of making a single mistake (e.g., 'Dr. Pat Jones incorrectly diagnosed the patient's illness').

■ single perf

16m.m. film with a row of perforations along one edge. On the film can this will be indicated by 1R appearing on the label.

■ single reel

in 35m.m. a reel is 1,000 feet of film (or usually a little less).

■ Single Sideband Radio (SSB)

a form of amplitude modulation of a radio signal in which only one of the two sidebands is transmitted. Either of the two sidebands may be transmitted while the carrier may be reduced or suppressed.

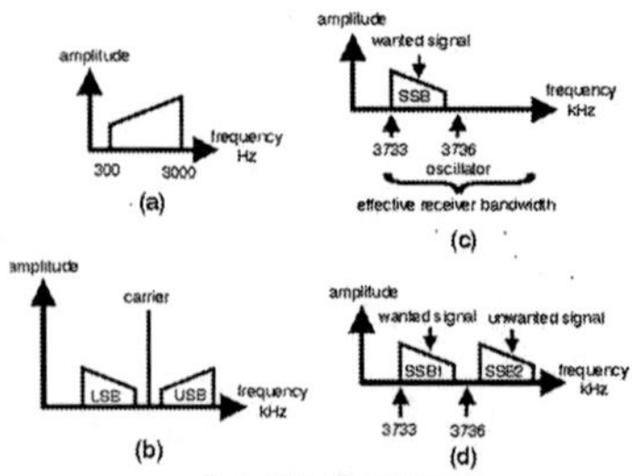

Spectrum diagrams

■ single system

single system refers to recording, editing or projecting sound and picture together on the same piece of film. Cameras used for TV news would record the sound on a magnetic stripe as well as photograph the picture. Also super-8 sound. Single system has some distinct editorial disadvantages, hence the more common use of Double System for shooting and editing.

■ SITOR

a commercial communications system very similar to AMTOR and used mainly for maritime and marine mobile communications.

■ sitting mike

a microphone on a table.

■ sizzle

dazzle or excitement, as opposed to substance. In its bid for consumers, some advertising plays up the 'sizzle' rather than the 'steak'.

■ slander

spoken defamation. (In many states, if a defamatory statement is broadcast, it is considered libel, even though technically the words are not written. Libel is considered more harmful and usually carries more serious penalties than does slander.)

■ slant

the emphasis of a campaign, advertisement, hook or peg.

■ slice-of-life

denoting any presentation that depicts naturalistic, everyday activities.

■ sliding scale

an arrangement between a motion picture exhibitor and a distributor that details how much box office revenue will be kept by the movie theatre.

■ **slogan**

short, memorable advertising phrase. When a product or company uses a slogan consistently, the slogan can become an important element of identification in the public's perception of the product.

■ **slop print**

an untimed black and white dupe print of your workprint, used for projection in a sound mix. A slop print is used because splices can jump and cause the film to go out of sync and a slop print will have no splices.

■ **slot time**

in the persistence method of collision avoidance slot time is the time delay before repeating the random number persistence calculation.

■ **slug**

a rather unattractive sounding name for Filler.

■ **smart terminal**

a Packet Radio terminal or computer capable of operating in either a conversational or a block mode, containing a full set of local editing capabilities without reliance on a controlling external computer.

■ **smartlink**

communication device between TV and VCR that ensures ultimate ease of use.

■ **smith act**

a federal law adopted in 1940 that makes it illegal to advocate the violent overthrow of the government.

■ **smoothness**

surface smoothness is determined by measuring the rate of air flow between the sheet surface and a flat reference surface. Smoothness usually is expressed in Sheffield or Bekk units.

■ **SMPTE**

abbreviation for the Society of Motion Pictures and Television Engineers.

■ **sniping**

the act of pasting up outdoor posters over billboards or on empty structures, walls and traffic poles, often without permission.

■ **social change**

a positive change in peoples' lives - as they themselves define such change. This section has summaries and full articles based on theories of social change.

■ **social construction**

a popular perspective in sociology that argues there is nothing natural or normal about the world we inhabit and that, rather, it consists of a series of conventions that are continually created by individuals who define situations and interact, albeit within broader contexts.

■ **social conventions**

customary verbal and non-verbal actions which constitute polite discourse. Examples include please, thank you, excuse me, may I introduce, etc.

social responsibility theory

the belief that the press has a responsibility to preserve democracy by properly informing the public and by responding to society's needs.

social utility

the media function that addresses an individual's need to affiliate with family, friends and others in society.

socialisation

the process whereby individuals are made aware of the behaviour that others expect of them as regards the norms, values and culture of their society. Agents of socialisation include the family, school, friendship groups, religious institutions and the mass media.

soft ground

an etching technique in which the plate is covered with malleable ground through which a variety textures can be pressed, allowing them to be etched into the plate. For example, a piece of paper laid on top of a soft grounded plate can be drawn upon with a pencil and the resulting etched image will resemble a pencil line drawn on paper. To be distinguished from 'hard ground' used for simple line etching.

soft light

a type of light with a built-in surface to act as a bounce card, providing soft, indirect light on the subject.

soft news

features that rely on human interest for their news value.

soft sell

subtle or unpressured advertising technique.

software

the place where media messages are stored. Intended for use with hardware. Software can take the form of computer diskettes, video cassettes, film, audio cassettes, etc.

sound blanket

basically just a quilted mover's blanket. Often it is thrown over the camera (and the camera operator) to cut down on camera noise, as a sort of improvised Barney.

sound effects

special effects using sound to suggest a story element such as background, time, place, character, etc. Also used to heighten and intensify action or evoke an emotional response.

sound fill

see **filler**.

sound reader

a playback head for reading mag stock, mounted on a bracket that snaps onto a synchroniser. It is pugged into the squawk box.

sound slug

see **filler**.

sound speed

24 frames per second. The normal

speed for filming and projecting.

■ **source**

person who initiates communication.

■ **source reduction**

source reduction means using less material to hold or package, a product in the first place. This reduces the amount of packaging material that must be recycled or discarded after use. Film contributes to source reduction by allowing thinner materials to be used without a loss in package integrity.

■ **space**

a page or section of a page bought for advertising purposes in a newspaper, magazine or catalogue.

■ **spacer**

a metal cylinder with a flat plate at one end and a hole through the centre, used between reels on the spindle of a rewind to space out the reels the same distance as the gangs of a synchroniser. Although it is a little shorter, in a pinch you can use cores as spacers.

■ **spam**

the electronic equivalent of junk mail.

■ **spatial resolution**

number of pixels horizontally and vertically in a digital image.

■ **spec**

short form of 'speculation'. Work done 'on spec' is done for no guaranteed remuneration, in hope of winning the job, campaign or account in question. Pitches to prospective clients used to be done almost exclusively on spec.

■ **special damages**

damages that can be awarded to a plaintiff in a lawsuit upon proof of specific monetary loss.

■ **special effects**

sound or video used in the editing process to heighten drama or suggest a time, place or story element. Often used as a transition.

■ **specialised publication**

industry-specific trade or professional publication (manufacturing, insurance, telecommunications, etc.)

■ **specifics**

in sound editing, these are any effects that directly relate to the picture, where we see a thing happen and hear it too. Backgrounds, ambiance and speech are not specifics.

■ **spectrum (electromagnetic spectrum)**

a means of charting the order of radio and television signals in terms of their physical wavelength. A continuous range of frequencies in the earth's atmosphere.

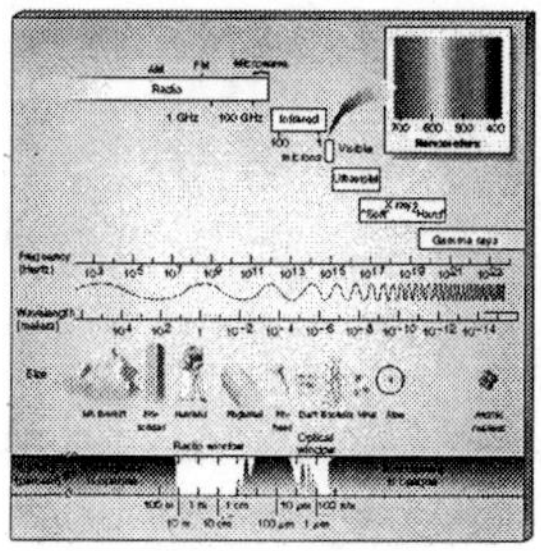

■ **spectrum scarcity**

broadcast spectrum space is limited, so not everyone who wants to broadcast can, those who are granted licenses must accept regulation.

■ **speed**

this is what the camera person or sound recordist will call out to acknowledge that they are rolling. It comes from the days when it took a few seconds for certain equipment to reach proper speed.

■ **spider**

another, less commonly used, term for Spreader.

■ **spikes**

spikes is a term that comes from theatre. They are little pieces of tape placed around the legs of furniture or the tripod legs, before they are moved, making it easy to return things to their original position.

■ **spin**

jargon for the point of view or bias you create in a story.

■ **spin**

jargon for the point of view or bias you create in a story.

■ **splice**

a method of joining two pieces of film so they can be projected as one continuous piece. There are three methods: the Tape Splice (usually used for editing), the Cement Splice (used for original material) and the far less common Ultra-Sonic Splice (used for Polyester Base film).

■ **splicing tape**

a special type of clear tape, not interchangeable with scotch tape, used to splice film. It comes in perforated (for use with a Rivas) and unperforated (for use with a Guillotine). Transparent splicing tape is used for picture and white splicing tape for sound.

■ **split reel**

a very handy reel, the two halves of which may be unscrewed and film on a core placed between. Once screwed back together (but not too tight or it will never open) your film on a core has quickly been converted into film on a reel.

■ **split screen**

Typically a split screen is a matte shot divided down the centre of the shot.

■ **split-run**

using two different advertisements in the same publication, where the publisher will run the copy in different parts of his press run. Split runs are used to test the effectiveness of copy or space. An A/B split means copy alternates also throughout the press run. There are geographic splits, four-way splits, etc.

■ **spokesperson**

a well-known person serving as a regular advocate of specific product or cause.

■ **sponsorship**

the purchase of more than one commercial within a programme, allowing advertisers to receive bonus time via billboards or exclusivity of advertising within the brand's product category or both.

■ spool down

winding an unexposed 400 foot roll down onto four 100 foot daylight spools for use in a camera that will only take 100 feet of film. Spooling down can only be done in complete darkness. 42 turns on a rewind per daylight spool will divide a 400 foot roll pretty evenly. Also, it is vitally important that the film be wound all the way through once and then spooled down, otherwise the edge numbers will be on the wrong side and not printed onto the workprint.

■ spot (spot announcement)

15- or 30-second radio or television commercial.

■ spot advertising

any advertising presented in selected locales rather than on a national level.

■ spot meter

a type of meter for taking a Reflective Light Reading with a short telescopic sight that enables you to take a very specific reflective reading of a small, well-defined area.

■ spot news

news of immediate interest.

■ spread

advertisement or other print presentation that takes two facing pages in a magazine or newspaper. A full-page 'spread' fills both pages and may take up the gutter in between as well.

■ spread spectrum

fundamental to telecommunications, a method of transmitting radio signals as a very wideband but low-powered signal that appears almost like noise. At the receiver all components of the desired signal are filtered from the noise and summed to recover a usable signal.

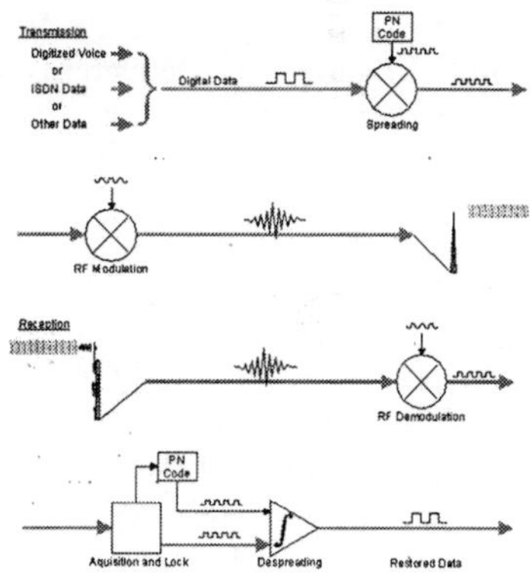

■ spring lock

a round spring-loaded clamp that

goes on the end of a rewind to allow several reels to turn together.

■ sprocket

the teeth on a roller designed to engage with the perforations in film. Sometimes sprocket holes are referred to as sprockets too.

■ sprocket holes

the same as perf.

■ spun

spun glass diffusion material. see diffusion.

■ squawk box

a small amplified speaker used on an editing bench and receiving sound from the Sound Reader.

■ SSID

the SSID is the specific number applied the call sign of a digipeater or second, third, etc...Packet stations. The acronym is derived from the term, 'Secondary Station Identification'. It is most often used with nodes of the The NET variety. In Packet radio, a call sign is normally used as an address. In a applications where an amateur requires more than one address on the air at a time the call sign may be used with an 'SSID'. There are 16 different possible SSIDs, 0 through 15. An SSID is used when applied to a personal mailbox or PBBS by adding the dash one suffix to the call. Most personal mailbox calls use -1 as the SSID. i.e. the Packet mailbox of K4ABT is K4ABT-1.

■ STA

Special Temporary Authorisation.: a special permit granted by the FCC to operate using a special application for experimental or test purposes. STA's are also issued to stations for use in applications that are not normally permitted or allowed.

■ stabile

display that is suspended or that rises from a pedestal at different levels and planes, none of which move.

■ stage manager

the individual on the set of a studio who cues the participants and otherwise provides liaison with the control room.

■ stand up

a commentary or report by a TV correspondent seen on camera, usually at the scene of the action. Used to open, close or bridge the elements of a report.

■ Standard Advertising Unit (S.A.U.)

system of standard dimensions for print display advertising based on six columns, each 2 1/16 inches wide, with a 1/8 inch 'gutter' between columns. Because nearly all broadsheet newspapers are now in SAU in their display pages, a single ad may be used in many places without resizing.

stand-up shot

the source is filmed standing in front of a wall, while a TV reporter asks questions. This kind of shot adds an authoritative source to a television story.

start bit

the leading bit of every asynchronous character, needed to trigger the receiver that a new character is starting, must intrinsically be a space (0) bit.

state

a state of a print includes all the impressions pulled without any change being made to the matrix. A first state print is one of the first group of impressions pulled. Different states of a print can reflect intentional or accidental changes to the matrix. States of a print should be distinguished from editions of a print. There can be several editions of a print which are the same state and there can be several states of a print in the same edition.

station

any user location on a Packet Radio network capable of sending or receiving Packet AX.25 transmissions.

station id

used on radio and television to identify the station frequency and call letters. Analogs to a company logo or a newspaper masthead.

station label

station label utilises information sent by individual broadcasters to automatically identify and label the stations.

status conferral

a process by which media attention bestows a degree of prominence on certain issues or individuals.

statute of limitations

a law that requires that a legal action must begin within a specified period of time (usually one to three years for a civil case) after the legal wrong was committed.

stereotypes

a form of media representation by which instantly recognised characteristics are used to label members of social or cultural groups. While often negative, stereotypes can contain an element of truth and are used by the media to establish an instant rapport with the audience.

stet

from Latin for 'let it stand'. Used in copyediting and proofreading to signify that the original copy, not the revision, should be used.

stick slip

the process in which (1) the tape sticks to the recording head because of high friction, (2) the tape tension builds because the tape is not moving at the head, (3) the tape tension reaches a critical level, causing the tape to release from and briefly slip past the read head at high speed, (4) the tape slows to normal speed and once again sticks to the recording head, (5) this process is repeated indefinitely. Characterised by jittery movement of the tape in the transport and/or audible squealing of the tape.

■ **sticky shed**

the gummy deposits left on tape path guides and heads after a sticky tape has been played. The phenomenon whereby a tape binder has deteriorated to such a degree that it lacks sufficient cohesive strength so that the magnetic coating sheds on playback. The shedding of particles by the tape as a result of binder deterioration that causes dropouts on VHS tapes.

■ **sticky tape**

tape characterised by a soft, gummy or tacky tape surface. Tape that has experienced a significant level of hydrolysis so that the magnetic coating is softer than normal. Tape characterised by resinous or oily deposits on the surface of the magnetic tape.

■ **stiffness**

how resistant print media is to bending or flexing.

■ **stone**

a lithographic stone is a slab of stone, usually limestone, used as a matrix for a print. Lithographic stones are used to make lithographs and chromolithographs.

■ **store and retrieve**

compiling information in some form of memory and recovering the data as required (e.g. storing sound and images on video tape and playing it back).

■ **store-and-forward**

this is the process employed in nodes and digipeaters where a packet is received, processed and retransmitted to the next node, digipeater or destination station.

■ **storyboard**

a series of panels roughly depicting scenes, copy and shots proposed for a television commercial. The storyboard gives the client a good idea of the agency's concept for a commercial, before extensive production charges are incurred.

■ **strategic partner**

a company or organisation that another company or organisation aligns itself with to benefit both parties.

■ **strategic thinking**

summaries of strategic thinking as the basis for communication, change and development policies and interventions.

■ **strategies**

methods used to accomplish objectives

■ **stream**

AX25 allows many connections to be made from several stations at the same time. Each connection is called a 'stream'. To test one's sanity, open more than one stream and allow two or more connections, then carry on separate QSO's with each separately connected station.

■ streamer

a grease pencil mark on the workprint indicating either a fade or a dissolve, called so because when projected it resembles a streamer trailing across the screen.

■ streaming

the simultaneous downloading and accessing (playing) of digital audio or video data

■ streaming video

method of sending TV over the Internet.

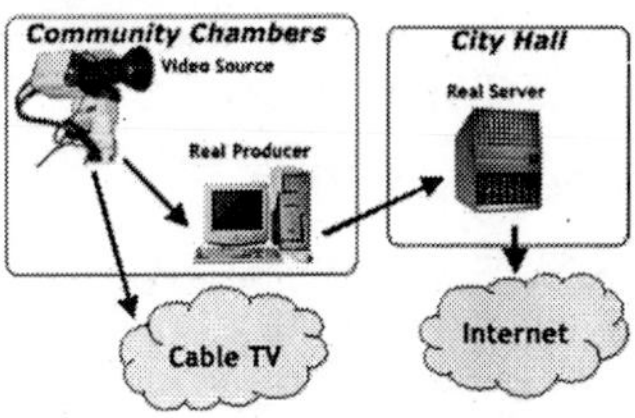

■ stress

force per unit area, such as pounds per square inch (psi). A tape wound on a reel with high tension results in a tape pack with a high interwinding stress. See **tension**.

■ stripe

35m.m. mag stock that contains a stripe of magnetic tape rather than the complete coating found on Fullcoat. Stripe mag will also have a balance stripe to prevent warping.

■ studio system

the factory-like production system in Hollywood by which movies were made from about 1925 to 1955.

■ stunt

a programming manoeuvre that moves a show from its usual time slot to a more advantageous slot or multiple time periods in order to boost ratings or introduce a new program. It also refers to unusual or sensational programming designed to grab attention during sweeps periods.

■ stylist

hair and/or makeup artist on a television shoot.

■ subliminal

literally, this adjective applies to anything that works by manipulation of the subconscious. Contemporary advertising is largely subliminal not because of hidden messages deliberately inserted, but because of a reliance on images that evoke positive associations at the subconscious level.

■ subliminal advertising

concealed appeal to consumers' unconscious awareness to buy product.

■ subscription

a system representing a contract between a television broadcaster and viewer for reception of a service at a fee agreed upon.

■ subsidiary rights

rights given by a publisher to others, allowing them to reproduce certain content.

substantiation

a Federal Trade Commission rule that requires an advertiser to prove the truth of advertising claims made about a product or service.

substitution

the process of replacing colours in a image with colours or patterns on the pallet for the image. this is implemented during colour format conversion and pallet correction

substrate

backing film layer that supports the magnetic layer in a magnetic tape.

subway card

an advertising poster attached to the interior of a subway car.

sulphur ground

a technique in which a caustic sulphur compound is painted directly on an etching plate or in which sulphur dust is otherwise applied to a plate. The resulting marks will hold ink and can be printed like an etching. The technique typically creates blotchy expanses of grey tones. This might be compared to printing rust marks on a steel or iron plate.

super

an image superimposed over another image. Often the subject of an interview will be 'supered' with identifying information. Also called 'titles' or 'lower thirds' because of the positioning of words.

super 16

a format using single perf 16m.m. film on which a wider image is exposed than is the case with regular 16m.m., using the area that would normally have the soundtrack. Super 16m.m. was conceived specifically for blow up to 35m.m. and is typically rather inconvenient for anything else.

super spectrum sound

another version of Full Spectrum Sound with improved vocal and bass frequency response with two additional high-frequency speakers. Guarantees perfect stereo reproduction.

super speed

just a fancy way for Zeiss to describe a fast prime lens, typically with a T-stop of 1.3.

superimposition

the same as Double Exposure, but often used expressly to describe a double exposure done through optical printing, as in superimposed titles, etc.

support

the material (usually paper) to which the image is transferred from the inked matrix and which provides the image's physical support and much of its tone.

surveillance

the news and information function of the mass media.

survey

a technique of gathering data that typically uses a questionnaire.

■ **SW**

Short Wave. A section of the electromagnetic frequency spectrum between 3 and 30 MHZ. Used for long distance radio communications since the signals are reflected from the ionosphere. Also known as the high frequency (HF) range.

■ **sweetening**

electronically improving the quality of an audio or video signal, such as adding sound effects, audio ambience or laugh tracks.

■ **switch**

mechanical, electromechanical or electronic devices for making, breaking or changing connections in circuits.

■ **switching**

any method (e.g. mechanical, electronic) used to turn the flow of energy on and off in a system (e.g. light switch, keyboard).

■ **symbol**

something that stands for something else in which there is no direct relationship except as defined by convention.

■ **sync**

the degree to which sound and picture are lined up, in-sync being lined up exactly and out-of-sync not so exactly. It can be applied to any specific sound and picture relationship, not just voices and not just sync-sound, but any type of specific effect too.

■ **sync mark**

1. the point at which the clapsticks come together at the beginning of a shot and the accompanying sound on the sound track.
2. an 'X' mark on a single frame at the beginning of a reel of picture that lined up with a second sync mark on a roll of sound (May also be used anywhere where needed). Sync marks are also used at the beginning of A&B rolls.

■ **sync sound**

sync sound is sound recorded while shooting picture. Usually it involves footage of people speaking and is thus sometimes called lip sync. It must be recorded with either crystal or cable sync to line up and not drift out of sync.

■ **synchronisation**

relating to Packet Radio, the function of terminal node controllers to reach equal clocking of data and recognised frames.

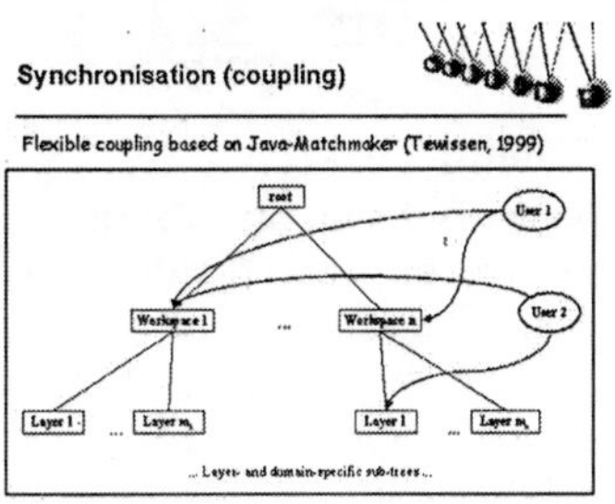

synchroniser

a very helpful tool of the editing room, a synchronser is a device with a centre axle and several sprocketed wheels attached to it. The wheels are called gangs. Film may be clamped into the gang, so that it can be measured with a footage counter on the front of the synchroniser. One revolution of the synchroniser equals one foot of film. Several elements, such as film and sound, A&B rolls, can be run in tandem can easily cut to the same length. It is used by the negative cutter for the assembly of A&B rolls, as well as for logging, measuring footage, syncing and checking sync in the editing room.

synchronous

a serial communications mode in which the data bits are sent in a continuous stream without character start and stop bits. The data stream is embedded with clocking bits for synchronisation at the receive end of the circuit. AX.25 packet communications use synchronous data transmissions.

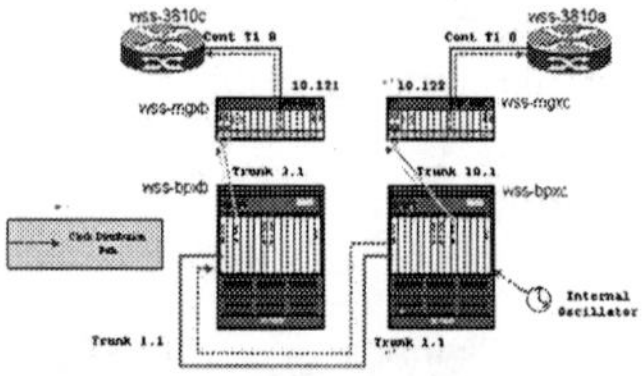

syncing

the actual lining up of sound and picture before editing a sync sound film. This also involves cutting the excess sound between takes and adding filler, so that the picture and sound are now in sync for beginning to end.

syndicated

report that appears in more than one media outlet simultaneously.

syndicated columnist

person hired by publications or broadcast organisations to produce written or spoken commentary about specific feature subjects. A syndicated print column is usually published in a wide variety of newspapers, magazines or on many local networks.

syndication

sale of radio or television content to stations on a market-by-market basis.

synergy

formerly used in the sense of an interaction among parts of a whole that renders the whole greater than the sum of the parts. At present, synergy is ascribed to the ability of media conglomerates to coordinate marketing with advertising campaigns involving multimedia processes from selling T-shirts to sales of video and CDs.

synthetic materials

materials created through chemical synthesis (e.g., plastics, fibreglass).

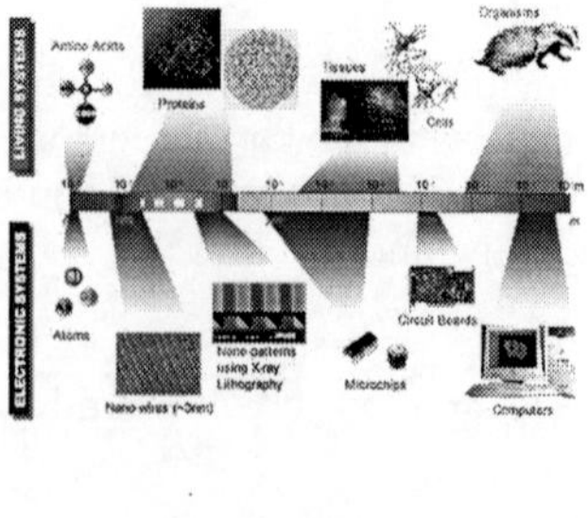

■ syquest

a manufacturer of SCSI removable cartridge hard drives. This drive specification has been widely used in pre-press and publishing situations.

■ SYSOP or BBS SYSOP

the person(s) responsible for the smooth operation of a BBS, including maintaining forwarding routes, redirecting misaddressed messages, checking for illegal or improper messages. SNO's are not sysop's.

■ system

a regularly interacting or interdependent group of items forming a unified whole.

■ System Node Operator (SNO)

the person(s) responsible for the growing operation of a network node. Duties include checking for legal operations. SNO's are not sysop's.

■ systemic discrimination

d*iscrimination* intrinsic to the normal functioning of an institution, contrasted with conventional discrimination, which openly and deliberately tries to exclude or deny. Systemic discrimination is embedded in a way that penalises minorities because of the logical consequences of even well-intentioned arrangements that are founded on faulty assumptions. Initiatives that seek to impose a 'one size fits all' application of rules, procedures or rewards may also be systemically discriminatory.

■ systemic stereotyping

that are not an error in individual perception but embedded within the structures, outputs and processes of media institutions. That is, media cannot help but stereotype, given their need to process information and codify reality within the boxed-in constraints of print or electronic media. The media are heavily if unconsciously dependent on stereotyping as a means of simplifying content for audiences.

■ systems and control

the application of devices and processes to manage, sort, control and organise.

■ tablet

a pressure sensitive input device used in conjunction with a pen to edit digital images.

■ tabloids

literally, newspapers that are half the size of broadsheets. Often used in a derogatory sense to convey the idea of dumbing down or sensationalism.

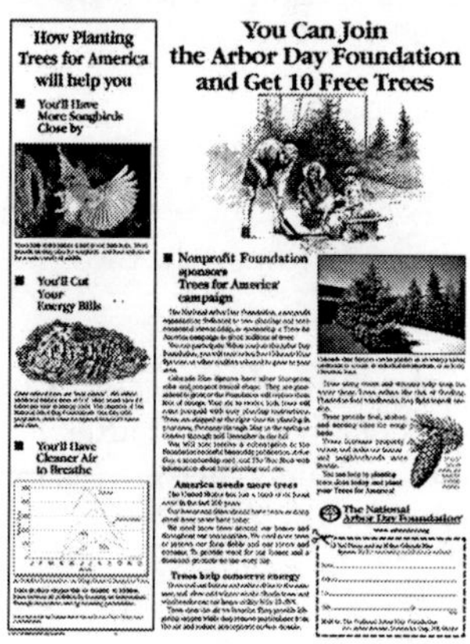

■ tachometer

a gauge on a camera measuring the film speed when the camera is running.

■ tag line

a sentence or phrase that provides a creative description of an organisation's position.

■ tag time

last statement of a show, spot or commercial.

■ tail

the end of a shot or a roll is called the tail.

■ tail slate

sometimes it is necessary to mark a shot at the end rather than at the beginning. When this is done it is called a tail slate. It is customary to call 'Tail Slate!' just before clapping the slate, so that the person syncing the film does not get confused. To easily distinguish a tail slate, the slate is held upside down when marking the shot.

■ take

multiple versions of the same shot are called takes.

■ take up reel

an empty reel, used on a projector to gather up the film after it has passed through the movement.

■ take up spool

an empty spool in a camera used to gather up the film after it has passed through the movement.

■ talent

actors, models and singers employed in advertisements.

■ talent agency

an organisation that represents actors and models appearing in advertisements.

■ talking head

television shot that shows only the upper shoulders, neck and face of the person being interviewed. Usually accompanied by a computer-generated sign that appears midchest identifying the person and his or her company

■ tape

the medium whereby images and sound are recorded on plastic through an electronic process. As a verb, 'to tape' means the production process which uses video or audio hardware to record images and/ or sound on tape.

■ tape baking

a process in which a magnetic tape is placed at an elevated temperature for a brief time in order to firm up the tape binder. This procedure is recommended as a temporary cure for the sticky shed or sticky tape syndrome.

■ tape noise

a magnetic signal on the tape resulting from the finite size and non-uniform distribution of magnetic particles in the magnetic layer of the tape. Tape noise is inherent in any magnetic tape but can be reduced by using smaller pigment sizes in tape formulations. The iron oxide pigments found in less expensive tapes have the largest tape noise level. Ranked in size iron oxide > chromium dioxide > metal particulate > barium ferrite. Therefore, ranked in order of tape noise iron oxide > chromium dioxide > metal particulate > barium ferrite.

■ **tape pack**

the structure formed by and comprised solely of tape wound on a hub or spindle, a tape reel consists of a tape pack, the metal, plastic or glass hub and flanges. Tape transport The mechanics used to guide and move the tape through the recording system and past the read and write heads of the recorder. Thc tape transport consists of the tape guide pins, capstan, rollers, tension controllers, etc.

■ **tape splice**

a method of joining two pieces of film so they can be projected as one continuous piece. Tape splices are used in the editing stage. To cut the negative Cement Splices are used.

■ **TAPR**

Tucson Amateur Packet Radio Corp: ' non-profit' research group best known for the TNC1 & TNC2 TNCs and their clones.

■ **target audience**

in advertising, the segment of the population for whom the product or service has an appeal.

■ **target market**

target audience.

■ **TCP/IP**

1. Transmission Control Protocol / Internet Protocol- the KISS mode activates this mode in some TNCs. This mode is not supported by software for all computers and Terminal Node Controllers (TNCs). The KISS protocol was used by Phil Karn KA9Q, to develop the Packet radio version of TCP/IP.

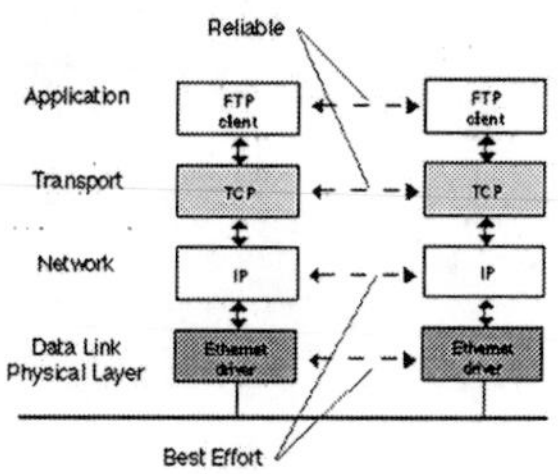

2. is a combined set of protocols that perform the transfers of data between two computers.

■ **TDM**

Time Division Multiplex. The management of multiple signals on one channel by alternately sending portions of each signal and assigning each portion to particular blocks of time.

■ **tearsheet**

a page on which an ad was placed in a publication and sent to an advertiser for proof of performance.

■ **teaser**

an attention-getting highlight of a television show presented before the show begins. It is intended to draw viewers to the program.

■ **technical drawings**

drawings that contain the detailed information required to produce an object or system (e.g., measurement, scale, material, finishing information).

■ technological determinism

the theory that contends technology drives historical change.

■ technology

hardware used to create and communicate with media, e.g., radio,

computers, telephones, satellites, printing presses, pencils, etc.

■ technology tools

hardware used to create and communicate with media, e.g., radio, computers, telephones, satellites, printing presses, pencils, etc. See also, hardware.

■ telecine

a machine for transferring film to video.

■ telecommunications

the transmission of voice and/or data through a medium by means of electrical impulses and includes all aspects of transmitting Packet Radio information.

■ Telecommunications Act of 1996

major revision of U.S. communication laws that affected broadcasting, cable and telephone industries.

■ telegraph

a system employing the interruption of or change in, the polarity of signalling to convey coded information. Many of to-days techniques in data communications follow precepts first established in telegraphy.

■ telemarketing

selling or advertising or market research done by telephone.

■ telemetry

discipline of measuring a quantity or quantities, transmitting the results to a distant point and there interpreting, indicating or recording the quantities measured.

■ telenet

a presentation protocol layer in the ARPA & TCP/IP suite used for keyboard to keyboard and keyboard to host communications.

■ telephoto

used as an equivalent to Long Lens, but for those who wish to be overly exact, a telephoto lens is a long lens that is physically shorter than its focal length.

■ teleprompter

a trademark used for the device that shows an actor or a speaker an enlarged line-by-line reproduction of a script, unseen by the audience.

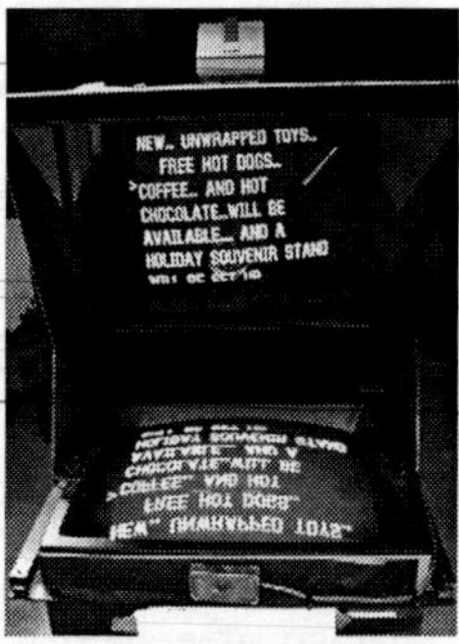

■ teletext

an electronic communications system in which printed text is broadcast by television signal to sets equipped with decoders.

■ tension

force or force per tape width. The force on a tape as it is transported through a recorder. A tape wound on a reel with high tension results in a tape pack with a high interwinding stress. See **stress**.

■ tent pole

a hit program of such strength that its audience will stay with the network for the rest of the evening.

■ terminal

relating to Packet Radio, a device capable of sending or receiving information over a Packet Radio frequency. A terminal or display input/output (I/O) device. A Cathode Ray Tube (CRT) normally referred to as a terminal. They are often referred to as 'dumb terminals'. In most Packet stations our computer is employed as a terminal. A terminal consists of a display screen and keyboard and a connected to an RS-232 port. When you type on the keyboard data is sent out of the Transmit Data pin of the RS-232 connector on the terminal. When Receive Data signals are detected on the RS-232 connector the text is displayed on the screen.

■ terminal equipment

devices, apparatus and their associated interfaces used to forward data along a Packet Radio network or to a target Packet station/terminal (DTE).

■ terrestrial

a term used to distinguish broadcasting from transmitters situated on the earth's surface from broadcasting from satellite (celestial).

■ test market

a consumer group interviewed to determine target audience.

■ test market spot

a spot used exclusively on the test market and monitored for its effectiveness.

■ testimonial

a statement, often given by a celebrity, affirming the value of a product, event or service. The authority, glamour, character or special knowledge of a celebrity can reflect on the advertised product. Customer testimonials are also commonly used.

■ testimonial appeals

appeals in which audiences are urged to support a cause, purchase a product or engage in certain behaviour because a celebrity figure is doing so. Audiences need to consider whether the celebrity figure has qualifications that are relevant to the persuasive effort. (Example: A sports figure urges viewers to purchase a particular cereal because he/she eats it.)

■ **texnet**

a networking node protocol developed by the Texas Packet Radio Society and used primarily in Texas and the southwest. TEXNET uses a custom three port node which supports 1200 or 9600 baud modems, as daughter cards. A notable feature of TEXNET is that it can support a local hard drive using the TEXNET board's on-board disk controller.

■ **text**

the individual results of media production: a movie, a TV episode, a book, an issue of a magazine or newspaper, an advertisement, an album, etc.

■ **TGI**

Target Group Index. Annual survey system of media usage and product/brand usage, broken down by demographic characteristics. The survey is conducted by a questionnaire placed and recovered by an interviewer.

■ **the call**

this is the sequence of directions that begin a take, typically: 'Roll Sound!' 'Roll Camera!' 'Mark it!' 'And... Action!'

■ **the clios**

annual awards given for excellence in radio and television advertising.

■ **the distribution system**

the actual cables that deliver the signals to subscribers.

■ **the drum beat**

selected programmes, data, materials, people and media sources from communication, development and change organisations.

■ **the groundglass**

a flat surface of etched glass in the viewfinding system of a camera that is the same distance from the lens as the film plane.

■ **the medium is the message**

one of those obscure sayings of the 60s media guru argues that no medium is neutral and what is said is profoundly affected by the medium in which it is said. The saying may also be taken to imply, in a sense, that the medium is 'more important' than the message. If interpreted in this way, then the saying can be seen to be close to the contemporary post-modern pre-occupation with the over-production of signs, the superficiality of media communication and the 'implosion of meaning'.

■ **the movement**

the parts of a camera or projector that move the film intermittently: the pull down claw, the rollers before and after the loops and the gears connecting these parts form the movement. If there is a registration pin, this is also part of the movement. Sometimes the shutter can also be considered part of the movement.

the slate

a board with two hinged sticks attached. The slate is used to record a scene number and sync point (via the clapstick) at the beginning of a shot.

the sticks

1. the tripod or the tripod legs.
2. the clapper on the slate.

the taking lens

on a turret, the lens that is actually in front of the gate, producing an image on the film.

TheNet

this is a networking software package created by Hans Giese, DFBAU and supported by NORD-LINK in Germany. TheNET implements a multi-port, multi-station packet radio network protocol. The latest release of theNET is the X1J4 revised by Dave Roberts G8KBB and is burned into a 27C512. TheNET X1J revision 4 series EPROMs implement a bank-switching technique to enable the use of a larger EPROM thus allowing more features to be added to theNET nodes.

TheNet parms

TheNET node EPROM's installed in TNCs, operate using timers and other parameters that are burned into the EPROM. Most of these parameters may be modified over the air by the SNO. A complete description of these parms are detailed elsewhere in this book.

theorising

a process of defining general principles that logically explain the relationship between seemingly unconnected patterns.

thermal

an effect related to changes in temperature. The thermal expansion coefficient of a tape refers to its change in length upon a change in the ambient temperature.

throughput

a measurement of the number of bits, blocks, characters, messages or interactive transactions passing though a Packet or data communications system. Throughput is usually a number that describes network performance. Baud rate describes only the number of bit transitions that leave a transmitter in a second. Throughput is a statistic that actually shows the delivery of data in a Packet network, end to end. Throughput is calculated by taking the original baud rate, given in bytes per second, subtracting the overhead and the time used to traverse the network. This includes the time lost due to network protocols, the lost time due to choking and collisions.

throwaway

a handbill or some other printed matter distributed free to residences and containing local advertising, a novelty item used to entice consumers into buying an item for sale.

tie-in

a campaign to link products, media or markets.

tie-in kit

a device for bypassing the fuse box and electrical wiring of a location by tapping power directly from the mains.

■ tight wind

a handy attachment sometimes found on an editing bench on the right rewind, used to wind film onto a core and giving it a very smooth edge. It can be quicker than opening and tightening split reels if you are just rewinding an entire roll.

■ tight wind hub

a tight wind is useless without it. This is the hub that holds a core on the spindle of a rewind.

■ tilt

a vertical camera move on an axis, up or down. Not to be used interchangeably with pan. It is not really correct to say 'pan up' or 'pan down', when you really mean tilt.

■ Time Division Multiple Access (TDMA)

a satellite communications technique for sharing use of a satellite transponder by dynamically allocating time slots among its users.

■ Time Division Multiplexing (TDM)

equipment enabling transmission of a number of independent signals over a common path by transmitting them sequentially at different instants of time.

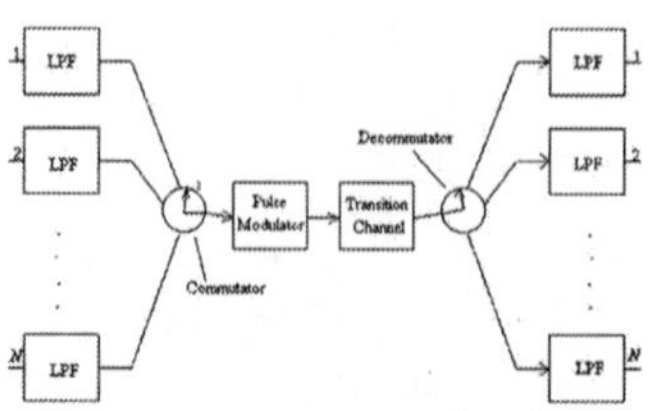

■ time lapse

time lapse is when single frame shooting is used to dramatically speed up the action over the course of a long period of time. Typically it is a process where a single frame is shot after a consistent pause. It could be one frame every ten seconds or one frame every hour and such.

■ time shifting

recording programs and playing them back at times other than when they were aired.

■ time slot

a specific time bought for airing a commercial on radio or television.

■ time, place and manner restrictions or rules

rules, when justified by a substantial government interest, that can regulate the time, place and manner of speaking or publishing and the distribution of printed material.

■ timed print

unlike a One Light Print, this is a print where the timer has gone through and timed every shot.

■ timeline

in non-linear editing the area in which audio and video clips are applied, typically giving duration in frames and seconds.

■ timeliness

news value that stresses when an event occurred.

■ timer

the person at the lab who goes

through your film, shot by shot and selects the printing lights.

time-sharing

the sharing of use of a processor among multiple simultaneous users.

time-to-live

when a packet is sent from one TheNET node to another TheNET node the packet contains several bytes of information which are useful at TheNET nodes along the path. One of these bytes of information is the time-to-live initialiser. Each time a node relays the packet one hop further the time-to-live is decremented one node. When it decrements to zero the message is discarded. Therefore, if the number of hops that the packet has to travel (hop) to reach it's specified destination is greater than the initial time-to-live the packet will never reach its destination. In addition, if the time-to-live on the return trip is not high enough an acknowledgment will not be returned.

timing

the lab's process of selecting printing lights to for the proper redition of exposure and colour when making a print. The term is a little consuming, as it has nothing at all to do with 'time' as in 'running time' or such.

timing lights or printing lights

these are the lamps of the contact printer at the lab. Their brightness can be controlled, which is measured in a scale of 1 to 50, 1 being the darkest and 50 the brightest. In colour there are three lights used together: Red – Green - Blue. When working with negative it is worth remembering that the values are reversed: the brighter the light, the darker the print will be.

timing report

a list of the timing lights and corresponding footages the lab used in making your print. The timing report can be very helpful for analysing the footage and judging the possibilities of further corrections. Any serious problems with the footage (out of focus, scratches, edge fog, etc.) are usually also noted on the timing report.

TNC

Terminal Node Controller is the combined modem and packet assembler and disassembler. The interface device between the computer terminal and RF transceiver. The TNC assembles and disassembles packets and provides error detection. The TNC's job is to take text typed on the terminal or computer and store it until the user hits a carriage return . At that time the text is sent to the destination station. Each line of text ending with a carriage return becomes a packet and is stored in the TNC until it can be sent to the destination station (channel clear).

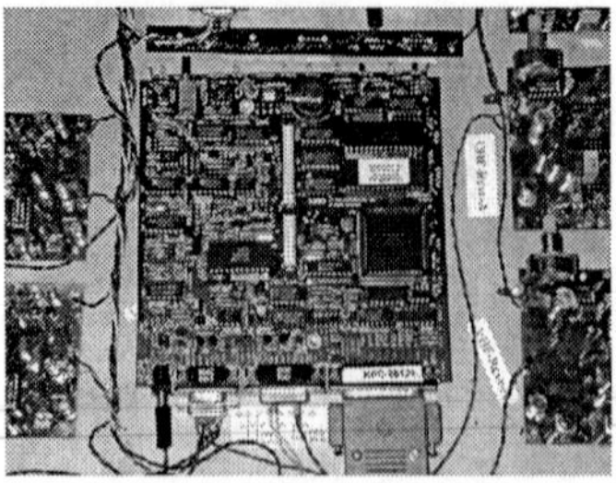

The TNC has commands that allow the user to set the timing parameters and install the operator's call-sign. Once the user has installed the licensed call-sign the TNC adopts its own personality and allows only connect requests directed to the installed call.

■ tone

1. a 1,000 Hz sine wave used at the beginning of a tape to provide consistent volume when transferring sound.
2. room tone.

■ topology

the logical or physical arrangement of nodes on a Packet Radio network in relation to each other. How well a network functions is more related to its topology (the quality of the links and paths) than to the software used to form a network.

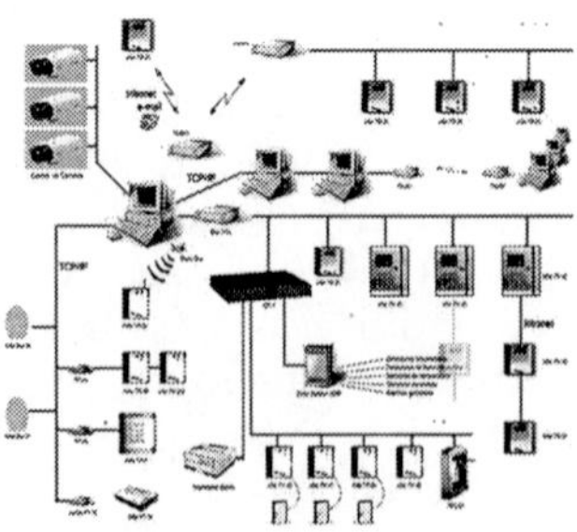

■ tort

a wrongful act resulting in an injury to another person's, property or reputation, for which the injured party is entitled to seek compensation.

■ touch-screen

a display monitor that is pressure sensitive to touch and is often used as a multimedia control instead or in conjunction with a keyboard. Better authoring systems should have touch-screen interface functions built in their software. Touch-screen displays vary widely and can be accomplished with special overlays or can come as integral screens with built-in touch-screen capabilities. The best screens also feature z-axis control, which allows screen response at different rates depending on the level of pressure applied.

■ trace packet

a special test packet in Packet Radio networks that causes a report to be sent back to the network control operator who originated the test packet.

■ track

a sequence of contiguous data, the beginning, length, mode and end of which are defined in the table of contents, which is held in the Q subcode channel of the lead-in area of the disc. The two types of tracks currently defined are the CD-DA track according to the CD-ROM specification that is also used in CD-I. In CD-DA the length of a track is related to playing times between four seconds and 72 minutes.

■ **track angle**

the angle that the track of a helical scan recording makes to the edge of the tape. This should correspond with the scan angle of the helical recorder - the angle that the tape makes to the equatorial plane of the rotating drum head. If the track angle and scan angle do not correspond, mistracking will occur.

■ **tracking shot**

a tracking shot is one where the camera is placed on a dolly and is moved while filming. Also known as a dolly shot.

■ **tracking studies**

study that examines how ads perform during or after a campaign.

■ **trade libel**

product disparagement and not considered true libel, disparaging a product as opposed to the manufacturer or maker of the product.

■ **trade magazine**

magazines edited to reach a member of a specific occupational group or business.

■ **trade name**

the name used by a company to describe and distinguish its brand of a generic product.

■ **trade publication**

a magazine, newspaper or newsletter published by members of a specific industry.

■ **trade regulation rules**

rules adopted by the Federal Trade Commission that prohibit specific advertising claims about an entire class of products. For example, makers of fruit drinks that contain less than 10 per cent fruit juice cannot advertise these products as fruit juice.

■ **trade show**

a convention at which advertising agencies or related companies show and compare products and ideas. Companies frequently underwrite elaborate displays, receptions, presentations and giveaways for trade shows in their industry.

■ **trade-out**

a barter arrangement for the exchange of commercial time, advertising space, products or services.

■ **traffic**

calls being sent and received over a communications network.

■ **training**

an international listing of training events, courses, distance-learning courses and web-based courses that might be of interest to people and organisations working in communication and development.

■ **transcription**

the process of copying all of the information on one tape to another tape of the same or different format. The term refreshing is commonly used by some archivists and librarians to refer to the process of copying information from one tape to a newer tape of the same format (e.g., VHS to VHS). When the information is copied to a different format, the terms reformatting and converting have been used.

■ **transition**

the production technique chosen to move from one scene to another in video or audio programming. Also production elements between programs. Some transitions are cuts, fades, dissolves, special effects, wipes, segues, etc.

■ **transmission**

the electrical transfer of a signal, message or other form of information from one location to another, most desirably in unaffected form at the receiver.

■ **transmission speed**

number of pulses or bits transmitted in a given period of time, expressed variably in Bits Per Second (BPS), Words Per Minute (WPM), Characters per Second (CPM), an occasionally as Lines per Minute (LPM) in WeFAX transmission.

■ **transparency**

the quality of a media text by which it appears to be natural rather than constructed.

■ **transparent**

to make the some forms of binary Packet Radio information invisible to other Packet operators. In Packet communications, a suspension of control character recognition in certain systems while information transfer is in progress. This mode prevents the TNC from reacting to special characters. Another mode of operation in a packet TNC that allows the sending of all possible binary characters without fear of actuating commands in the TNC. The transparent mode is primarily used for the transfer of binary data files.

■ **transport layer**

the fourth layer of the ISO Open Systems Interconnection Reference Model. The 'transport' layer performs the function of end-to-end control of transmitted Packet Radio information and is responsible for optimised use of the Packet Radio network resources. It controls the transfer of datagrams between two level 3 nodes via a number of intervening L3 nodes.

■ **trapezoidal error**

a change in the angle of a recorded helical scan track. Can result in mistracking.

■ **trends**

full articles and summaries of regional and global trends in communication media - television, radio, print media, publications and internet. Also includes some trends in development issues - both regional and global.

■ **trial court(s)**

normally the first court to hear a lawsuit. This court is the forum in which the facts are determined and the law is initially applied, as opposed to an appellate court, to which decisions are appealed.

■ **trim bin or editing bin or bin**

a trim bin is a bin on wheels lined

with a fabric bag and topped off with a frame with a row pins on which to hang film while editing. Oddly enough, a trim bin is not used for trims, which are small, but for selects and outtakes. Not to be confused with a waste basket!

■ trims

trims are outtakes of a few frames, usually a foot or less. To keep them from getting lost they are usually stored separately from longer outtakes, either in their own vault box or in a trim book.

■ tripod head

the part of the tripod with the pan and tilt mechanism to which the camera is attached.

■ trunk

a Packet Radio or Packet link between two nodes that are used as backbones. The trunk is normally a limited access path that allows only nodes or System Node Operator (SNO) access.

■ trustee model

in broadcast regulation, the idea that broadcasters serve as the public's trustees or fiduciaries

■ t-stop

similar to an F-Stop, some lenses, particularly zoom lenses, will have f-stops on one side of the aperture ring and t-stops on the other. To differentiate the two, the t-stops will be red and the f-stops white. T-stops are used in place of f-stops for setting exposure. Lenses with a lot of glass elements will often lose a little bit of light. The t-stops are calibrated to the actual amount of light that is hitting the film, rather than arrived at mathematically, as is the case with f-stops. However, the f-stops are still relevant, because while the t-stop should be used to set the exposure, the resulting f-stop will indicate how much Depth of Field you have.

■ TTL

Transistor-To-Transistor Logic. An internal transfer standard for electronics devices in which a 1 state is +5 Volts and a zero state is 0 volts. Some TNCs will not accommodate this form of interface. A separate signal converter is required when a TNC does not support TTL. Some TNCs have built-in TTL strapping options or connectors.

■ tungsten

the colour temperature of artificial light which is 3,200K on the colour temperature scale. Quartz Lights use a tungsten filament, which burns at 3,200K and gives us this term. Colour film for indoor shooting is balanced for tungsten light, otherwise the image would appear orange in hue. If tungsten balanced film is used out-of-doors without a correction filter the image will have a washed-out blue hue.

■ tuning

the group term for a number of image editing activities including colour and grey balancing, hue & saturation, gamma, histogram and contrast adjusting etc.

■ **turnaround time**

time required to reverse the direction on a half-duplex communications channel.

■ **turret**

a rotating lens mount allowing for the mounting of three or sometimes four lenses on a camera, allowing for the quick change from one lens to another. Only one is in use at any given time and this is known as the taking lens.

■ **TV listing**

television schedules found in print media such as newspapers, TV Guide or magazines. TV listings can also be found as part of television and radio programming.

■ **TVRO**

Television, Receive Only: The acronym is used to denote the home satellite receiving system.

■ **two-step flow**

the term used to describe the observation that media messages flow from the media to opinion leaders to the rest of the audience. The important point is that their research demonstrated that media effects are mediated by the pattern of our social contacts. They concluded that the media have limited effects.

■ **TXData**

Transmit Data stream fed to a modem modulator.

■ **TxDelay**

the period of time (usually 350 mSec/TXD 35) when TNC issues a transmit command and the actual time the packet data stream begins.

■ **typeface**

printing type (e.g. Helvetica, Times New Roman, Courier)

■ **UA**

Unnumbered Acknowledgment frame- a packet frame sent in unconnected (un-proto) mode to acknowledge a connect or disconnect request.

■ **UART**

Universal Asynchronous Receiver-Transmitter. An electronic circuit contained within the communications port(s) of the computer that decodes and encodes data in the fashion required by the specific machine for receiving and transmitting purposes. The UART also performs the actual data transmission to the communication device, once it has been encoded and is ready to send.

■ **UHF**

the ultra-high-frequency band of the electromagnetic spectrum, channels 14 through 69 on the TV set.

■ **UI**

Unnumbered information frame. An Information frame without a frame number that is sent as a broadcast during a beacon, nodes broadcast, CQ and other similar frames. It is not acknowledged and there is no assurance that it will be received.

■ **ultra-sonic cleaner**

a sophisticated cleaning machine

found at labs to clean negatives prior to printing or transfer to video. It uses sound waves to shake loose dust.

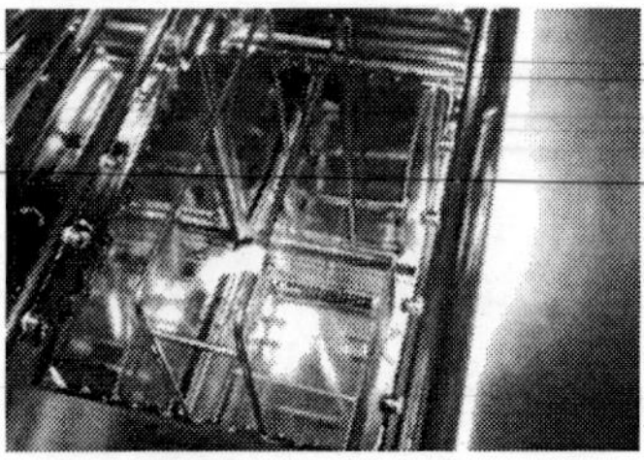

■ **ultra-sonic splicer**

an expensive and sophisticated splicing machine used for splicing Polyester Base stock.

■ **unattended operation**

transmission automatically controlled or not requiring a Packet Radio operator to function.

■ **undercrank**

to run the camera slower, producing fast motion. The term has survived from the time when you would crank a camera.

■ **underexposure**

filming a scene with less light than the emulsion of the film needs for a correct exposure. The image will be too dark. If compensated for in printing, the image will appear grainy and very muddy.

■ **underground press**

a type of specialised reporting that emerged in the mid- to late 1960s, with emphasis on politically liberal news and opinion and cultural topics such as music, art and film.

■ **unfair competition**

see misappropriation.

■ **Unique Selling Proposition (USP)**

an one-line description of your company's products or services that differentiates it among your market from the offerings of its competitors.

■ **unique users**

the number of individual users that visit a site within a certain time frame.

■ **university degrees**

a listing of university and other academic institutions that offer programmes related to communication, change and development.

■ **unprofessional**

an insult hurled at someone during a crisis when they have broken some unwritten rule of professional conduct. Commonly the term is used with the most frequency by people to whom it would just as easily apply.

■ **UNPROTO**

an 'un-proto' packet is a packet transmitted without expecting a response. Technically it is called a UI frame which means Unnumbered Information. A packet station issuing a beacon for all to see or calling CQ, would use an unproto packet.

■ **upconverting**

process which increases the number of pixels or frame rate or scanning format used to represent an image by interpolating existing pixels to create new ones at closer spacing. Process does not increase the resolution of image.

Upconverting is done from standard definition to high definition.

■ **uplink**

that portion of a communications link reaching upward from the Earth to a satellite. In some Packet nodes (X-1J/X2) the 'user' command will display the uplink and downlink stations.

■ **upright moviola or upright**

an editing machine with arms in back to hold the take up and supply reels. The film moves up and around to a screen on the front. Foot petals control motors for sound speed and variable speed viewing.

■ **UPS**

Uninterruptible Power Supply. A battery reserve system for computer power installed to supply power in the event of outage. These systems protect against data loss during power outage.

■ **upscale**

having a look, feel or price designed to appeal to a well-to-do urban market.

■ **URL**

Uniform Resource Locator- generally denotes the web site address

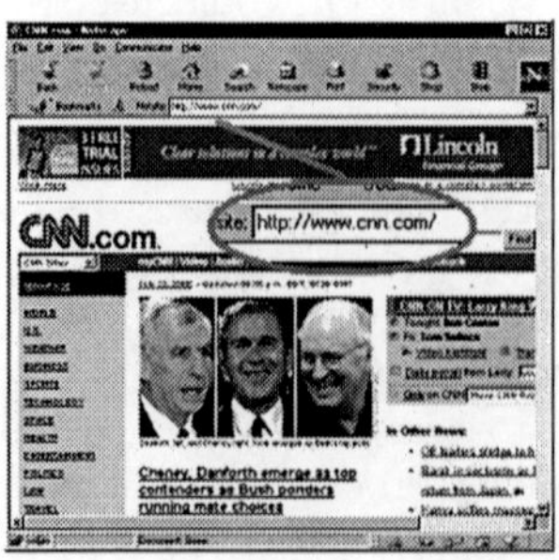

■ **user registration**

some Web sites request or require, users to fill in an online form before accessing the service. The information on the form is usually used to compile demographic data.

■ **uses and gratifications approaches**

to the media emphasise the active use made of media by audience members to seek gratification of a variety of needs. The standard adage is that, where effects research asks 'what do the media do to audiences?', the uses and gratifications approach asks 'what do audiences do with the media?'. Audiences are said to *use* the media to *gratify* needs. The needs most commonly identified are: surveillance (i.e. monitoring what's going on in the world), personal relationships, personal identity and diversion (i.e. entertainment and escapism).

■ **uses-and-gratifications model**

a model proposing that audience members have certain needs or drives that are satisfied by using both non-media and media sources.

■ **utility**

ethical principle that stresses the greatest good for the greatest number.

■ **vari speed**

a motor or the control for a motor which will run a camera or an editing machine at speed faster or slower than sound speed.

■ **variable obscenity statutes**

a Supreme Court doctrine that permits states to prohibit the sale, distribution or exhibition of certain kinds of non-obscene matter to children, so long as these laws do not interfere with the accessibility of this material to adults.

■ **variety**

the entertainment industry trade publication.

■ **vault box**

a white, flat, square cardboard box designed to hold 1,000 feet of 35mm or two 1,000 foot rolls of 16mm.

■ **v-chip**

a device installed in a TV set that restricts the reception of violent or objectionable material.

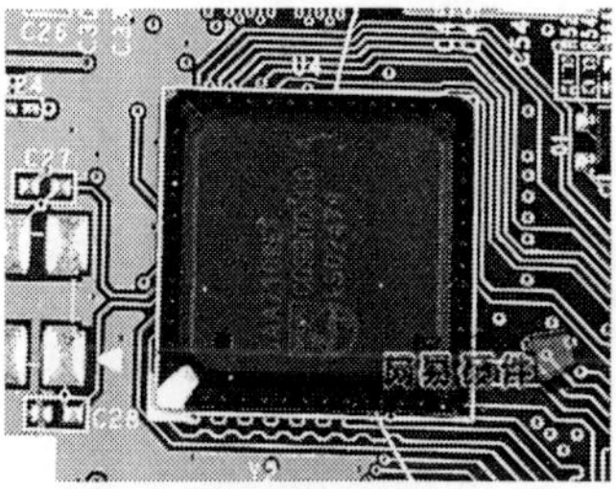

■ **veil of ignorance**

ethical principle that argues that everyone should be treated equally.

■ **verdict**

the decision of a trial jury based on the instructions given to it by the judge.

■ **vertical integration**

the process by which a media company acquires another elsewhere in the production process.

■ **vertical publication**

a publication dealing with one specific topic and appealing to a particular audience, in contrast to horizontal publications which are more broad.

■ **VHF**

the Very-High-Frequency band of the electromagnetic spectrum, channels 2 through 13 on the TV set.

■ **video capture**

the term for converting analog video signal to digital stills and Motion files.

■ **videocassette**

the software required to record and play back video content. Also called a videotape.

■ **vinegar syndrome**

characteristic of the decomposition of acetate based magnetic tape where acetic acid is a substantial by-product that gives the tape a vinegar-like odour. After the onset of the vinegar syndrome, acetate tape backings degrade at an accelerated rate - the hydrolysis of the acetate is catalysed further by the presence of acetic acid by product.

■ **virtual**

something which is a representation rather than the real thing. In advertising, the word 'virtually' means 'almost'.

■ **visible minorities**

a popular term for people of

colour or racial minorities. It refers to an official government category of persons who are native- or foreign-born, non-white and non-Caucasoid, including Chinese, Africans, etc. In the 1996 census, 11.2 per cent of Canada's population identified themselves or were identified, as visible minorities.

■ visual literacy

the ability to look at visual information with perception. A visually literate person understands how visual elements contribute to the meaning of the whole.

■ VNR

Video New Release. The television equivalent of a news release.

■ Voice-Over (V.O.)

recorded off screen voice heard on a television or radio commercial.

■ voir dire

a preliminary examination the court makes of persons chosen to serve as jurors in a trial. Persons can be challenged for cause or on the basis of a peremptory challenge by either side in the legal dispute.

■ want ad

classified recruitment ad, an advertisement for personnel, also known as 'help wanted' ads. The Motto agency utilises an eight-point check list of criteria that maximise response to help-wanted ads.

■ warp

a special effect sequence of morph images that simulate smooth transitions of dissimilar frames.

■ waste paper

a generic term used for post-consumer waste and some pre-consumer waste.

■ watermark

an impression made in a wet sheet of paper as it is being manufactured. Watermarks are visible when the sheet is held up to light. They appear as a word, symbol or other impression.

■ wax pick

characterises the resistance of the surface layer of a sheet to the breakaway of surface fragments. Expressed in Dennison units.

■ web page

a hypertext page contained within a website.

■ web radio

the delivery of radio over the Internet directly to individual listeners

■ website

a set of hypertext pages linked to each other that contain information about a common topic.

■ wet gate

a contact printing method, made on a specially equipped printing machine, where the film is in a liquid that temporarily fills in any scratches on the base, preventing them from refracting light and showing up in the print. Commonly, answer prints are printed with a wet gate. Labs often charge a little extra for wet gate printing.

■ **WHMIS**

Workplace Hazardous Materials Information Systems.

■ **wide lens**

a lens with a focal length smaller than 25mm in 16mm or 50mm in 35mm, which, like looking into the wrong end of a pair of binoculars, provides an extended view of a large area.

■ **wild**

not sync. A wild motor is one that runs close to 24 frames per second, but not close enough for sync sound. Also applies in a few other cases, such as, if you are filming a rear screen projection scene and the projector and camera are not Interlocked they can be said to be running wild.

■ **wild sound**

non-sync sound, recorded without the camera running, usually recorded to supplement the sync takes.

■ **wild spot**

a radio spot, appearing in various slots and locales, neither regional nor national or on a non-network station.

■ **windows**

a technique whereby a broadcast from another place is slotted into a transmission from the principal source of the transmission.

■ **wire service**

news stories, features, etc., sent by direct line to subscribing or member newspapers and radio and television stations.

■ **wireless telegraph**

early efforts at long-distance communication that led to development of radio.

■ **wireless telephony**

early efforts at long-distance voice communication that led to development of radio.

■ **wood engraving**

a relief print carved in the end grain of a block of wood whose thickness is the same as the height as a piece of movable type ('type high'). This was traditionally a commercial technique practiced by specialists and used in magazines and book illustrations.

■ **woodcut**

the relief image is carved from a wooden block.

■ **woodcut**

a relief print usually carved in the plank grain of a piece of wood. After the relief image has been carved in the plank with knives or gouges it is inked with a dauber or roller. It can then be printed by hand (in which case a sheet of paper is laid down on the inked plank and rubbed from the back with a smooth surface such as the palm of the hand or a wooden spoon) or with the help of a mechanical press.

■ **word-of-mouth**

informal way in which media products become known by audiences.

■ **workprint**

a positive copy of the original negative that is cut during the editing process. At the end of editing the original negative is then cut by the negative cutter to match the workprint shot for shot and an answer print struck from the cut negative. A workprint can also be made from reversal original.

■ **World Wide Web (WWW)**

an Internet tool that links users to audio, video and graphical information. It also provides a means for accessing information on computers connected via the Internet.

■ **WYSBYGI**

'What You See Before You Get it'. An extension of WYSIWYG interface design allowing the user to view and edit selected smaller areas from a preview dialogue box prior to committing special effects with the processing load of only a portion of the entire file.

■ **WYSIWYG**

'What You See Is What You Get'. A working interface of many authoring systems where an author sees the screens as he develops them exactly as they will appear to the user.

■ **xenon**

a very bright, daylight balanced projection lamp or a projector with a xenon lamp. A xenon lamp is not interchangeable with a tungsten lamp or arch lamp, but requires a different lamp housing on the projector. Because xenon lamps are daylight balanced it is sometimes advisable with colour film to have the lab make a print that is balanced for xenon. This is sometimes called a 5,400K print, the colour temperature of daylight.

■ **yellow journalism**

sensationalised journalism, appearing during the 1890s, noted for its emphasis on sex, murder, popularised medicine, pseudoscience, self-promotion and human-interest stories.

■ **zapple rule**

a corollary to the equal time rule that states that when the supporters of a legally qualified candidate are given time on a radio or television broadcast, the supporters of all other legally qualified candidates for the same office must also be given equal opportunity.

■ **zero cut**

a method of negative cutting specifically for blow up, where every shot is given. Frame handles so that the registration pin of the printer is never engaging with a splice, which can cause the image to wobble at the cut. It is most commonly used when you are blowing up from 16mm to 35mm. Zero cut should be done only if really necessary, because the lab can only print the film as an optical, which is far more expensive than a contact print. Zero cutting is a little more complicated than standard A&B rolls, so the negative cutter also charges more for it.

■ **zincograph**

a lithograph done on a zinc plate instead of on a stone. The term is also used to designate a photo-etched relief print.

zoned edition

newspaper that has special sections for specific geographic areas.

zoom

a smooth movement by the camera lens from far away to close up or from close up to farther away.

zoom lens

a variable focal length lens. A zoom lens will have a third ring, besides ones controlling focus and iris, that will allow you to change the focal length within a range of wide to long.